Mass Customisation and Personalisation in Architecture and Construction

Challenged by the recent economic crisis, the building and construction industry is currently seeking new orientation and strategies. In this book, mass customisation is uncovered as a key strategy in helping to meet this challenge. The term 'mass customisation' denotes an offering that meets the demands of each individual customer, whilst still being produced with mass production efficiency. Today mass customisation is emerging from a pilot stage into a scalable and sustainable strategy.

This book is the first dedicated publication of its kind that provides a forum for the concept within an applied and highly innovative context. Including contributions from some of the most prominent thinkers and practitioners in this field from across the world, including Denmark, Germany, Hong Kong, Italy, Sweden, Taiwan, the UK and the US, this book brings together a panel of experts who have carried out research both in academia and practice. It provides an overview of state-of-the-art practice related to the concept of customisation and personalisation within the built environment.

Poorang A.E. Piroozfar is a Senior Lecturer in Architectural Technology and Co-director of @BEACON (Advanced Technologies in the Built Environment, Architecture & CONstruction) at the School of Environment and Technology, University of Brighton, UK.

Frank T. Piller is a Professor of Management and Director of the Technology & Innovation Management Group of RWTH Aachen University, Germany. He is also a Faculty Member of the MIT Smart Customization Group at the MIT Media Lab, Massachusetts Institute of Technology, USA.

MASS CUSTOMISATION AND PERSONALISATION IN ARCHITECTURE AND CONSTRUCTION

**Edited by
Poorang A.E. Piroozfar
and Frank T. Piller**

LONDON AND NEW YORK

First published 2013
by Routledge
2 Park Square, Milton Park, Abingdon, Oxon OX14 4RN

Simultaneously published in the USA and Canada
by Routledge
711 Third Avenue, New York, NY 10017

Routledge is an imprint of the Taylor & Francis Group, an informa business

British Library Cataloguing in Publication Data
A catalogue record for this book is available from the British Library

Library of Congress Cataloging in Publication Data
Mass customisation and personalisation in architecture and
    construction/edited by Poorang A.E. Piroozfar and Frank T. Piller.
    pages cm
    Includes index.
    1. Architects and builders. 2. Mass customisation.
    I. Piroozfar, Poorang A. E., editor of compilation. II. Piller, Frank T.,
    1969– editor of compilation.
    NA2543.B84M37 2013
    720.28 – dc23   2012041948

ISBN: 978-0-415-62283-7 (hbk)
ISBN: 978-0-415-62284-4 (pbk)
ISBN: 978-0-203-43773-5 (ebk)

Typeset in Stone Sans and Franklin Gothic
by Florence Production Ltd, Stoodleigh, Devon, UK

Printed and bound in Great Britain
by Bell & Bain Ltd, Glasgow

Contents

Illustrations

FIGURES

TABLES

Contributors

Assa Ashuach completed his MA at the Royal College of Art, London, in 2003 following his BA in product design at Betzalel Academy of Art & Design in Jerusalem. He established Assa Ashuach Studio in London, where he focuses on research and consultancy in industrial design and manufacturing innovation, specialising in a wide range of additive manufacturing technologies and coding of unique 3D software methodologies. His internationally awarded works are included in permanent exhibitions, public and private collections. Assa invented the Digital Forming concept as a new product design method and later co-founded Digital Forming & UCODO Ltd in London.

Martin Bechthold is a professor of architectural technology at the Harvard Graduate School of Design, director of the Design Robotics Group and co-director of the Master in Design Studies Program. His work has been dis-seminated widely in the form of books, articles and public lectures. His research primarily deals with computer-aided design and manufacturing applications in architecture, with a focus on construction automation in the pursuit of component customisation, design robotics and emerging material systems.

Thomas Bock is a professor and the chair of building realisation and robotics at the Technische Universität München (TUM). His research focuses on automation and robotics in building construction, ranging from planning, building, production and utilisation through to reorganisation, deconstruction and disassembly. After studying architecture at the University of Stuttgart and the IIT Chicago, he did his doctorate at the University of Tokyo. He sits on the editorial boards of top journals such as *Robotica*, *Automation in Construction* and *International Journal of Construction Management*. Recently he became coordin-ator of CIB's newly founded W119 (Customised Industrial Construction).

Eric R.P. Farr is a researcher and critic with a MArch/MUD and a PhD in architecture and urban studies. He specialises in theorising fuzzy logic for plan-ning decision-making, as well as sustainable architecture and architectural theory. His experience is backed by his work as an international design consul-tant. He has been invited to give talks and lectures in universities and professional organisations worldwide. He advocates mass customisation and personalisation of urban spaces and his work on ICT has recently found a merger with his interests and involvements with mass customisation and co-creation in the AEC Industry.

Stefan Christoffer Gottlieb is a senior researcher at the Danish Building Research Institute, Aalborg University. His research focuses on critical studies of innovation and organisation in the built environment. He has authored books and articles on construction reform and development, including the role of mass customisation and industrialised production principles in the sector development agenda.

Anders Haug is an associate professor at the Department of Entrepreneurship and Relationship Management at the University of Southern Denmark. His main research areas are information management, knowledge management, knowledge representation and knowledge engineering. He has a PhD in knowledge representation in the context of creating product configurators, and has produced a number of international publications that deal with the development of product configurators, representation of complex industrial knowledge, sharing of product information and more. He also teaches in courses on managing information systems, product configuration and theory of science.

Lars Hvam is a professor in operations management at the Technical University of Denmark and the head of the Centre for Product Modelling (http://www.productmodels.org). He has worked as a consultant in several major companies within the areas of mass customisation and product configuration and has managed major research projects and supervised numerous PhD students in the fields of mass customisation and product configuration.

Jens Stissing Jensen is a post-doc researcher at Aalborg University. His research focuses on the governance of industrial transformation in the construction sector including the role of mass customisation. Currently a core topic of his research is the role of service-oriented technical component suppliers in the emerging co-transformation of the construction industry and an energy system based on increasing shares of renewable energy. He has authored articles and book chapters on the governance of sector development in the Danish construction sector and on sectoral energy efficiency strategies.

Stephen H. Kendall is a professor of architecture at Ball State University in the United States, with a PhD in design theory and methods from MIT. His research focuses on open building, which recognises that built environment is under constant change, and suggests that professionals guiding the design and construction of built environment need to assure a clear role for building inhabitants in this on-going process. He is the author of many books, technical reports and papers on this subject, encompassing both housing and healthcare architecture. He is joint coordinator of the CIB commission W104 Open Building Implementation.

Thomas Linner is a research assistant in building realisation and robotics at the Technische Universität München (TUM). During the last few years he has supervised some major research projects, with a focus on generation of mass customisable buildings and building sub-systems. He is a specialist in the area of automated production of building products as well as in the enhancement of the performance of building products by advanced technologies. Today, more and more, the generation of new business models, value system and manufacturing organisations complementary with mechatronic assisted living technologies is becoming the central issue in his research.

Niels Henrik Mortensen is a professor at the Technical University of Denmark and holds a PhD and an MSc in mechanical engineering. He is the head of the Product Architecture Group at the Technical University of Denmark, DTU management, where the main focus of research is on procedures and methods supporting development of product families based on product architectures and platforms. Niels Henrik is also, through the Institute of Product Development, an active consultant to Danish and international industrial companies within the areas of platform-based product development and product configuration.

Masa Noguchi is a reader in architectural technology at Mackintosh School of Architecture, The Glasgow School of Art, where he also serves as a co-director of MEARU (ZEMCH R&D Group). He established the world's first Zero Energy Mass Customised Housing (ZEMCH) course within the postgraduate programme. As well as inventing a Mass Custom Design® approach to sustainable affordable housing, he developed an interactive mass custom design rendering/communication tool and designed Canada's first net zero-energy house for Alouette Homes – i.e. ÉcoTerra house. As the co-founder of ZEMCH Network, he also contributed to initiating the international conference.

Ingrid Paoletti is an assistant professor at Politecnico di Milano, 'Best' Department and also the coordinator of the Cluster on Innovative Technologies and Construction Industry. Her research focuses on innovation in construction with a particular focus on mass customisation, industrialisation and digital fabrication. She is the author of several books, international papers and articles and coordinator of prizes and conferences on innovative technologies in architecture.

Frank Piller is a professor of management at RWTH Aachen University and the director of RWTH's Technology and Innovation Management Group. His research focuses on interfaces in the innovation process and customer-centric value creation. He is the author of several books and numerous articles on mass customisation, and has been the co-initiator of the MCPC conference series, a biannual conference on mass customisation, personalisation and co-creation.

Ghashang Piroozfar is a PhD student in the Department of Mathematics and Statistics at the University of Calgary. She received her MSc degree in mathematics in 2009 from Uppsala University, followed by an MSc degree in economics from KTH Royal Institute of Technology in 2010. Her research in the field of economics focuses on the applications of game theory to different subjects, including the building construction and mass customisation area.

Poorang Piroozfar is a senior lecturer in architectural technology and researcher, @BEACON, School of Environment and Technology, University of Brighton. His research spans over rule-based expert systems, ICT, building facades, as well as process, production and information management in the AEC industry. His interest in customer-centric approaches to design, fabrication and implementation in the construction industry has converged with other new concepts, resulting in introduction of new interdisciplinary and multidisciplinary research projects during recent years. He has been working proactively to promote mass customisation and personalisation in architecture, construction and the built environment internationally since 2005.

Olga Popovic Larsen is a professor of structures in architecture at the School of Architecture, Royal Danish Academy of Fine Arts, Copenhagen, Denmark. She is an architect by training, holds an MSc in earthquake engineering and a PhD in reciprocal structures. She leads the research/education group in structures at the school covering all the teaching and research in the broad field of load-bearing structures. Her research bridges over architectural technology and structural engineering; more specifically: demountable lightweight structures, design for disassembly, design for re-use, mass customisation, also reciprocal frames, gridshells, tensegrities and their application in architecture.

Lawrence Sass is an associate professor in the Department of Architecture at MIT, teaching courses specifically in digital fabrication and design computing since 2002, after earning a PhD in 2000 and an SMArchS in 1994 also at MIT. He has a BArch from Pratt Institute in NYC, has published widely and has exhibited his work at the Modern Museum of Art in New York City.

Daniel Smithwick is a PhD candidate in the MIT Department of Architecture as well as an affiliate researcher with the MIT Smart Customisation Group. His research focuses on web-based platforms and design tools for user-generated architecture and digital fabrication. Prior to his PhD studies, he co-founded a start-up aimed at providing consumers with mass customisable backyard structures, and he was a researcher at the MIT Media Lab where he led numerous classes and workshops and authored papers on mass customisation for architectural design.

Guohua Tang is a PhD candidate in the Department of Industrial Engineering and Logistics Management at Hong Kong University of Science and Technology, where he received his MPhil degree in the same field in 2010. Prior to that, he received a BSc degree in automation engineering in Zhejiang University, PRC. His research focuses on mass customisation and its applications in various industries, the interface between sales and marketing and supply chain management, and demand management for manufacturing firms.

Christian Thuesen holds a PhD from DTU (Technical University of Denmark), where he is employed in the Department for Management Engineering as a senior researcher within innovation, business development, mass customisation and project-based production. His collaboration with the industry is currently maintained through the development of a Master's program on 'Design and Management of Projects in Networks' and membership of the Innovation Network for Energy Efficient and Sustainable Construction (InnoBYG.dk) where he is a member of the steering committee and project manager on a research project on sustainable business models.

Mitchell M. Tseng is a professor and director of the Zhejiang Advanced Manufacturing Institute, Hong Kong University of Science and Technology, which he joined in 1993 as the founding department head of industrial engineering after holding executive positions at Xerox and DEC. He previously held faculty positions at the University of Illinois at Urbana–Champaign and the Massachusetts Institute of Technology. Mitchell received an MSc and a PhD in industrial engineering from Purdue University and a BSc degree from National Tsing Hua University. He is a fellow of the International Academy of Production Engineers (CIRP) and ASME.

Kung-Jen Tu is an assistant professor in the Department of Architecture, National Taiwan University of Science and Technology. Currently, he also serves as the Secretary General of the Taiwan Institute of Property Management. He specialises in the areas of open building design and facility management. His research focuses on adopting open building as an effective building design strategy in offering flexible building infrastructure to accommodate diverse spatial needs and to allow users to customise their spaces.

Kasper Sánchez Vibæk is an associate professor at CINARK – Centre for Industrialised Architecture at the Royal Danish Academy of Fine Arts, School of Architecture. In January 2012 he received his PhD in the subject of systems in architecture. As well as a Master in Architecture he also holds a supplementary degree in sociology. Since 2004 he has conducted research in the conditions for and processes of contemporary architectural creation and realisation. This includes how the benefits of industrial production can be combined with context-sensitive architectural solutions through hybrids like mass customisation and integrated product deliveries.

Hao-Yang Wei was an associate professor in the Department of Architecture, National Taiwan University of Science and Technology. He specialised in the areas of materials and methods in building construction and open building design. His research focused on implementing the open building concept in building design and developing the support and the components of various infill systems that aim to offer flexible building infrastructure for mass customisation.

Tomas Westerholm is a founder and CEO of 3D Render Ltd. His career in digital content and experience creation is shaped by true life problem solving, and web configurators are a pure example of it. He believes in the power of visual sensation on a human observer and keeps seeking the better, more powerful and more efficient way of interactive visual communication with space users.

Foreword

From mass customisation of goods and services to mass customised cities: a global imperative

Kent Larson, MIT Media Lab

With dark and crowded tenements rapidly filling cities, the great architects of the early twentieth century focused on reinventing urban design, architecture, and transportation systems to solve looming societal problems. They imagined that their new tools – electricity, motors, steel, concrete, plate glass, mass production, and fresh ideas about design – could be used to make cities healthier and more productive.

Le Corbusier, the most influential architect of the first half of the twentieth century, developed an audacious plan in a 1925 proposal to bulldoze most of central Paris north of the Seine, and replace it with sixty-storey glass-clad skyscrapers set surrounded by parks where 'the air is clean and pure' and 'there is hardly any noise'. Funded by Avions Voisin, a French luxury automobile brand, Le Corbusier's 'Plan Voisin' naturally celebrated private automobiles – the ultimate technology to provide freedom and autonomy to (affluent) people prior to the Great Depression. Walter Gropius, founder of the Bauhaus and an early advocate of a form of mass customisation, hoped that industrial design and construction processes could 'meet the public's desire for individuality and offer the client the pleasure of personal choice'.

Though not their intention, the modernist towers and shift from on-site craft to mass production of major building components after World War II resulted in relentless monotony with anonymous places of living, working, and commerce separated by roads filled with private automobiles. The mass produced, not the mass customised city evolved.

Today, Corbusier's ideas for cities are alive and well in Asia, with hundreds of new cities under development being planned largely on his 1925 model. In China alone, 300 million rural inhabitants will move to urban areas over the next 15 years – requiring the construction of the equivalent of the entire built environment of the United States.

Cities matter! They will account for approximately 90 per cent of global population growth, 80 per cent of wealth creation, and 60 per cent of total energy consumption. Unfortunately, most new cities are made up of grim, energy-intensive, sprawling and isolated 'super blocks' connected by congested and polluted highways. We strongly believe that we need to reinvent our thinking about cities by applying 'mass customisation thinking' to this domain.

MASS CUSTOMISATION FOR NEW CITIES

Great cities typically evolved organically over hundreds of years. They are the unique combination of countless creative acts by entrepreneurs, patrons, civil servants, artists, and architects. The great question for our time is: can we deploy the new tools of our digital era to create healthy, high-performance 'instant cities' with some of the richness and diversity of the urban places that we all love.

We can begin to see a path forward. The following outlines a kind of mass customisation process for creating new cities that, like a great theatrical script, provides a strong top-down framework to enable bottom-up creative interpretation, improvisation, and execution.

Compact, service-rich neighborhoods. A map of Paris that Corbusier proposed to destroy shows the 20 neighborhoods, or arrondissements, spaced about one mile apart. Each was a distinct village with a unique identity, providing most of what people need in life within a 10 to 15 minute walk. Each maintained their village structure even as they merged together over time. We propose to create cities from nested 'compact city cells' of about 1 mile in diameter, each with a neighborhood center and mix of places of living, shopping, work, and play within a short walk. A compact city cell is also an autonomous electrical microgrid and communication network, and contains systems for local energy production, waste management, etc. We envision a tool where the attributes of each neighborhood can be adjusted parametrically according to the climate, cultural values, demographics of the residents, and desired street and commercial activity. Cells are nested and connected to each center by trams or subway, to create a kind of resilient urban mesh network.

Parametric density/vibrancy. With a network of compact city cells defined, we can then 'dial in' the desired street life, which is largely a function of density. In a city cell of one mile in diameter, there would be 12,700 people at the density of Cambridge, MA, 46,000 people if Paris, and 55,000 people if Manhattan. We envision a tool that would allow designers and the community to dynamically visualise the impact increased density on building heights at the street wall, functional towers in background, widths of streets, and the number of cafes, shops, galleries, and public amenities that could be supported by the local population.

Mobility-on-demand. Increasing density, with its positive impact on street life, is not practical if it also increases the number of automobiles on the street with the attendant pollution, congestion, noise, and wastage of valuable land for parking. Mobility-on-demand (MoD) systems, created at the Media Lab, consist of lightweight electric vehicles located at charging stations throughout an urban service area. The convenience of such a shared-vehicle system, in which users can walk to the closest pick-up point and drop off at any other charging station, reduces the need for private automobiles and creates a system with high levels of vehicle and parking space utilisation and reduced carbon footprint and energy use. Coupled and coordinated with existing mass transit systems, shared-use personal mobility systems address the 'First and Last Mile' problem of reaching and departing from mass-transit stations. We envision a configuration tool that makes use of a typology of streetscape designs, vehicle pathway types, shared mobility hubs, charging infrastructure, etc. to rapidly configure the compact city cell in response to density and local conditions. We believe that optimised pathways for shared-use electric cars, electric scooters, 3-wheel bike lane vehicles, and electric and conventional bicycles will result a 10x reduction of congestion, pollution, and noise while allowing for a dramatic increase in density/vibrancy.

Personal space-on-demand. With ubiquitous communication and information technologies, the home is now a center of learning, entertainment, shopping. With almost free computation and powerful sensing, the home will soon become a center of health care delivery to address a rapidly aging society. With distributed renewable energy production costs in rapid decline and oil prices rising, residential buildings will become centers of energy production. With work becoming distributed and mobile, many companies report that more employees are working from home than in the office at any given time – making the home as important a workplace as the office. We envision the separation of the process of creating urban housing into two district steps. First, builders efficiently create open-loft spaces with standardised power, data, and mechanical connection interfaces. Second, occupants configure their personalised 'infill' using sophisticated interfaces running on smart phones and tablets – making use of automated fabrication technology, sophisticated supply chains, and powerful computational design tools. This will make it possible to meet the consumer demand for personalised environments and products that express an individual's unique identity – and satisfy the complex activities and family structures of contemporary life.

Urban farming. With a rapidly growing urban population, conventional methods of growing and distributing food are proving to be highly wasteful and unsustainable. Emerging high-tech aeroponic technologies for cities are proving to have extraordinary advantages, but requiring a fraction of the water, no pesticides, no long-distance transportation, and reduced spoilage. We envision urban apartments with standardised water and nutrient distribution systems, allowing each resident to delineate the types of crops they wish to grow in the south-facing facade garden. The components and related sensing devices and networks would be configured, installed, and remotely monitored, allowing each family to grow up to 50 per cent of their high-value food adjacent to where food is prepared.

THE PATH FORWARD

These are just some of many elements resulting from the application of mass customisation thinking towards the creation of new cities. The chapters assembled in this volume provide many further ideas and points of inspiration. The editors have curated a wonderful collection of papers that move our current thinking on mass customisation in the built environment to a new level. I am sure that the ideas, research, and blueprints of the authors of this book will inspire your thinking about mass customisation, architecture, and new cities as much as they have inspired mine.

Kent Larson
MIT Media Lab, Massachusetts Institute of Technology
Cambridge, MA, March 2013

Abbreviations

AI	Artificial Intelligence
AM	Additive Manufacturing
BIM	Building Information Modelling
CA	Customised Apartment
CAD-CAM	Computer Aided Design–Computer Aided Manufacturing
CAMP	Computer-Aided Manufacturing Planning
CNC	Computer Numerical Control
CODO	Co-Designed Object
DCF	Discounted Cash Flow
DF	Digital Forming
EOS	Electro Optical Systems
ERP	Enterprise Resource Planning
ETFE	Ethylene/Tetra-Fluoro-Ethylene Copolymer
GFA	Gross Floor Area
GPU	Graphic Processing Unit
GUI	Graphical User Interface
HAPPS	Heim Automated Parts Pickup System
HVAC	Heating, Ventilation and Air Conditioning
ICT	Information and Communication Technology
IFS	Integrated Façade System
IOBRS	Integrated Open Building Remodeling System
IPD	Integrated Product Delivery
KA	Royal Danish Academy of Fine Arts, School of Architecture
LC	Life Cycle
MC	Mass Customisation
MEP	Mechanical, Electrical and Plumbing/Piping
NC	Numerical Control
NCC	Nordic Construction Company
OBRS	Open Building Remodeling System
ODO	Original Designed Object
PCS	Panelised Cabinet System
PDM	Product Data Management

PQI	Performance Quality Indicators
RC	Reinforced Concrete
RCA	Royal College of Art
RF	Reciprocal Frame
RFID	Radio-frequency Identification
SaaS	Software as a Service
SAR	The Foundation for Architects' Research
SLS	Selective Laser Sintering
SME	Small and Medium Enterprises
TEKES	The Finnish Funding Agency for Technology and Innovation
TPS	Toyota Production System
UVAV	User Value-Added Viewpoints

INTRODUCTION

1

Mass customisation and personalisation in architecture and construction: an introduction

Poorang Piroozfar and Frank T. Piller

ABSTRACT

Challenged by a global crisis, the building industry is currently seeking new orientation and strategies. Stakeholders in the built environment are being forced at an extensive and unprecedented pace to improve a set of conflicting objectives. On one hand, they want to enhance the cost efficiency and economic sustainability of their constructions. On the other hand, the market demands that the functional performance, indoor quality, comfort levels and social sustainability of the buildings shall be increased. And at the same time, building professionals concentrate on the reduction of energy consumption, the ecological footprint of a building process and its carbon emission, boosting the environmental sustainability. Finally, designers also have distinct aesthetic values they would like to realise in their design. This apparently conflicting set of goals demands a new industrial paradigm in the built environment. In industrial markets, mass customisation emerged more than two decades ago as a paradigm for exactly this purpose – offering highly customised products with mass production efficiency. From its origins in machinery and IT hardware mass customisation recently gained growing popularity in consumer goods industries. In particular, the advent of the internet enabled its introduction in many markets. This chapter briefly recaps this development and provides a common understanding of the elements of mass customisation as a business paradigm. In addition, the individual chapters in this handbook are introduced.

WHAT IS MASS CUSTOMISATION?

The recent economic crisis has placed efficiency and cost-cutting back on the agenda of executives and entrepreneurs worldwide. Yet, cost cuts should not be blindly pursued at the risk of damaging the long-term strategy and value proposition of an organisation. As in the end, the famous saying by Peter Drucker still holds true: 'It is the customer who determines what a business is' (Drucker, 1954). In the very sense of this statement, the ability to manage a value chain from the customers' point of view determines the competitiveness of many companies. In many industries, firms today are faced by an uninterrupted trend toward heterogeneity of demand (Franke et al., 2009; Zuboff & Maxmin, 2003). In particular, consumers with great purchasing power are increasingly attempting to express their personality through individual products. Thus, manufacturers are forced to create product portfolios with an increasing wealth of variants, right down to the production of units of one. As a final consequence, many companies have to process their customers' demand individually. To address this opportunity, new technologies today provide several opportunities that have not been available before. Flexible manufacturing technologies have reduced the typical trade-off between individuality and efficiency. Modern information technology has enabled pervasive connectivity and direct interaction possibilities among individual customers and between customers and suppliers. This connectivity offers an enormous amount of additional flexibility. Yet despite all the technological advances, this is by no means a straightforward task. Particularly in today's highly competitive business environment, activities for serving customers have to be performed both efficiently and effectively at the same time.

Since the early 1990s, mass customisation has emerged as one leading idea for achieving precisely this objective. Davis, who initially coined the term in 1987, refers to mass customisation when 'the same large number of customers can be reached as in mass markets of the industrial economy, and simultaneously [. . .] be treated individually as in the customized markets of preindustrial economies' (Davis, 1987: 169). A more pragmatic definition was introduced by Tseng and Jiao (2001). According to them, mass customisation corresponds to 'the technologies and systems to deliver goods and services that meet individual customers' needs with near mass production efficiency' (Tseng & Jiao, 2001: 685). In the following, we define mass customisation in accordance with Joseph Pine (1993) as 'developing, producing, marketing, and delivering affordable goods and services with enough variety and customisation that nearly everyone finds exactly what they want'.

When the subject of mass customisation is raised, the successful business model of the computer supplier Dell is often cited as one of the most impressive examples. The growth and success of Dell is based on this firm's ability to produce custom computers on demand, meeting precisely the needs of each individual customer and producing these items, with no finished goods inventory risk, only after an order has been placed (and paid for).

But beyond Dell, there are many other examples of companies that have employed mass customisation successfully. Consider the following examples:

- Pandora Radio relieves people of having to channel surf through radio stations to find the music they like. Customers submit an initial set of their preferred songs, and from that information Pandora identifies a broader set of music that fits their preference profile and then broadcasts those songs as a custom radio channel. As of summer 2010, Pandora.com had 48 million listeners who created more than half a billion radio stations from the 700,000 tracks in its library and who listened for 11.6 hours per month on average.
- BMW customers can use an online toolkit to design the roof of a Mini Cooper with their very own graphics or picture, which is then reproduced with an advanced digital printing system on a special foil. The toolkit has enabled BMW to tap into the custom after-sales market, which was previously owned by niche companies. In addition, Mini Cooper customers can also choose from among hundreds of options for many of the car's components, as BMW is able to manufacture all cars on demand according to each buyer's individual order.
- American Power Conversion (APC) sells, designs, produces, and installs complex infrastructure systems for data centers (Hvam et al., 2008). Obviously, these systems need a large degree of customisation, with regard to the building environment where the data center is deployed and the performance and functional features of a particular technical setup. After changing from an engineer-to-order to a mass customisation strategy, APC saw a reduction of its overall delivery time for a complete system from around 400 to 16 days. Also, production costs were significantly reduced (by factors of 30–40 per cent). These drastic improvements were the result of implementing a modular product architecture and the mandatory use of a product configuration system for sales and order processing. In addition, modularisation also allowed the company to split its manufacturing into a mass production of standard components in the Far East, and an order-based final assembly at various production sites around the world within close customer proximity.

What do these examples have in common? Regardless of product category or industry, they have all turned customers' heterogeneous needs into an opportunity to create value, rather than regarding heterogeneity as a problem that has to be minimised, challenging the 'one size fits all' assumption of traditional mass production (Salvador et al., 2009). This is the essence of mass customisation and its foremost idea.

FROM CARS TO BUILDINGS

And how about buildings, architecture and urban systems? The individual creative architect, designing a unique solution for a client and the specific requirements and opportunities of a dedicated site for a specific project in a particular setting, can be considered as one of the fundamental applications of customised value creation. The same holds true for the design of urban spaces and structures as well as commercial premises and civil infrastructures which have always been driven by an ultimate, almost extreme degree of customisation.

So why a book about mass customisation in the built environment, defined as the building, construction, interior design, architecture and urban planning? Challenged by a global crisis, this industry is currently seeking new orientation and strategies. Stakeholders in the built environment are being forced at an extensive and unprecedented pace to improve a set of conflicting objectives. On one hand, they shall enhance the cost efficiency and economic sustainability of their constructions. As every builder and home owner will confirm, the robustness and efficiency of the building processes are often not given up on. There is a lot of (process) customisation, but no 'mass production efficiency'. On the other hand, the market demands that the functional performance, indoor quality, comfort levels and social sustainability of the buildings shall be increased. And at the same time, builders shall concentrate on the reduction of energy consumption, the ecological footprint of a building process and its carbon emission, boosting the environmental sustainability. This apparently conflicting set of goals demands a new industrial paradigm in the built environment.

In addition, the public is getting increasingly annoyed by the dominant design traditions which are reused over and over again, changing traditionally unique patterns of city landscapes into an exchangeable and increasingly standardised (not to say boring) system. So we do not need less, but more customisation in the built environment – but customisation that is delivered in a new and innovative way. Mass customisation could become the key strategy to meet this challenge and has been discussed recently in larger intensity in the communities of architecture and urban planning. Digital CAD technologies, the requirement for sustainable buildings, the advent of the 'New Pre-Fab' movement (illustrated by the successful exhibition in the MoMa New York), and new interaction technologies at the customer interface have enabled innovative entrepreneurs to establish new strategies for the larger built environment.

Consider the following examples of mass customisation in the built environment:

- Backed by the proprietary Toyota Production System, Toyota Homes was launched in the 1970s and soon afterwards developed and transferred the car production models and strategies to off-site production of housing. Toyota homes can be considered as a full application of the mass customisation system. Benefitting from a fully vertical integration of the production process, Toyota Homes have managed to accommodate all the expertise required for design, production and assembly of residential buildings. The market forefront of the system is a semi-self-contained configuration system which can be started off by the customers or in close collaboration with the sales team at Toyota Homes to help the customers customise their homes based on their needs and within the range of the configurable elements/options. The configuration is then automatically transferred into the production system (off-site manufacturing of all components on an assembly line).
- Shading devices on the outer facades of the Bibliothèque Nationale de France in Paris represent an example of customisable facade, where the users can choose to open or close the laminated vertical timber louvers to strike a balance between the desired level of natural lighting inside the building and the heat gain of the internal spaces, thereby maintaining the indoor comfort light and heat levels. When open, the light and the heat from the sun gets into the building, and when closed, the internal secondary facade performs as the internal layer of a double-skin facade, and the trapped heat can be ventilated out of the building. This facade is a typical application of an adaptable, hence customisable, building design.
- UK-based Yorkon is a manufacturer of steel-framed modular buildings. Extensively relying on its mother company Portakabin, a provider of modular buildings, Yorkon has established itself as a major player in the market of systemised, yet niche constructions. Portakabin's extensive system of mass produced modular units, construction site accommodation and events buildings has given Yorkon the opportunity to offer its clients more choice, while benefitting from economies of scale of the corresponding mass produced units. For example, Yorkon can offer a full range of the cladding options including regional stone, York stone, timber, brick, terracotta, render, metal and composite panels; or roof options including flat, pitched, vaulted and glazed, giving its client many design options. All these options, however, are being delivered at much lower cost than a traditional builder.

Yet despite these examples and the growing need for change in the construction industry, there has been no dedicated publication focusing on the topic of mass customisation in the built environment. Our book is a first start to provide a platform for a more focused discussion of its kind. We hope it will become a forum to illustrate applications and conceptual contributions on mass customisation and personalisation in the built environment, which have been around for some time, but where no documentation and intellectual debate has existed.

AN OVERVIEW OF THIS BOOK

Focusing on the customer or the end-user in the built environment, our book presents innovative strategies building on the idea of mass customisation and personalisation in the built environment. We want to equip service providers in, or facilitators of, the construction processes, from conception to completion and in its post-occupancy stages, with fresh ideas of what could be possible and of what is already there. Furthermore, this publication also seeks to address new concerns with reference to its main theme, including sustainability, zero-carbon construction and green design, information management and life cycle assessment. The scope also goes further to encompass innovative ideas and concepts which can potentially facilitate the application not only in the targeted context of this book, but also as a general strategy for other disciplines. The book is structured around four different areas.

PART I: PRINCIPLES OF MASS CUSTOMISATION

This part addresses the principles of mass customisation both as a production model and strategy and with reference to the built environment. In Chapter 2, Frank Piller provides a general introduction to the mass customisation concept, its background and its underlying fundamental capabilities: solution space definition, the design of robust processes and choice navigation. Focusing not on the domain of the built environment, but rather on the traditional fields of application of mass customisation, the chapter documents the state of the art of mass customisation in today's economy per se.

Chapter 3 transfers some of the advancements of mass customisation in service and manufacturing industries into the built environment. Poorang Piroozfar draws a comparative analysis between the two sectors to point out similarities and differences. This will enable a debate whether mass customisation and personalisation could successfully be applied in the building industry. While the answer apparently is 'yes', the chapter concludes with some practical guidelines for successful employment of customisation and personalisation strategies in the built environment in the future.

In Chapter 4, Steven Kendall provides an introduction into a core application of personalisation in the built environment, customised residential fit-out. Customisation of dwellings is intrinsic in built environments whose health results from acts of control by inhabitants, balancing acts of control by community powers. At the same time, property developers, government agencies and even citizen associations suppress customisation because they believe it is inefficient or 'out of (their) control'. Kendall explores this challenge and discusses how to make customisation efficient and harmonious. Residential fit-out is one solution.

In the last chapter of Part I, Eric Farr extends the scope of the discussion of moves from building to urban spaces and spatial entities. Chapter 5 explores why and how mass customisation of urban spaces and entities, coined 'spatial mass customisation', can be supported. The chapter investigates the types of urban spaces that can absorb mass as well as those urban entities with capacities for being customised. It then identifies the customisability of those urban entities that can be used to design, enhance or modify urban spaces, providing also a number of case examples.

PART II: ENABLING TECHNOLOGIES, DESIGNS, AND BUSINESS MODELS

The second part of the book focuses on the fundamental systems, technologies and economic models that form the intellectual underpinning of mass customisation in the built environment. This section consists of the following chapters.

In Chapter 6, Lars Hvam, Niels H. Mortensen, Christian Thuesen and Anders Haug describe system products and system deliveries as the core outcomes of product modularisation and product configuration – two of the key concepts of mass customisation. These concepts are discussed based on examples from both the construction industry and related industry. The description focuses partly on the product architecture and partly of the setup of the business processes by using 'Configure to Order' and 'Engineer to Order' processes.

Martin Bechthold, in Chapter 7, compares different products and processes along the stages of industrial development of the built environment, starting with the highly deterministic mass production paradigm. Next, strategies of how to achieve a limited amount of product variety with standard architectural and consumer products are reviewed. Then the product and process view will be extended to mass customisation. The chapter concludes with an overview about mass customisation as a business strategy for the future.

Chapter 8, by Kasper S. Vibæk, extends the perspective from modular components and manufacturing approaches towards architectural systems, an emerging type of integrated product delivery (IPD) systems in the building industry. IPDs are proposed as a means for handling design complexity by integrating design decisions into discrete industrialised products of matter, process and thought that can be configured and customised for a specific delivery and form part of unique construction projects. This can facilitate a more strategically focused design attention, and the combination of such discrete subsystems into 'assemblages' can theoretically form complete buildings.

Olga Popovic Larsen provides an example of a customisable building technology, 3D lightweight timber grid structures. In Chapter 9, she discusses the architectural potential and design/construction opportunities that these structures offer for the implementation of a mass customisation system. The chapter presents a case study with two lightweight timber structures involving the construction of two full-scale physical models: a gridshell and a multiple reciprocal frame structure, demonstrating the applications for customised buildings.

An alternative method to conventional construction is the large-scale deployment of industrialisation, enabled by applying automation and robotics based processes and technologies throughout all phases of the life cycle of built environments. Chapter 10, by Thomas Bock and Thomas Linner, provides an introduction to these systems. The authors present a number of best-practice projects which have been tested or applied successfully in larger scale during the last decades. The chapter concludes with a framework for combined on/off-site building production as an approach for managing sustainable and resource efficient construction processes.

Chapter 11 finally discusses some economic models that explain the economic benefits of applying mass customisation to the built environment. Guohua Tang and Mitchell M. Tseng use the case of customisable apartments in high-rise buildings in Hong Kong. With customised housing, customers have wider choices beyond the monolithic decision in traditional apartment housing. At the same time, however, developers are facing new challenges in deciding different business alternatives, such as what is the right mix of customisable attributes offered to customers, the appropriate range of choices, etc. This chapter addresses this challenge from an economic perspective by developing a decision framework based on discounted cash flows.

PART III: PRACTICAL APPLICATIONS, PROTOTYPES, AND EXPERIENCES

The third part of the book provides a more in-depth insight into some of the most prominent case studies of mass customisation and personalisation in the built environment. Some of these cases have developed into large-scale practical applications; others are still at the stage of a prototype or pilot. But in its entirety, the part provides a good overview of how mass customisation and personalisation is currently developing in buildings and urban planning.

Chapter 12 looks into some emerging trends and concepts of mass customisation in Taiwan's housing industry. Kung-Jen Tu and Hao-Yang Wei show two different examples of the application of mass customisation. The construction of new apartment buildings is moving from 'pure standardisation' towards 'segmented standardisation', while the housing remodeling industry is moving from 'pure customisation' towards 'tailored customisation'. The chapter hence illustrates two of the core paths towards mass customisation: increasing the efficiency of pure (craft) customisation by a more robust process design and enabling greater customer-centricity by adding customisation options to a previously standardised system.

Asia has been one of the strongest fields of application of mass customisation, as Chapter 13 demonstrates using the example of the Japanese building industry. Here a large-scale mass customisation system has evolved since the 1970s. Japanese prefabrication and construction automation are often considered as some of the most advanced strategies in the field. Thomas Linner and Thomas Bock provide an evolutionary view on the Japanese off-site construction industry and discuss why large-scale industrialisation and automated construction have been applied in Japan so successfully, while other environments did not manage to build up similar structures.

Chapter 14 stays in the context of Japan, but provides a more functional perspective on using mass customisation as a vehicle to deliver low-carbon housing. As Masa Noguchi argues, Japanese housing manufacturers have been at the forefront of the commercialisation of mass customisable homes which correspond with today's market needs for low to zero carbon dioxide (CO_2) emissions. The chapter provide an insight into the design, production and marketing approaches of this application.

Lawrence Sass and Daniel Smithwick provide an extreme case of mass customisation in the building industry in Chapter 15: the provision of mass customised structures for temporary relief shelters (or 'housing') for the population in need in post-Katrina New Orleans, produced via digital fabrication. This design system supports an interactive working process between building design, manufacture and assembly of small structures. Implicit in the work described in this chapter is the proposal that the process may be applied to any environment in need of new structures. From a technological perspective, the chapter provides a theoretical overview of a rule-based system used to convert a 3D digital design model into easy-to-assemble, interlocking wooden components.

Chapter 16 provides two final case studies of mass customisation in the building sector. Ingrid Paoletti describes the cases of Gehry's IAC New York office building and Gramazio and Kohler's Winery in Switzerland, where customisation and parametric design has enabled innovative building envelopes.

PART IV: FUTURE TOPICS, NEW POTENTIALS, AND EMERGING CHALLENGES

The contributions for this part provide an outlook of future topics and also discuss some of the challenges in applying mass customisation in the building discipline.

The 'Stylemachine' by Tomas Westerholm, presented in Chapter 17, is an innovative approach for mass customisation of block apartments via the internet. Web-based services as a data model of the business process, a database and a virtual back-end interface for managing the related information can form an ultimate solution for customisation and personalisation in the building industry. The chapter provides the perspective of a solution provider to assist both clients from the construction industry and end-users (consumers custom-ising their individual homes) in formulating their ideas in a web-based interface. The experiences of a current pilot application are being used to develop a roadmap of further research and potential applications.

Chapter 18, by Christian Thuesen, Jens S. Jensen and Stefan C. Gottlieb, takes a theoretical perspective and projects from a review of construction management practices during the past 50 years into the future of mass customisation in the built environment. Theoretically, the chapter builds on two fundamental insights: the Pareto principle and the Thomas theorem. The chapter concludes that if we allow ourselves to view buildings as both unique but also as standardised we can create a new platform for developing the construction industry.

Chapter 19 applies game theory as an established mathematical theory in economics to develop a further understanding of customisation strategies in the construction industry. Ghashang Piroozfar and Poorang Piroozfar show how informal rules can decrease the willingness to take shortcuts in fulfilling rules, regulations and requirements while enhancing customisation options. This approach may become the foundation of a future analysis of the field.

Chapter 20 provides an outlook into a future that already is here in the form of prototypes and first applications: the concept of 'digital forming'.

Assa Ashuach shows how this idea developed from a concept in 2005 into a commercial company in 2009 with the aim of unlocking product design and co-creativity online. Digital forming facilitates the design of everyday products, using synthesis of innovative 3D software solutions and additive manufacturing methods. With an on-demand production process, the conventional storage and logistic issues for mass produced items are removed.

IMPLEMENTING MASS CUSTOMISATION

In conclusion, the contributions in this book show that, when properly implemented, mass customisation delivers across-the-board improvements in all dimensions of operations strategy: responsiveness, price, quality and service (Ismail et al., 2007). Admittedly, the development of the corresponding capabilities to make this happen (refer to Chapter 2 for a more detailed discussion of these capabilities) mandates for organisational changes which are often difficult. In many organisations, powerful inertial forces often prevent the change towards a new business model. Managers and their employees often get accustomed to a dominant logic shaped by the attitudes, behaviors and assumptions that they have witnessed in their environments over a long time. Their mindset remains conditioned by managerial routines, systems and incentives created under the mass production framework. However, shifting the locus of value creation towards mass customisation and personalisation requires no less than a radical change in the management mindset (Forza & Salvador, 2006). Beyond all technological and economic tasks, overcoming this inertia to change may be the largest challenge of profiting from mass customisation thinking in the built environment. Here, we still see plenty of future work needing to be done in the field. So read on, this is just the beginning . . .

ACKNOWLEDGEMENTS

This book could have not been finalised without the help and contributions of numerous people. First of all, we would like to thank the authors of the individual chapters for their contributions. The book has been the result of a rather long process, and we thank you all for your patience and efforts to meet our deadlines and ever-changing requirements. Many of the original contributions in this book relate back to the special sessions on mass customisation in architecture at the 2007 (MIT, Cambridge, MA), 2009 (Alto University, Helsinki) and 2011 (UC Berkeley, CA) conferences on Mass Customisation, Personalisation and Co-Creation (MCPC). We thank all contributors to these tracks who have laid the foundation of this book.

We also thank the anonymous reviewers of the book proposal for their feedback, and the reviewers of all individual chapters who spent a large amount of their precious time in suggesting ideas for improvement and refinement.

We also owe a debt of gratitude to all people at Routledge/Taylor and Francis who provided support for this project. Especially Francesca Ford, the commissioning editor, and Laura Williamson, senior editorial assistant were always prepared to help us through with this challenging project. At RWTH Aachen, we thank Hanan El-Khouri who provided great editorial assistance in the final stage of the project.

Finally, we want to remember William J. Mitchell of MIT's School of Architecture and the Media Lab, and also the founding director of the MIT Smart Customisation Group. He envisioned the application of mass customisation and personalisation in architecture and urban planning long before these terms became buzzwords in the business press, and contributed many of the fundamental ideas and concepts that today are being put into practice in larger scale.

REFERENCES

Davis, S. (1987). *Future Perfect*. Reading, MA: Addison-Wesley.

Drucker, P. F. (1954). *The Practice of Management*. New York: Harper & Row.

Forza, C. and Salvador, F. (2006). *Product Information Management for Mass Customization: Connecting Customer, Front-office and Back-office for Fast and Efficient Customization*. London: Palgrave Macmillan.

Franke, N., Keinz, P. and Steger, C. (2009). Testing the value of customisation: When do customers really prefer products tailored to their preferences? *Journal of Marketing*, 73(5), 103–121.

Hvam, L., Mortensen, N. & Riis, J. (2008). Product customisation. New York: Springer.

Ismail, H., Reid, I. R., Mooney, J., Poolton, J. and Arokiam, I. (2007). How small and medium enterprises effectively participate in the mass customization game. *IEEE Transactions on Engineering Management*, 54(1), 86–97.

Pine, B. J. (1993). *Mass Customisation*. Boston: Harvard Business School Press.

Salvador, F., de Holan, M. and Piller, F. (2009). Cracking the code of mass customization. *MIT Sloan Management Review*, 50(3), 70–79.

Tseng, M. and Jiao, J. (2001). Mass customisation. In G. Salvendy (ed.), *Handbook of Industrial Engineering*. New York: Wiley, pp. 684–709.

Zuboff, S. and Maxmin, J. (2003). *The Support Economy*. London: Viking Penguin.

PART I

PRINCIPLES OF MASS CUSTOMISATION

2

Three capabilities that make mass customisation work

Frank T. Piller

ABSTRACT

Within the last two decades, mass customisation has emerged as a dominant business strategy. The goal of mass customisation is to efficiently provide customers what they want, when they want it. This chapter provides a general introduction to the mass customisation concept, its background, and its underlying fundamental capabilities: solution space definition, the design of robust processes, and choice navigation. The focus of this chapter will be less on the domain of architecture and the built environment, but rather on the traditional fields of applications. The chapter hence will serve as a framework for the analysis of mass customisation systems and the elements of such a system to make it work.

INTRODUCTION

The goal of mass customisation is to provide customers what they want, when they want it (Pine, 1993). However, to apply this apparently simple statement in practice is quite complex. As a business paradigm, mass customisation provides an attractive business proposition to add value by directly addressing customer needs and in the meantime utilising resources efficiently without incurring excessive cost. This is particularly important at a time where competition is no longer just based on price and conformance of dimensional quality. In our research we have found that the key to profiting from mass customisation is to see it as a set of organisational capabilities that can supplement and enrich an existing system. Companies mastering mass customisation successfully have built competences around a set of capabilities which are driving a sustainable mass customisation business. While specific answers on the nature and characteristics of these capabilities are clearly dependent on industry context or product characteristics, we found that from an aggregated view there are three fundamental groups of capabilities which determine the ability of a firm to mass customise (Salvador et al. 2008, 2009):

- *Solution space development.* First and foremost, a company seeking to adopt mass customisation has to be able to understand what the idiosyncratic needs of its customers are. This is in contrast to the approach of a mass producer, where the company focuses on identifying 'central tendencies' among its customers' needs, and targets them with a limited number of standard products. Conversely, a mass customiser has to identify the product attributes along which customer needs diverge the most. Once this is understood, the firm knows what is required to properly cover the needs of its customers. Consequently, it can draw up the so-called solution space, clearly defining what it is going to offer and what it is not.
- *Robust process design.* A second critical requirement for mass customisation is related to the relative performance of the value chain. Specifically, it is crucial that the increased variability in customers' requirements does not lead to significant deterioration in the firm's operations and supply chain (Pine et al., 1993). This demands a robust value chain design – defined as the capability to reuse or recombine existing organisational and value chain resources to fulfill differentiated customers' needs. With robust process design customised solutions can be delivered with near mass production efficiency and reliability.
- *Choice navigation.* Finally, the firm must be able to support customers in identifying their own problems and solutions, while minimising complexity and burden of choice. When a customer is exposed to too many choices, the cognitive cost of evaluation can easily outweigh the increased utility from having more choices (Huffman & Kahn, 1998; Piller, 2005). As such, offering more product choices can easily prompt customers to postpone or suspend their buying decisions. Therefore, the third requirement is the organisational capability to simplify the navigation of the company's product assortment from the customers' perspective.

The methods behind these capabilities are often not new. Some of them have been around for years. But successful mass customisation demands to combine these methods into capabilities in a meaningful and integrated way, to design a value chain that creates value from serving individual customers differently. In the following, we will discuss the three fundamental capabilities of mass customisation in larger detail.

SOLUTION SPACE DEVELOPMENT

A mass customiser must first identify the idiosyncratic needs of its customers, specifically, the product attributes along which customer needs diverge the most. This is in stark contrast to a mass producer, which must focus on serving universal needs, ideally shared by all the target customers. Once that information is known and understood, a business can define its 'solution space', clearly delineating what it will offer – and what it will not. This space determines what universe of benefits an offer is intended to provide to customers and then within that universe what specific permutations of functionality can be provided (Pine, 1995). To define the solution space, the company has to identify those needs where customers are different – and where they care about these differences. Matching the options represented by the solution space with the needs of the targeted market segment is a major success factor of mass customisation (Hvam et al., 2008). The core requirement at this stage is to access need information, i.e. information about preferences, needs, desires, satisfaction, motives, etc. of the potential customers and users of the product or service offering. Need information builds on an in-depth understanding and appreciation of the customers' requirements, operations, and systems. Spotting untapped differences across customers is not an easy task, because information about customers' unfulfilled needs is 'sticky' – that is, difficult to access and codify for the solutions provider (von Hippel, 1998). While this problem is shared by both mass producers and mass customisers, it is more demanding for the latter, because of the extreme fragmentation of customers' preferences. Understanding heterogeneous customer needs in terms of identifying differentiating attributes, validating product concepts, and collecting customer feedback can be a costly and complex endeavor, but several approaches can help.

The first is to engage in conventional market research techniques, i.e. to meticulously gather data from representative customers on a chosen market sector (e.g. Griffin & Hauser, 1993; Dahan & Hauser, 2002). This model is dominating especially in the world of consumer goods, where market research methodology such as focus groups, conjoint analysis, customer surveys, and analyses of customer complaints are used regularly to identify and evaluate customer needs and desires. Conjoint analysis in particular can be regarded as a tool suited to define a company's solution space in a mass customisation environment. The term denotes a set of methods to measure and analyse consumers' preferences by assessing their perception of the value of various attributes of a product (Green & Srinivasan, 1990). Previous research has developed methods for solution space definition in mass customisation which build on a conjoint analysis methodology (Chen & Tseng, 2005; Du et al., 2003; Siddique & Rosen, 2003). The main problem with conjoint analysis, and market research methods in general, however, is that it is well suited to gather market feedback about the potential value of proposed customisation options. But it is less suited to find which are the best options for customisation in the first place.

Another approach is to employ some form of 'customer experience intelligence', i.e. to apply methods for continuously collecting data on customer transactions, behaviors, or experiences and analysing that information to determine customer preferences. Social media and user generated content, e.g. on customer opinion forums, community websites, or user groups, are a very valuable source of information for latent needs that may not be fulfilled by the current 'mass produced' offerings. Methods like Netnography (Kozinets, 2002) allow the mass customiser to listen in to this voice of the customer at the beginning of the development of a solution space, or during its continuous refinement. This also includes incorporating data not just from customers, but also from people who might have taken their business elsewhere. Consider, for example, information about products that someone has evaluated, but did not order. A mass customiser often easily can obtain such data from log files generated by the browsing behavior of people using its online configurator (Piller et al., 2004; Squire et al., 2004). By systematically analysing that information, managers can learn much about customer preferences, ultimately leading to a refined solution space. A company could, for instance, eliminate options that are rarely explored or selected, and it could add more choices for the popular components.

Once the relevant options to be represented in a solution space have been identified (an iterative, continuous process that will continue as long as the mass customisation offering exists), it has to be transferred into a product architecture that will transform these needs into solutions for the customer. It is important to note that mass customisation does not mean to offer limitless choice, but to offer choice that is restricted to options that are already represented in the fulfillment system. In the case of digital goods (or components), customisation possibilities may be infinite. In the case of physical goods, however, they are limited and may be represented by a modular product architecture.

Modularity is an essential part of any mass customisation strategy (Duray, 2002; Gilmore & Pine, 1997; Kumar, 2005; Piller, 2005; Salvador, 2007). Each module serves one or more well-defined functions of the product and is available in several options that deliver a different performance level for the function(s) the product is intended to serve. This principle shows that mass customisation demands compromise: not all notional customisation options are being offered, but only those that are consistent with the capabilities of the processes, the given product architecture, and the given degree of variety.

The product family approach has been recognised as an effective means to accommodate an increasing product variety across diverse market niches while still being able to achieve economies of scale (Tseng & Jiao, 2001; Zhang & Tseng, 2007). In addition to leveraging the costs of delivering variety, product family design can reduce development risks by reusing proven elements in a firm's activities and offerings. The backdrop of a product family is a well-planned architecture – the conceptual structure and overall logical organisation of generating a family of products – providing a generic umbrella to capture and utilise commonality. Within this architecture, each new product is instantiated and extends to anchor future designs to a common product line structure. The rationale of such a product family architecture lies not only in unburdening the knowledge base from keeping variant forms of the same solution, but also in modeling the design process of a class of products that can widely variegate designs based on individual customisation requirements within a coherent framework (Tseng & Jiao, 2001). Setting the modular product family structure of a mass customisation system, and thus its solution space, becomes one of the foremost competitive capabilities of a mass customisation company.

ROBUST PROCESS DESIGN

A core idea of mass customisation is to ensure that an increased variability in customers' requirements will not significantly impair the firm's operational efficiency (Pine et al., 1993). This can be achieved through robust process design – the capability to reuse or recombine existing organisational and value-chain resources to deliver customised solutions with high efficiency and reliability. A successful mass customisation system hence is characterised by stable, but still flexible, responsive processes that provide a dynamic flow of products (Badurdeen & Masel, 2007; Pine, 1995; Salvador et al., 2004; Tu et al., 2001). Value creation within robust processes is the major differentiation of mass customisation versus conventional (craft) customisation. Traditional (craft) customisers reinvent not only their products, but also their processes for each individual customer. This comes at a high cost.

The core objective of robust process design is to counterbalance the additional cost resulting from the flexibility a company needs to serve its customers individually. We can differentiate two sources of additional cost of flexibility (Su et al., 2005): (i) increased complexity and (ii) increased uncertainty in business operations, which by implication results in higher operational cost. A higher level of product customisation requires greater product variety, which in turn entails greater number of parts, processes, suppliers, retailers, and distribution channels. A direct consequence of such proliferations is an increased complexity in managing all aspects of business from raw material procurement to production and eventually to distribution. Further, an increase in product variety has the effect of introducing greater uncertainty in demand realisations, increase in manufacturing cycle times, and increase in shipment lead times (Kumar & Piller, 2006; Yao et al., 2007). Increased system complexity and uncertainties (in demand and lead time) drive the operational cost upward due to more complex planning, greater hedging, increased resource usage, more complex production setups, diseconomies of scope, and higher distribution cost spread throughout the supply chain (Tseng & Piller, 2003).

Mass customisers use stable processes to deliver high-variety goods (Pine et al., 1993), which allows them to achieve 'near mass production efficiency', but it also implies that the customisation options are somehow limited. Customers are being served within a list of predefined options or components, the company's solution space. Building and executing in robust processes also is one of the dominant characteristics of mass customisation in the built environment where traditionally the nature of site fabrication has led to a highly crafted, often unstable and inventive approach to value creation. The idea of mass customisation is to provide a continuous stream of customised outcomes with a stable and efficient number of process elements.

A number of different methods can be employed to reduce these additional costs, or even to prevent their occurrence at all. A primary mechanism to create robust processes in mass customisation is the application of delayed product differentiation (postponement). Delayed product differentiation refers to partitioning the supply chain into two stages (Yang and Burns, 2003; Yang et al., 2004) A standardised portion of the product is produced based on forecasts, while the 'differentiated' portion of the product is based on each customer's preferences in the second stage. An example of delayed product differentiation in the automotive industry would be to send a standard version of the car (a stripped or partially equipped version) to dealers and then allow the dealer to install, on the basis of customer-specific requests, options like a CD/DVD player, the interior leather or fabric, and the cruise control system, etc. Prior to the point of differentiation, product parts are re-engineered so that as many parts or components of the products as possible are common to each configuration. Cost savings result from the risk-pooling effect and reduction in inventory stocking costs (Yang et al., 2004). Additionally, as common performance levels of functionalities are selected by a number of customers, economies of scale can be achieved at the modular level for each version of the module, generating cost savings not available in pure customisation-oriented production systems.

While postponement starts at the design of the offerings, another possibility to achieve robust processes is through flexible automation (Koste et al., 2004; Tu et al., 2001; Zhang et al., 2003). Although the words 'flexible' and 'automation' might have been contradictory in the past, that's no longer the case. In the auto industry, robots and automation are compatible with high levels of versatility and customisation. Even process industries (pharmaceuticals, food, and so on), once synonymous with rigid automation and large batches, nowadays enjoy levels of flexibility once considered unattainable. Similarly, many intangible goods and services also lend themselves to flexible automated solutions, oftentimes based on the internet. In the case of the entertainment industry, increasing digitalisation is turning the entire product system over from the real to the virtual world.

A complementary approach to flexible automation is process modularity, which can be achieved by thinking of operational and value-chain processes as segments, each one linked to a specific source of variability in the customers' needs (Pine et al., 1993). As such, the company can serve different customer requirements by appropriately recombining the process segments, without the need to create costly ad-hoc modules (Zhang et al., 2003). BMW's Mini factory, for instance, relies on individual mobile production cells with standard-ised robotic units. BMW can integrate the cells into an existing system in the plant within a few days, thus enabling the company to quickly adapt to un-expected swings in customer preferences without extensive modifications of its production areas. Process modularity can also be applied to service industries. IBM, for example, has been redesigning its consulting unit around configurable processes (called 'engagement models'). The objective is to fix the overall architecture of even complex projects while retaining enough adaptability to respond to the specific needs of a client.

To ensure the success of robust process designs, companies also need to invest in adaptive human capital (Bhattacharya et al., 2005). Specifically, employees and managers have to be capable of dealing with novel and ambiguous tasks in order to offset any potential rigidness that is embedded in process structures and technologies. Previous research revealed that, for example, individuals need a broad knowledge base that stretches beyond their immediate functional specialisation, in order to be able to proficiently interact with other functions in the process of identifying and delivering tailored solutions to the customer (Salvador et al., 2009). Such a broad knowledge base has to be complemented with relational attitudes that allow the individual to easily connect with other employees on an ad-hoc basis.

CHOICE NAVIGATION

Lastly, a mass customiser must support customers in identifying their own needs and creating solutions while minimising complexity and the burden of choice.

When a customer is exposed to myriad choices, the cost of evaluating those options can easily outweigh the additional benefit from having so many alternatives. The resulting syndrome has been called the 'paradox of choice' (Schwartz, 2004) in which too many options can actually reduce customer value instead of increasing it (Desmueles, 2002; Huffman & Kahn, 1998). In such situations, customers might postpone their buying decisions and, worse, classify the vendor as difficult and undesirable. Recent research in marketing has addressed this issue in more detail and has found that the perceived cognitive cost is one of the largest hurdles towards a larger adaption of mass customisation from the consumer perspective (Dellaert & Stremersch, 2005). To avoid that, companies have to provide means of choice navigation to simplify the ways in which people explore their offerings.

The traditional measure for navigating the customer's choice in a mass customisation system has been product configuration systems, also referred to as 'co-design toolkits' (Franke & Piller, 2003, 2004). Co-design activities are performed in an act of company-to-customer interaction and cooperation (Khalid & Helander, 2003). As early as 1991, Udwadia and Kumar were envisioning customers and manufacturers becoming 'co-constructors' (i.e. co-designers) of those products intended for each customer's individual use. In their view, co-construction would occur when customers had only a nebulous sense of what they wanted. Without the customers' deep involvement, the manufacturer would be unable to cater to each individualised product demand adequately. After this seminal publication, computer technology, particularly the capacity to simulate potential product designs before a purchase, has strongly enabled the collaborative effort (Haug & Hvam, 2007; Ulrich et al., 2003).

In mass customisation, co-design activities are in general performed with the help of dedicated systems. These systems are known as configurators, choice boards, design systems, toolkits, or co-design platforms (Forza & Salvador, 2006; Hvam et al., 2008). They are responsible for guiding the user through the elicitation process. Whenever the term configurator or configuration system is quoted in the literature, for the most part, it is used in a technical sense, usually addressing a software tool. The success of such an interaction system, however, is by no means defined solely by its technological capabilities but also by its integration into the sales environment, its ability to allow for learning, its ability to provide experience and process satisfaction, and its integration into the brand concept. Tools for user integration in a mass customisation system contain much more than arithmetic algorithms for combining modular components. Taking up an expression from von Hippel (2001), the more generic term 'toolkits for customer co-design' might better describe the diverse activities taking place (Franke & Piller, 2003). In a toolkit, different variants are represented, visualised, assessed, and priced with an accompanying learning-by-doing process for the user. The core idea is to engage customers into fast-cycle, trial-and-error learning processes (von Hippel, 1998). By engaging in multiple sequential experiments, customers can test the match between the available options, a particular configuration of these options, and their needs.

Choice navigation, however, does not just refer to preventing 'complexity of choice' and the negative effects of variety from the customers' perspective. Offering choice to customers in a meaningful way, on the contrary, can become a way for new profit opportunities (Franke & Schreier, 2010). Recent research has shown that up to 50 per cent of the additional willingness to pay for customised (consumer) products can be explained by the positive perception of the co-design process itself (Franke & Piller, 2004; Franke & Schreier, 2010; Merle et al., 2010; Schreier, 2006). Products co-designed by customers may also provide symbolic (intrinsic and social) benefits for them, resulting from the actual *process* of co-design rather than its outcome. Schreier (2006) quotes, for example, a pride-of-authorship effect. Customers may co-create something by themselves, which may add value due to the sheer enthusiasm about the result. This effect relates to the desire for uniqueness, as discussed before, but here it is based on a unique task and not the outcome. In addition to enjoyment, task accomplishment has a sense of creativity. Participating in a co-design process may be considered a highly creative problem-solving process by the individuals engaged in this task, thus becoming a motivator to purchase a mass custom-isation product.

An important precondition for customer satisfaction derived from co-design is that the process itself should be felicitous and successful. The customer has to be capable of performing the task. This competency issue involves flow, a construct often used by researchers to explain how customer participation in a process increases satisfaction (Csikszentmihalyi, 1990). Flow is the process of optimal experience achieved when motivated users perceive a balance between their skills and the challenge at hand during an interaction process (Novak et al., 2000). Interacting with a co-design toolkit may lead exactly to this state, as recent research in marketing indicates (e.g., Dellaert & Stremersch, 2005; Fuchs et al., 2010; Franke et al., 2008). Accordingly, recent research has recom-mended several design parameters of a configurator that should facilitate this effect of process satisfaction (Dellaert & Dabholkar, 2009; Franke et al., 2009; Randall et al., 2005).

Besides the application of toolkits, a number of other approaches exist, too. One effective approach is a need-based matching strategy (Salvador et al., 2009), in which software automatically builds configurations for customers by matching models of their needs with characteristics of existing solution spaces (i.e. sets of options). Then customers only have to evaluate the predefined configurations, which saves considerable effort and time in the search process.

But customers might not always be ready to make a decision after they've received recommendations. They might not be sure about their real preferences, or the recommendations may not appear to fit their needs. In such cases, combining a recommendation system with a co-design toolkit is a perfect solution.

A number of companies are engaging in even more innovative and drastic approaches to choice navigation. Choice navigation has been completely automated in recent products that 'understand' how they should adapt to the user and then reconfigure themselves accordingly. Equipped with so-called 'embedded configuration capability', the products paradoxically become stand-ard items for the manufacturer while the user experiences a customised solution (Piller et al., 2010). Such is the case with Adidas One, a running shoe equipped with a magnetic sensor, a system to adjust the cushioning and a microprocessor to control the process. When the shoe's heel strikes the ground, the sensor measures the amount of compression in its mid-sole and the microprocessor calculates whether the shoe is too soft or too firm for the wearer. A tiny motor then shortens or lengthens a cable attached to a plastic cushioning element, making it more rigid or pliable. With this system, the sport shoe is continuously adapting to different user needs during its usage stage – without any custom-isation in the manufacturing process.

CONCLUSIONS

Mass customisation has provided a viable framework in diverse industries to address the opportunity to turn heterogeneous customer demands into a profit driver. But the three capabilities presented in this chapter should be considered a journey rather than a destination. There is not a 'perfect' state of mass custom-isation (Salvador et al., 2009). What matters to most companies instead is to continuously increase their overall capabilities to define the solution space, to design robust processes, and to help customers navigate through available choices. A company may already profit tremendously from just implementing better, say, choice navigation capabilities to match diverse requests of customers not familiar with the product category. We have called this understanding *mass customisation thinking* (Piller & Tseng, 2010). It provides a way to profit from heterogeneities of a firm's customers. Mass customisation thinking means to build the three capabilities outlined before and to apply them for designing a value chain that creates value from serving customers individually. The follow-ing chapters of this book will explore and discuss how mass customisation thinking can be transferred to architecture, construction, and the built environ-ment, which are good cases to illustrate this transfer, and what are the open challenges.

NOTE

This chapter builds on the argumentation developed in Piller (2008) and Salvador et al. (2009).

BIBLIOGRAPHY

Badurdeen, F. and Masel, D. (2007). A modular minicell configuration for mass customization manufacturing. *International Journal of Mass Customization*, 2(1/2), 39–56.

Bhattacharya, M., Gibson, D. E., and Doty, H. (2005). The effects of flexibility in employee skills, employee behaviors, and human resource practices on firm performance. *Journal of Management*, 31(4), 622–640.

Chen, S. and Tseng, M. (2005). Defining specifications for custom products: a multi-attribute negotiation approach. *CIRP Annals*, 54(1), 299–304.

Csikszentmihalyi, M. (1990). *Flow: The Psychology of Optimal Experience*. New York: Harper and Row.

Dahan, E. and Hauser, J. (2002). The virtual customer. *Journal of Product Innovation Management*, 19(5), 332–353.

Dellaert, B. G. and Dabholkar, P. (2009). Increasing the attractiveness of mass customization: the role of complementary online services and range of options. *International Journal of Electronic Commerce*, 13 (2), 43–70.

Dellaert, B. G. C. and Stremersch, S. (2005). Marketing mass customized products: striking the balance between utility and complexity. *Journal of Marketing Research*, 43(2), 219–227.

Desmueles, R. (2002). The impact of variety on consumer happiness: marketing and the tyranny of freedom. *Academy of Marketing Science Review*, 12, 1–18. Available online at: http://www.amsreview.org/articles/desmeules12-2002.pdf (last accessed on 12 December 2012).

Du, X., Jiao, J., and Tseng, M. (2003). Identifying customer need patterns for customization and personalization. *Integrated Manufacturing Systems*, 14(5), 387–396.

Duray, R. (2002). Mass customization origins: mass or custom manufacturing? *International Journal of Operations and Production Management*, 22(3), 314–330.

Forza, C. and Salvador, F. (2006). *Product Information Management for Mass Customization: Connecting Customer, Front-office and Back-office for Fast and Efficient Customization.* London: Palgrave Macmillan.

Franke, N. and Piller, F. (2003). Key research issues in user interaction with configuration toolkits in a mass customization system. *International Journal of Technology Management*, 26, 578–599.

Franke, N. and Piller, F. (2004). Toolkits for user innovation and design: an exploration of user interaction and value creation. *Journal of Product Innovation Management*, 21(6), 401–415.

Franke, N. and Schreier, M. (2010). Why customers value self-designed products: the importance of process effort and enjoyment. *Journal of Product Innovation Management*, 27(7), 1020–1031.

Franke, N., Keinz, P., and Schreier, M. (2008). Complementing mass customization toolkits with user communities: how peer input improves customer self-design. *Journal of Product Innovation Management*, 25(6), 546–559.

Franke, N., Keinz, P., and Steger, C. (2009). Testing the value of customization: when do customers really prefer products tailored to their preferences? *Journal of Marketing*, 73(5), 103–121.

Fuchs, C., Schreier, M., and Prandelli, E. (2010). The psychological effects of empowerment strategies on consumers' product demand. *Journal of Marketing*, 74(1), 65–79.

Gilmore, J. H. and Pine, B. J. (1997). The four faces of mass customization. *Harvard Business Review*, 75(1), 91–101.

Green, P. and Srinivasan, V. (1990). Conjoint analysis in marketing research. *Journal of Marketing*, 54(4), 3–19.

Griffin, A. and Hauser, J. (1993). The voice of the customer. *Marketing Science*, 12(1), 1–27.

Haug, A. and Hvam, L. (2007). Modeling techniques of a documentation system that supports the development and maintenance of product configuration systems. *International Journal of Mass Customization*, 2(1/2), 1–18.

Huffman, C. and Kahn, B. (1998). Variety for sale: mass customization or mass confusion? *Journal of Retailing*, 74(4), 491–513.

Hvam, L., Mortensen, N., and Riis, J. (2008). *Product Customization*. New York: Springer.

Ismail, H., Reid, I. R., Mooney, J., Poolton, J., and Arokiam, I. (2007). How small and medium enterprises effectively participate in the mass customization game. *IEEE Transactions on Engineering Management*, 54(1), 86–97.

Khalid, H. M. and Helander, M. G. (2003). Web-based do-it-yourself product design. In M. Tseng and F. Piller (eds), *The Customer Centric Enterprise: Advances in Mass Customization and Personalization*. New York: Springer, pp. 247–266.

Kozinets, R. (2002). The field behind the screen: using Netnography for marketing research in online communities. *Journal of Marketing Research*, 39(1), 61–72.

Koste, L. L., Malhotra, M. K., and Sharma, S. (2004). Measuring dimensions of manufacturing flexibility. *Journal of Operations Management*, 22(2), 171–196.

Kumar, A. (2005). Mass customization: metrics and modularity. *International Journal of Flexible Manufacturing Systems*, 16(4), 287–312.

Kumar, A. and Piller, F. (2006). Mass customization and financial services. *Journal of Financial Transformation*, 18(3), 125–131.

Merle, A., Chandon, J., Roux, E., and Alizon, F. (2010). Perceived value of the mass-customized product and mass customization experience for individual consumers. *Production and Operations Management*, 19(5), 503–514.

Novak, T., Hoffmann, D., and Yung, Y. (2000). Measuring the customer experience in online environments: a structural modeling approach. *Marketing Science*, 19(1), 22–42.

Piller, F. (2005). Mass customization: reflections on the state of the concept. *International Journal of Flexible Manufacturing Systems*, 16(4), 313–334.

Piller, F. (2008). Mass customization. In C. Wankel (ed.), *The Handbook of 21st Century Management*, Thousands Oaks, CA: Sage Publications, pp. 420–430.

Piller, F., Ihl, C., and Steiner, F. (2010). Embedded toolkits for user co-design: a technology acceptance study of product adaptability in the usage stage. *Proceedings of the 43th Hawaii International Conference on System Science (HICSS)*, 43(1), 1–10.

Piller, F., Möslein, K., and Stotko, C. (2004). Does mass customization pay? An economic approach to evaluate customer integration. *Production Planning and Control*, 15(4), 435–444.

Piller, F., Reichwald, R., and Tseng, M. (2006). Competitive advantage through customer centric enterprises. *International Journal of Mass Customization (IJMassC)*, 1(2/3), 157–165.

Piller, F. and Tseng, M. (2010). Mass customization thinking: moving from pilot stage to an established business strategy. In F. Piller and M. Tseng (eds), *Handbook of Research in Mass Customization and Personalization, Part 1: Strategies and Concepts.* New York and Singapore: World Scientific Publishing, pp. 1–18.

Pine, B. J. (1993). *Mass Customization.* Boston: Harvard Business School Press.

Pine, B. J. (1995). Challenges to total quality management in manufacturing. In J. W. Cortada and J. A. Woods (eds), *The Quality Yearbook.* New York: McGraw-Hill, pp. 69–75.

Pine, B. J., Victor, B., and Boynton, A.C. (1993). Making mass customization work. *Harvard Business Review*, 71(5), 108–119.

Randall, T., Terwiesch, C., and Ulrich, K. (2005). Principles for user design of customized products. *California Management Review*, 47(4), 68–85.

Salvador, F. (2007). Towards a product modularity construct: literature review and reconceptualization. *IEEE Transactions on Engineering Management*, 54(2), 219–240.

Salvador, F. and Forza, C. (2007). Principles for efficient and effective sales configuration design. *International Journal of Mass Customization*, 2(1/2), 114–127.

Salvador, F., de Holan, M., and Piller, F. (2009). Cracking the code of mass customization. *MIT Sloan Management Review*, 50(3), 70–79.

Salvador, F., Rungtusanatham, M., and Forza, C. (2004). Supply-chain configurations for mass customization. *Production Planning and Control*, 15(4), 381–397.

Salvador, F., Rungtusanatham, M., Akpinar, S., and Forza, C. (2008). Strategic capabilities for mass customization: theoretical synthesis and empirical evidence. *Proceedings of Academy of Management Annual Meeting* (August 2008), 1–6.

Schreier, M. (2006). The value increment of mass-customized products: an empirical assessment. *Journal of Consumer Behavior*, 5(4), 317–327.

Schwartz, B. (2004). *The Paradox of Choice: Why More is Less.* New York: Ecco.

Sheth, J. N., Sisodia, R. S., and Sharma, A. (2000). The antecedents and consequences of customer-centric marketing. *Journal of the Academy of Marketing Science*, 28(1), 55–66.

Siddique, Z. and Rosen, D. (2003). Common platform architecture: identification for a set of similar products. In M. Tseng and F. Piller (eds), *The Customer Centric Enterprise: Advances in Mass Customization and Personalization.* New York: Springer, pp. 163–182.

Squire, B., Readman, J., Brown, S., and Bessant, J. (2004). Mass customization: the key to customer value? *Production Planning and Control*, 15(4), 459–471.

Su, J. C. P., Chang, Y., and Ferguson, M. (2005). Evaluation of postponement structures to accommodate mass customization. *Journal of Operations Management*, 23(3/4), 305–318.

Tseng, M. and Jiao, J. (2001). Mass customization. In G. Salvendy (ed.), *Handbook of Industrial Engineering.* New York: Wiley, pp. 684–709.

Tseng, M. M., Jiao, R. J., and Wang, C. (2010). Design for mass personalization. *CIRP Annals Manufacturing Technology*, 59(1), 175–179.

Tseng, M. and Piller, F. (2003). The customer centric enterprise. In M. Tseng and F. Piller (eds), *The Customer Centric Enterprise: Advances in Mass Customization and Personalization.* New York: Springer, pp. 1–18.

Tu, Q., Vonderembse, M. A., and Ragu-Nathan, T. S. (2001). The impact of time-based manufacturing practices on mass customization and value to customer. *Journal of Operations Management*, 19(2), 201–217.

Udwadia F. E. and Kumar, R. (1991). Impact of customer co-construction in product/service markets. *International Journal of Technological Forecasting and Social Change*, 40, 261–272.

Ulrich, P., Anderson-Connell, L., and Wu, W. (2003). Consumer co-design of apparel for mass customization. *Journal of Fashion Marketing and Management*, 7(4), 398–412.

von Hippel, E. (1998). Economics of product development by users: the impact of 'sticky' local information. *Management Science*, 44(5), 629–644.

von Hippel, E. (2001). Perspective: user toolkits for innovation. *Journal of Product Innovation Management*, 18(4), 247–257.

Yang, B. and Burns, N. D. (2003). Implications of postponement for the supply chain. *International Journal of Production Research*, 41(9), 2075–2090.

Yang, B., Burns, N. D., and Backhouse, C. J. (2004). Postponement: a review and an integrated framework. *International Journal of Operations and Production Management*, 24(5), 468–487.

Yao, S., Han, X., Yang, Y., and Rong, Y. (2007). Computer-aided manufacturing planning for mass customization. *International Journal of Advanced Manufacturing Technology*, 32(1/2), 194–204.

Zhang, M. and Tseng, M. (2007). A product and process modeling based approach to study cost implications of product variety in mass customization. *IEEE Transactions on Engineering Management*, 54(1), 130–144.

Zhang, Q., Vonderembse, M. A., and Lim, J-S. (2003) Manufacturing flexibility: defining and analyzing relationships among competence, capability, and customer satisfaction. *Journal of Operations Management*, 21(2), 173–191.

3

Advancements of mass customisation in service and manufacturing industries: lessons for the built environment

Poorang Piroozfar

ABSTRACT

Mass customisation is a well-known strategy in manufacturing and service industries but still has to be investigated in the built environment, architecture and construction with reference to the specifics of those disciplines. The two mainstreams – the manufacture/service industries and the building industry – are fundamentally different in terms of the final product, the production process, the cash flow and the value chain amongst many other aspects. Building upon the existing literature of mass customisation in the pioneering industries, this chapter investigates those achievements with an aim to facilitate their transfer and employment in the construction industry. It draws a comparative analysis between the two sectors to point out similarities and differences. This helps show the way forward if any attempt towards mass customisation and personalisation is to be successfully made in the building industry. It subsequently outlines the feasibilities and obstacles in the way of application of those strategies in the built environment. Finally the chapter concludes with some practical guidelines for successful employment of customisation and personalisation strategies in the built environment in the future.

INTRODUCTION

The construction industry is less receptive to new ideas and emerging concepts than its sister industries, hence slower to embrace change, evolve and improve (Piroozfar 2008). The need for learning from other sectors of industry has now long been acknowledged (Herbert 1984; Latham 1994; Egan 1998; Kieran and Timberlake 2004; Willis and Woodward 2006; Celento 2007). In response to these calls, numerous research projects have been undertaken to pace up the construction industry with new technologies and cutting edge concepts in pioneering industries. With a reasonable boost in research during the recent years, mass customisation (with particular focus on the production/fabrication process) has been no exception (see for instance the works of the contributors to this book). This chapter outlines what has already started in this process of learning and what more needs to be learnt.

CUSTOMISATION 'AS IS'

Prone to have all the requirements of a 'paradigm shift' (Barker 1993), mass customisation was initially described as such (Pine 1993). However, much more detailed epistemological deliberation would be needed, had mass customisation been aimed to be introduced as a real 'paradigm shift'. Beyond any philosophical discussion, the immediate implication of customisation is the cost. Jiao and Tseng (2004) study design customisability, process customisability and perceived value of customisation as required features for justification of cost effectiveness of customisation. Market study shows that customers are willing to pay a premium of 10–30 per cent on customised shoes (Piller and Muller 2004) and up to 100 per cent premium for customised watches (Franke and Piller 2004). Kaplan et al. (2007) show that there is a significant direct influence of base category consumption frequency and need satisfaction on customers' behavioural intention to adopt a customised product.

Personalisation vs. customisation

Vesanen and Raulas (2006) draw analytical comparison between personalisation and customisation, suggest that customisation is an element of personalisation and show how the different phases of personalisation – customer interactions, analyses of customer data, customisation based on customer profiles and targeting of marketing activities – are linked. This, however, does not invalidate the fact that customisation relies highly on customer–firm collaboration as a strategy to create value by some form of company–customer interaction at the fabrication/assembly stage of the operations level to create customised products with production cost and monetary price similar to those of mass produced products (Kaplan and Haenlein 2006).

Customer/user collaboration

Collaboration and participation of users/customers have been celebrated through user innovation (von Hippel 1978, 1986, 1988; Bogers et al. 2010), learning from customers (Payne et al. 2007, 2009) and web-based and advanced ICT (Prandelli et al. 2006; Lichtenthaler 2008) which have facilitated new forms of co-creation (Prahalad and Ramaswamy 2000, 2004) and open innovation (Chesbrough 2003, 2006). Piller et al. (2004) suggested five degrees of customer integration with regard to their contribution to value creation.

Irrespective of different theories and concepts in/of management behind the concepts of collaboration and innovation or those directly formed to model collaboration (for instance Payne et al. 2007; Etgar 2008; Ojanen and Hallikas 2009), if any collaboration is to be successful in addition to what is required at customer/user level, there are requirements at other levels:

- At external level: driving (or restraining) forces of, for instance, the market (which in this study is posited as constant),
- At product level: at design, production and post-production stages (such as the platform, modularity, product families, etc.),
- At process level: factors such as process management, organisation, flexibility, etc.; and finally,
- At intermediary level: ICT, and knowledge and information management strategies, etc.

Platform design and product families

There is a notable difference between definitions of what constitutes a platform even between different members of one manufacturing sector, for instance between Ford and VW (Dahmus et al. 2001). Muffatto (1999) refers to Meyer and Lehnerd's (1997) broad definition of a platform as a relatively large set of product components that are physically connected as a stable sub-assembly and are common to different final models. He then provides a brief yet systemic overview of its associated core concepts such as product architecture, modularisation and standardisation (Muffatto 1999). Product platform, product family and design alternatives have been investigated by Yan et al. (2005) as the definition stage in design development to delve into customisation stage; transforming the specific customer information into the devised platform. Alizon et al. (2009) assert that not only did Ford use a platform for Model T (which is now adopted by today's leading car manufacturers such as in GM's Skateboard Platform or in VW's A-Platform), but it has also been a perfect exemplar of a fully mass customised product thanks to its average five new products per year, its 5000 optional gadgets and its specific models tailored to final customers' needs. According to Simpson (2004) designers are able to handle variety within a platform through modular-based design or scale-based design. The role of a platform in facilitating customisation should not be limited to a physical platform since user-centred Web 2.0 services also provide a platform for participation in content development since buyers and sellers are actively involved in value creation (Helms et al. 2008).

Modularisation and product architecture

According to Pine (1993) modularity is a key to achieving mass customisation. It provides a means for standardisation of repetitive components. As a result, parts of the product can be mass produced as standard modules and niche products as a combination or modification of the modules. Six types of modularity are very well known across the customisation domain (Abernathy and Utterback 1978; Ulrich and Tung 1991; Pine 1993 and others). Duray et al. (2000) argue that the essence of mass customisation lies, first, in mass customisers having a means for including each customer's specifications in the product design and, second, in utilising modular design to achieve manufacturing efficiencies to approximate standard mass produced products. They developed a conceptual typology of customisation based on customer involvement and type of modularity in different stages of design, fabrication,

3.1 Module-based product family design for mass customisation (Zha and Sriram 2006)

assembly and use. This includes fabricators, involvers, modularisers and assemblers, with fabricators most closely resembling craft producers and assemblers most similar to mass producers. Dahmus et al. (2001) suggest that system architecture involves clustering various components in a product such that the resulting modules are effective for the company. An ideal architecture is one that partitions the product into practical and useful modules. Stone et al. (1998) introduced a set of three heuristics to identify product modules on a function structure: dominant flow, branching flows and conversion–transmission. Zha and Sriram (2006) suggest module-based product family design for mass customisation as indicated in Figure 3.1.

ICT

The process design should precede (Davenport et al. 2004; Sommer 2004) or at least coincide with (Vesanen and Raulas 2006) IT provision. Utilisation of ICT to assist customisation through participation (i.e. open innovation, co-creation, etc.) is well documented (von Hippel and Katz 2002; von Hippel 2005; Leimeister et al. 2009; Zwass 2010). Fuller et al. (2010) highlighted the importance of virtual tools and technologies in consumer empowerment which in return will enhance the trust in the firms who offer co-creation and enhance customers' willingness to participate. ICT, therefore, guarantees the delivery of value to customers who are motivated to participate through monetary reward, recognition, challenge or intrinsic interest (Fuller 2010). Yao et al. (2007) demonstrate how computer-aided manufacturing planning (CAMP) can be used for mass customisation as a computerised tool to support rapid design and simulation of manufacturing systems.

Knowledge and information management

Knowledge management is invaluable to mass customisation for it helps provide frameworks and infrastructure for knowledge creation, knowledge distribution and knowledge-based innovation regarding customers (Helms et al. 2008). Franke and Piller (2004), Franke et al. (2006) and Elofson and Robinson (2007) have explored the effects of customer knowledge and capabilities on new product design. However, the traditional knowledge acquisition process is not always the best choice because of lack of a standardised and systemic approach, inflexibility and also incapability of handling tacit knowledge. What was suggested by Rugg and McGeorge (1995) as 'Laddering' was an early alternative. Raman (2006) suggests Web 2.0 applications, including wikis and blogs, are receiving much attention for their use as a collaboration tool. Warkentin et al.'s study (2001) indicates e-knowledge networks as key in inter-organisational collaborative e-businesses, linking knowledge management and e-commerce. However, it is important to ensure that knowledge management technologies deliver the right (amount of) information to the right person at the right time (Malhotra 2000).

FRAME OF REFERENCE

Piaget (1973) in his model of 'assimilation' and 'accommodation' used the notion of schemata and sense-data; the internal world in one's mind and the mind dependent external world. While in 'assimilation' the external perception will need to transform to fit into the internal dimensions of the mind, in 'accommodation', by contrast, the mind's preconception normally needs to lend itself to modification to be able to accommodate the external (mind dependent) existence. The two, however, are almost always in a dialectical relationship. Schemata may be referred to as a subordinate analogy of 'frame of reference'. Our discussion here follows the same dialectic to assimilate and accommodate mass customisation – as an external sense-data – in our internal frame of reference or schemata; i.e. the built environment.

CUSTOMISATION-TO-BE

In an earlier paper I compared the construction industry with its pioneering sister industries (see Figure 3.2) and marked out 11 differences which would have influenced the ways mass customisation could be applied in architecture and the built environment. These include: size, customers' proportional and dimensional interaction with the product, mobility, the concept of variation, product life cycle, costs, economies of scale, customers' needs and expectations, the ownership (first customers vs. future owners), the supply chain (or the sequence of procurement–order–design–fabrication–assembly–delivery–use–disassembly) and finally the concept of modularisation in the building industry (Piroozfar 2005).

Taking into account all the inherent differences between the building and other industries, if mass customisation (or any process-oriented, off-site or modern method of construction) is to be successfully implemented in the built environment, architecture and construction, the new movement which has already started in the building discipline needs to be invigorated and established through:

- Closer inter-, cross- and intra-professional participation
- A vertical integration of the production, fabrication and assembly processes

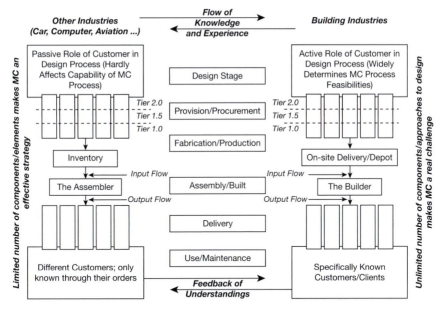

3.2 Comparative flow of work in building and other industries (Piroozfar 2005)

- A new multi-layered approach to building
- A new modular concept and a new definition of modularity
- A clearly defined type and level of customisation with regard to building type, functionality, use, life span, user classification, level of flexibility needed, as well as level of complexity of the project (both process-wise and product-wise)
- A new approach to zoning of structures and building services
- A new component and products clustering method/system
- A new definition of interface and interface design
- Application of the concept of platform and platform design
- Setting a new evaluation framework based on Performance Quality Indicators (PQI) and User Value-Added Viewpoints (UVAV)
- A bottom-up approach rather than a top-down one
- Clarification of what can be customised at design, fabrication, assembly and post-occupancy stages of a building
- Wider, smarter and more responsive use of ICT (such as online real-time networked platforms, BIM applications, parametric design, digital fabrication, cloud-based applications etc.) and new manufacturing technologies (such as rapid prototyping, digital craftsmanship, digital fabrication, generative component design, CNC technologies, etc.).

DISCUSSION AND CONCLUSION

There are discrepancies between the industry standard jargons in construction and other major industries. Hence the perception, deployment, application and expectations of personalisation and customisation in the two are and should be different. There is a crucial need for re-reading what is involved and an interpretation mechanism when and if those borrowed concepts are to be implemented successfully in the built environment, architecture and construction.

Customisation should be comprehended accordingly in different sectors of the building industry. This is controversial because for instance in the domestic sector, in which a deeper and higher level of customisation is normally desired, the ownership term may defeat the purpose. While in the non-domestic sector where restriction on configurations is higher, hence the level of customisation is understood to be lower, the use periods may easily exceed that of the domestic sector.

Customisation in the building industry should be implemented incrementally and using a bottom-up approach. Now that a proper perspective of the concept has been developed, a reflection on what has gone right and what has not, and a catch-up plan with the latest achievements, emerging concepts and future opportunities in service and manufacturing industries can help the construction industry to build on those strengths. This has a potential advantage which might be worthwhile contemplating as the construction industry could be deemed traditionally strong in some of the latest strategies fuelled or initiated by customisation. This could help, had we had a good collective memory and been willing to retrieve and learn from our own past.

The type of personalisation and customisation, or any of their correlated concepts or strategies, needs to be seen, worked out and decided based on a multi-criteria decision support system. This does not necessarily call for a complex computer application as this may result in loss of the required soft technology in the process. By contrast, this is a very human-oriented mechanism which needs to take into account what was introduced in this chapter yet should be open to personal interpretation and prioritisation of specifications, requirements and resources. It is possible to devise a rule-based toolkit to assist the decision maker (at any particular level) but such a toolkit would not be an ordinary one which blindly gives certain rigid answers.

And last but not least, personalisation and customisation should be personalised and/or customised, should they be aimed to be employed in the built environment, architecture and construction successfully.

REFERENCES

Abernathy, W. J. and Utterback, J. M. (1978), 'Patterns of industrial innovation', *Technology Review*, June/July 1978.

Alizon, F., Shooter, S. B. and Simpson, T. W. (2009), 'Henry Ford and the Model T: Lessons for product platforming and mass customization', *Design Studies*, 30(5): 588–605.

Barker, J. A. (1993), *Paradigms: The Business of Discovering the Future*, New York, HarperBusiness.

Bogers, M., Afuah, A. and Bastian, B. (2010), 'Users as innovators: a review, critique, and future research directions', *Journal of Management*, 36: 857–875.

Celento, D. (2007), 'Innovate or perish: new ways of designing and building in the coming marketplace for architecture', *Harvard Design Magazine*, Winter/Spring 2007.

Chesbrough, H. W. (2003), *Open Innovation: The New Imperative for Creating and Profiting from Technology*. Boston, MA: Harvard Business School Press.

Chesbrough, H. W. (2006), 'New puzzles and new findings', in: H. Chesbrough, W. Vanhaverbeke and J. West (eds), *Open Innovation: Researching a New Paradigm*, Oxford University Press, Oxford.

Dahmus, J. B., Gonzalez-Zugasti, J. P. and Otto, K. N. (2001), 'Modular product architecture', *Design Studies*, 22(5): 409–424.

Davenport, T. H., Harris, J. G. and Cantrell, S. (2004), 'Enterprise systems and ongoing process change', *Business Process Management Journal*, 10(1): 16–26.

Duray, R., Ward, P. T., Milligan, G. W. and Berry, W. L. (2000), 'Approaches to mass customization: configurations and empirical validation', *Journal of Operations Management*, 18: 605–625.

Egan, J. (1998), *Rethinking Construction: Report of the Construction Task Force*, London, HMSO.

Elofson, G. and Robinson, W. N. (2007), 'Collective customer collaboration impacts on supply-chain performance', *International Journal of Production Research*, 45: 2567–2594.

Etgar, M. (2008), 'A descriptive model of the consumer co-production process', *Journal of the Academy of Marketing Science*, 36(1): 97–108.

Franke, N. and Piller, F. (2004), 'Value creation by toolkits for user innovation and design: the case of the watch market', *Journal of Product Innovation Management*, 21: 401–415.

Franke, N., von Hippel, E. and Schreier, M. (2006), 'Finding commercially attractive user innovations: a test of leaduser theory', *Journal of Product Innovation Management*, 23: 301–315.

Fuller, J. (2010), 'Refining virtual co-creation from a consumer perspective', *California Management Review*, 52(2): 98–123.

Fuller, J., Muhlbacher, H., Matzler, K. and Jawecki, G. (2010), 'Consumer empowerment through Internet-based co-creation', *Journal of Management Information Systems*, 26(3): 71–102.

Helms, M. M., Ahmadi, M., Jih, W. J. K. and Ettkin, L. P. (2008), 'Technologies in support of mass customization strategy: exploring the linkages between e-commerce and knowledge management', *Computers in Industry*, 59(4): 351–363.

Herbert, G. (1984), *The Dream of the Factory-made House: Walter Gropius and Konrad Wachsmann*, Cambridge, Mass, MIT Press.

Jiao, J. and Tseng, M. M. (2004), 'Customizability analysis in design for mass customization', *Computer-Aided Design*, 36: 745–757.

Kaplan, A. M. and Haenlein, M. (2006), 'Toward a parsimonious definition of traditional and electronic mass customization', *Journal of Product Innovation Management*, 23(2): 168–182.

Kaplan, A. M., Schoder, D. and Haenlein, M. (2007), 'Factors influencing the adoption of mass customization: the impact of base category consumption frequency and need satisfaction', *Journal of Product Innovation Management*, 24(2): 101–116.

Kieran, S. and Timberlake, J. (2004), *Refabricating Architecture: How Manufacturing Methodologies are Poised to Transform Building Construction*, New York, McGraw-Hill.

Latham, M. (1994), *Constructing the Team*, London, HMSO.

Leimeister, J. M., Huber, M., Bretschneider, U. and Krcmar, H. (2009), 'Leveraging crowd-sourcing: activation-supporting components for IT-based ideas competition', *Journal of Management Information Systems*, 26(1): 197–224.

Lichtenthaler, U. (2008), 'Open innovation in practice: an analysis of strategic approaches to technology transactions', *IEEE Transactions of Engineering Management*, 55: 148–157.

Malhotra, Y. (2000), 'Knowledge management for e-business performance: advancing inform-ation strategy to "internet time" information strategy', *The Executive's Journal*, 16(4): 5–16.

Meyer, M. H. and Lehnerd, A. H. (1997), *The Power of Product Platform*, New York, The Free Press.

Muffatto, M. (1999), 'Introducing a platform strategy in product development', *International Journal of Production Economics*, 60–61: 145–153.

Ojanen V. and Hallikas, J. (2009), 'Inter-organisational routines and transformation of cus-tomer relationships in collaborative innovation', *International Journal of Technology Management*, 45(3/4): 306–322.

Payne, A., Storbacka, K. and Frow, P. (2007), 'Managing the co-creation of value', *Journal of the Academy of Marketing Science*, 36: 83–90.

Payne, A., Storbacka, K., Frow, P. and Knox, S. (2009), 'Co-creating brands: diagnosing and designing the relationship experience', *Journal of Business Research*, 62(3): 379–389.

Piaget, J. (1973), *The Child's Conception of the World*, London, Paladin.

Piller, F. T., Moeslein, K. and Stotko, C. M. (2004), 'Does mass customization pay? An economic approach to evaluate customer integration', *Production Planning & Control*, 15(4): 435–444.

Piller, F. T. and Muller, M. (2004), 'A new marketing approach to mass customization', *International Journal of Computer Integrated Manufacturing*, 17(7): 583–593.

Pine, B. J. (1993), *Mass Customization: The New Frontier in Business Competition*, Boston, Mass., Harvard Business School Press.

Piroozfar, A. E. (2005), 'Mass-customisation: applicability and complications in building industry', in: F. Piller and M. Tseng (eds), *3rd International World Congress on Mass Customization and Personalization (MCPC 2005)*, Hong Kong.

Piroozfar, A. E. (2008), 'Mass customization: the application on design, fabrication and implementation (DFI) processes of building envelopes', PhD, University of Sheffield.

Prahalad, C. K. and Ramaswamy, V. (2000), 'Co-opting customer competence', *Harvard Business Review*, 78(1): 79–87.

Prahalad, C. K. and Ramaswamy, V. (2004), *The Future of Competition: Co-creating Unique Value with Customers*, Boston, Massachsetts, Harvard Business School Publication.

Prandelli, E., Verona, G. and Raccagni, D. (2006), 'Diffusion of web-based product innovation', *California Management Review*, 48: 109–135.

Raman, M. (2006), 'Wiki technology as a free collaborative tool within an organizational setting', *Information Systems Management*, 23(4): 59–67.

Rugg, G. and McGeorge, P. (1995), 'Laddering', *Expert Systems*, 12(4): 279–291.

Simpson, T. W. (2004), 'Product platform design and customization: status and promise', *Artificial Intelligence for Engineering Design, Analysis & Manufacturing*, 18(1): 3–20.

Sommer, R. A. (2004), 'Architecting cross-functional business processes: new views on traditional business process reengineering', *International Journal of Management and Enterprise Development*, 1(4): 345–356.

Stone, R., Wood, K. and Crawford, R. (1998), 'A heuristic method to identify modules from a functional description of a product', *Proceedings of ASME Design Engineering Technical Conferences*, Atlanta, Georgia, USA. DTM-5642.

Ulrich, K. and Tung, K. (1991), 'Fundamentals of product modularity', *Proceedings of the 1991 ASME Winter Annual Meeting Symposium on Issues in Design/Manufacturing Integration*, Atlanta, Georgia, USA.

Vesanen, J. and Raulas, M. (2006), 'Building bridges for personalization: a process model for marketing', *Journal of Interactive Marketing*, 20(1): 5–20.

von Hippel, E. (1978), 'Successful industrial products from customer ideas: presentation of a new customer-active paradigm with evidence and implications', *Journal of Marketing*, 42: 39–49.

von Hippel, E. (1986), 'Lead users: a source of novel product concepts', *Management Science*, 32: 791–805.

von Hippel, E. (1988), *The Sources of Innovation*, New York, Oxford University Press. Available online at: http://web.mit.edu/evhippel/www/sources.htm (last accessed 20-07-2011).

von Hippel, E. (2005), *Democratizing Innovation. Cambridge*, MA., MIT Press, Available online at: http://web.mit.edu/evhippel/www/democ1.htm (last accessed 20-07-2011).

von Hippel, E. and Katz, R. (2002), 'Shifting innovation to users via toolkits', *Management Science*, 48(7): 821–833.

Warkentin, M., Bapna, R. and Sugumaran, V. (2001), 'E-knowledge networks for inter-organizational collaborative e-business', *Logistics Information Management*, 14(1/2): 149–163.

Willis, D. and Woodward, T. (2006), 'Diminishing difficulty: mass customization and the digital production of architecture', *Harvard Design Magazine*, Fall/Winter 2006.

Yan, W., Chen, C. H. and Khoo, L. P. (2005), 'A Web-enabled product definition and customization system for product conceptualization', *Expert Systems*, 22: 241–253.

Yao, S., Han, X., Yang, Y., Rong, Y., Huang, S. H., Yen, D. W. and Zhang, G. (2007), 'Computer-aided manufacturing planning for mass customization: part 1, framework', *International Journal of Advanced Manufacturing Technology*, 32(1–2): 194–204.

Zha, X. F. and Sriram, R. D. (2006), 'Platform-based product design and development: a knowledge-intensive support approach', *Knowledge-Based Systems*, 19(7): 524–543.

Zwass, V. (2010), 'Co-creation: toward a taxonomy and an integrated research perspective', *International Journal of Electronic Commerce*, 15(1): 11–48.

4

The next wave in housing personalisation: customised residential fit-out

Stephen H. Kendall

ABSTRACT

Customisation of dwellings is intrinsic in built environments whose health results from acts of control by inhabitants, balancing acts of control by community powers. At the same time, property developers, government agencies and even citizen associations suppress customisation because they believe it is inefficient or "out of (their) control." Yet without incremental customisation, the everyday environment cannot be healthy. The challenge is to make customisation efficient and harmonious. Residential fit-out is one solution.

PERSONALISATION IN HOUSING IS NOT NEW

Households have always personalised their dwellings, independent of wealth, climate or building culture. In owned dwellings, families do more extensive things because they are empowered; but even in rented dwellings, households manage to exercise control. And in time, large developments of initially uniform dwellings – detached or in multiunit buildings – reveal personalisation, inside and outside.

Individually, these signs of control are nearly invisible. In the aggregate, however, these acts of inhabitation constitute an important and very large economic reality. Residential upgrading is a very large part of the building industry and in some countries exceeds new construction (US Census Bureau 2010, Itard and Meijer 2008, Ministry of Land, Infrastructure, Transportation and Tourism 2009).

Given these realities, what lies ahead for housing personalisation? I hope to show that the next wave in dwelling personalisation lies in new product/ service companies delivering fully coordinated residential fit-out. Such services will be applied first in newly built or converted multiunit buildings and townhouses (row houses), and will include everything needed to make empty space inside habitable. While the details will vary from place to place, the basic outlines can be sketched, based on observations in Europe, the United States and Japan.

DWELLINGS ARE NOT AUTOMOBILES

The concept that the production of automobiles is a suitable model for housing personalisation has a long history. Yet, while automobile production is moving toward mass customisation (van den Thillart 2004, Nambiar 2009), it is a poor model to describe housing personalisation, not principally because of technical differences, nor with the complexity or disaggregation of the supply chains, but because automobiles are placeless. Unlike dwellings, automobiles are known by their detachment from place. This is part of their appeal, but makes analogies with dwellings and housing personalisation deeply flawed.

A more helpful analogy is a complete system of automobile transport inclusive of vehicles and roadways. Highways are designed with capacity for a range of vehicle types. They are an infrastructure approved in regulatory processes connected to a specific political jurisdiction. Highway specialists build them. The vehicles using highways are produced by an independent industry, regulated by other bodies and subject to periodic enhancement and innovation. The highway and the vehicle thus have a symbiotic relationship, but with a high degree of autonomy.

THE SOCIAL CONSTRUCTION OF DWELLING PERSONALISATION

In the same way that highways (infrastructure) and vehicles (what is served by the infrastructure) need each other, multiunit residential buildings are usefully construed as having two spheres of control: a real estate asset serving many (a base building) and shorter-lived dwellings each serving a household (the fit-out). This is the principle of open building and is the basis for the emergence of a fit-out industry discussed here.

Analogies have their limits, but the dialectic between highways and the vehicles using them has had its parallel in the real estate industry for more than 50 years in the construction of office buildings and shopping centers. Empty "base buildings" (core and shell) are successively filled in by tenants who have their preferred fit-out installed, meeting standards set by the base building investor and the future occupant. The fit-out (tenant work or tenant improvements) changes from time to time, without disturbing other fit-out or the base building, using standard processes and products from a wide range of local and global suppliers.

Residential open buildings are now built this way around the world, meeting developer or "common" interests and waiting for inhabitation by households. We know that no dwelling can exist without action by both "the community" and the individual (Habraken 1970). There is always a common physical and organisational infrastructure within which each dwelling is situated – a symbiosis as fundamental as the highway and the vehicles using it. While this distinction is familiar in the law (see amongst others USCONDOS 2012), multiunit buildings are subject to more disputes than other building types because of poor acoustical separation of units, and entangled utility systems that often do not correspond technically to the organisational/legal distinction between what is shared – and what should last longer – and what is individually controlled and, normally, of a shorter use-life.

TECHNICAL MATTERS MAKE PERSONALISATION DIFFICULT

In large part, the technical – and thus organisational – problems in housing personalisation stem from the troubled state of entanglement in design and construction processes (see Figure 4.1). The problem is exacerbated by the belief that "integration" of all decisions and parts will lead to a better result – integration meaning unification or centralisation of decisions. But in a complex system such as housing, decisions are distributed – some decisions are common and others are individual – stretching over time. The public utilities are a case in point. Each operates with its own technical standards, its own equipment, pricing, and installation rules and each crosses many territorial boundaries. For example, a home electrical appliance attaches to an outlet in the wall, served by a cable buried in the wall that connects, via an electrical meter, to a cable in the building and then to a cable in the street and eventually to a power generation plant. Similarly, the toilet connects to a drainpipe in the wall or floor that connects to the building's drainage pipes that connects to the city sewage system. All such systems cross multiple territorial boundaries and are often funded by different funding mechanisms, causing potentially complex and disruptive interfaces both during construction and also later during upgrading of any part of the pathway of such systems.

The socio/technical construction of housing personalisation thus points to the importance of clarifying the distinction between the common and individual spheres of control. When this distinction is made, new processes, companies' technical systems and methods will inevitably be – and in fact are – emerging worldwide to support personalisation. The most important of these

4.1 Entangled wiring, piping and ducts in a typical dwelling in the United States

processes to emerge is "kitting" and the new business forms and supply chains attendant to it.

KITTING: A NEW KIND OF READY-TO-ASSEMBLE SERVICE

In the international market for building products and services, companies add value and profit by preparing "kits" of RTA (ready-to-assemble) products. Value is added off-site, in delivery, and in assembling or installing the kit on-site. For example, electrical contractors often pre-wire all the junction boxes and terminations off-site, put these assemblies and associated parts into boxes and bring them to the job site to be installed. Other examples of kits include sunrooms, delivered in boxes ready for assembly, and kitchens from IKEA (Normann and Ramirez 1993). Bar coding is often used to track these parts and assemblies and sensors are now embedded to track long-term performance and access for replacement. We also see such mundane products as plastic-wrapped toilet flush valve replacement kits. Often, these products or kits are not made entirely (or at all) by the company providing the kit label, but may be brought together from a variety of manufacturers or suppliers. Many contain parts enabling the kit to be applied in a variety of situations, with some parts discarded when not used. This is not new, with examples appearing before industrial production in the building sector (Fitchen 1986).

KITTING AND PRODUCT SERVICE SYSTEMS

Kitting has reached a high level of complexity in the housing sector most notably in "whole house kits." Leading architects have toyed with this idea, many failing to move beyond the prototype stage (Herbert 1984). The Japanese success with whole house kits (Sekisui, National, Daiwa, Toyota, Mitsui, Misawa), first introduced in the 1960s (McGrath 1996), demonstrates an understanding that design and technology by themselves are not enough – service is key and is delivered with great care by the large companies in this market. To be sure, this understanding was nascent in earlier whole house kitting companies in the late nineteenth century (Sears houses) and continues to thrive in the United States (e.g. Bensonwood Homes), in Japan and in some European countries. Interestingly, most successful businesses providing whole house kits use building technologies, products and architectural designs found more generally in the building sector (Cobbers et al. 2010).

It is clear that to survive in the global market, kit manufacturers and suppliers must market a combination of products and services. Consumers increasingly focus on benefits. By shifting to include benefits and products, companies are gaining competitive advantage, aligning production systems with emergent complex demand (Morelli 2002). These companies are learning to understand consumer needs, enabling the provision of knowledge-intensive solutions, or product service systems (PSS), a service-led competitive strategy that is the basis to differentiate from competitors who simply offer lower priced products (Mont 2008). By considering product life cycle, companies increase value in use for consumers by taking the risks, responsibilities and costs traditionally associated with ownership, while (in some cases) retaining asset ownership that can enhance utilisation, reliability, design and protection. The same new way of thinking has led to the consideration of all stages of product life cycle, as well as synergies with other products and services. This is the concept of "through-life management" (Koskela et al. 2008), encompassing product design and production, producing services through those artifacts, and planning for deconstruction (or disposal). The central idea is to create an understanding of all those stages as one unit of analysis and as one integral object of management.

A TURNING POINT: PERSONALISATION OF BUILDINGS BY USE OF FIT-OUT KITS

With this background, I will explain how a residential fit-out company would provide housing personalisation services using the concept of *fit-out kits*. But today, comprehensive personalisation in multiunit housing is either impossible or very expensive. The reason is that the conception of the "whole house" or "integrated building" is dominant – the separation of the whole into two spheres of decision-making (the base building and the fit-out) has not yet permeated the residential market as it has the office and retail market. The rest of this chapter attempts to explain how such an open building model would operate in the real world.

STEP ONE: DESIGNING AND PREPARING THE FIT-OUT KIT

In the residential market, design centers, showrooms and model dwellings are already familiar. In the showroom, a prospective buyer can view floor plans, touch materials, and become informed about costs and schedules. Trained staff are available to "build" the dwelling in a computer model.

Dimensions and specifications of the space to be fitted out are provided to the fit-out adviser. Space layout and equipment alternatives for the new dwelling are discussed and visualised using advanced software. Once decisions are made about the dwelling's layout, specifications, equipment and amenities, the cost and schedule are settled and the order goes to the company's fabrication and distribution center. Some companies – for example PLUS HOME in Finland and Stadgenoot in the Netherlands – enable much of this process to occur on-line, each household having access to a web space where large menus of options and links to suppliers are available. At the fabrication/distribution center, each fit-out kit is prepared as a separate "project" with a contract, warrantee, delivery schedule and installation instructions, and a user's manual.

STEP TWO: LOADING THE CONTAINERS

Following the parts inventory, the bar-coded parts – in boxes or bundles – are loaded into containers in the reverse order of their installation. Some products may be delivered directly from the manufacturer to the installation site; others may be delivered to the distribution facility already palletised (see Figure 4.2).

STEP THREE: DELIVERING THE CONTAINERS

The containers are delivered to the base building, in the correct sequence and timing. If more than one unit is being fitted out at once, as will often be the case, on-site logistics is key to success, but is inherently better organised than present delivery methods. A trained multi-skilled installation team for each fit-out project arrives with the first container. This means that many teams may be operating in a building at the same time (see Figure 4.3).

4.2 Showroom display; fabrication facility and loading/delivering of containers

4.3 Delivery and unloading of contents into the unit to be fitted out

STEP FOUR: UNLOADING THE CONTAINERS

When the container reaches the base building, it is either deposited for unloading into the service elevator, or below the balcony door of the unit to be fitted out. Boom trucks can lift containers as high as ten floors (as in Korea), or roof-mounted boom arms running on parapet-mounted rails can lift containers to be temporarily fastened to the building while the parts are off-loaded into the empty space. Everything must be small enough to pass through a standard opening.

STEP FIVE: INSTALLATION

The multi-skilled fit-out installers follow detailed instructions, working as a team sharing most tasks rather than waiting for specialists to do their work in sequence. Since each fit-out kit is different (but part of a given company's system), the team is able to perform as a learning unit, taking full responsibility for completing each fit-out kit, one at a time, before being assigned to another fit-out project (see Figure 4.4).

STEP SIX: HANDING OVER THE USER'S MANUAL

The entire process – from signing the contract to handing over the key to the new occupant – should take approximately three to four weeks for an average (1200 square foot) dwelling unit. When, in the future, the unit must be completely stripped and a new fit-out kit installed, containers can once again be used to remove the old parts.

4.4 Multi-skilled installers at work; fit-out piping installation; finished dwellings ready for occupancy one month after the fit-out work began

CONCLUSIONS

A key roadblock to further maturation of personalisation in housing has been the problem of obsolete classification or categories of work in the building sector. Buildings are understood as "lumpy" economic goods (real estate assets) or as made of a very long list of parts. But with the emergence of open building, and the precedent of the office and retail markets, there is the opportunity for a classification of work to emerge in housing (Ekholm 1996) following the demand for dwelling unit personalisation.

While housing projects have become larger, residential life tends to become more individualised. For generations, large-scale multiunit residential or mixed-use projects have created tensions between the demands of building logistics and economy, and users' individual (and evolving) preferences. We are now beginning to understand how such projects can be well served by the introduction of a fit-out level.

This approach to residential construction has often been considered desirable but not economical. But it is important to realise that recent projects are commercially driven. Examples include the Plus Home/MOOR projects in Helsinki, promoted by the Sato Development Company; the SOLIDS projects in Amsterdam, developed by Stadgenoot; the Warsaw "standard" in Poland; a large number of "free-plan core and shell" apartments in Moscow; many S/I (Skeleton/Infill) projects in Japan; several S/I projects by the SUNTY Development Company in Taipei, and several S/I projects in Beijing. Similar projects have recently been built in Canada, Germany, Spain, and in the United States, where, for instance, production builders think in terms of producing "volume" (largely empty shells). In addition, the adaptive reuse of old warehouses and office buildings for residential occupancy is familiar in many countries, mirroring open building principles.

Technical subsystems and products that can be used in fit-out kits are increasingly available in the international building supply market. In the Netherlands, MATURA, an early fit-out system – introduced into the market in 1990 ahead of its time – is now coming back in a modified form (Kendall

1994). (For some other examples see Infillsystemsus (2012), among many others.) In Japan, fit-out companies have been launched, targeting 1980s era residential apartments as well as newly built projects. Examples include REBITA and INTELLEX, both real estate companies seeing profit in reactivating the existing building stock (Matsumura 2011, Sakurai 2011). A new Japanese law passed in 2008 provides incentives to developers to build 200-year housing, resulting in projects in Tokyo and Osaka developed by Haseko and Kajima (Minami 2011).

It is well understood that industrial manufacturing has been most effective and dynamic where individual users are directly served (Habraken 1998). Witness the automotive, electronics and telecommunications industries. As is usually the case, release of tension between conflicting demands on the small and large scale can unleash new energies and innovation. Designing base buildings understood as infrastructures for living will stimulate the evolution of a fit-out industry that will accelerate innovation and distribution of new domestic fit-out services and systems. We can say that the release of these tensions is the most important aspect of the trend toward a fit-out approach to personalisation in housing.

The shift towards a new way of delivering large projects challenges traditional design and construction management methods, as well as financial, legal and regulatory tools. New legal and economic frameworks are thus needed. In other words, the true challenge is toward professional habits and conventions that must adjust to new ways of working.

Residential application of the fit-out concept, although based on the same principles as observed in office buildings and shopping centers, is particularly important because it affects a very large market whose potential is not yet understood or exploited. Although no systematic market analysis has been done, it is reasonable to assert that the potential market for residential fit-out is at least as large as that of the automobile industry. Roughly speaking, the cost of a fit-out kit for a dwelling approximates the cost of the cars its occupants use. This shows the magnitude of the shift identified here – an entirely new industry of impressive scope, based on industrial manufacturing of parts and delivering what is best called a durable consumer good. In this perspective, the trends outlined here allow the building industry to effectively come to terms with industrial production – and mass customisation – in its most creative mode.

BIBLIOGRAPHY

Cobbers, A., Jahn, O. and Gössel, P. (eds) (2010) *Prefab Houses: Building Kits for a Better Life*, Köln: Taschen.

Ekholm, A. (1996) 'A conceptual framework for classification of construction works', *Electronic Journal of Information Technology in Construction (ITcon)*, vol. 1, Stockholm: Royal Institute of Technology.

Fitchen, J. (1986) *Building Construction before Mechanization*, Cambridge: MIT Press.

Habraken, N.J. (1970) *Three Rs for Housing*, Amsterdam: Scheltema & Holkema (originally published in *FORUM*, 20(1), 1966).

Habraken, N.J. (1998) *The Structure of the Ordinary: Form and Control in the Built Environment*, Cambridge: MIT Press.

Herbert, G. (1978) *Pioneers of Prefabrication: The British Contribution to the Nineteenth Century*, Baltimore: Johns Hopkins Press.

Herbert, G. (1984) *The Dream of the Factory Made House: Walter Gropius and Konrad Wachsman*, Cambridge: MIT Press.

Infillsystemsus (2012) *Cablestud*, Infill Systems US: Products and services for efficient and customized interior fit-out. Available online at: http://infillsystemsus.com/cablestud (last accessed 12-12-2012).

Itard, L. and Meijer, F. (2008) *Towards a Sustainable Northern European Housing Stock: Figures, Facts and Future*, Delft: IOS Press BV (Delft University Press).

Kendall, S. (1990) 'Control of parts: parts making in the building industry', unpublished PhD Dissertation, Cambridge, MIT.

Kendall, S. (1994) 'The Entangled American House', *Blueprints*, Washington DC, The National Building Museum: 2–7.

Koskela, L.J., Rooke, J. and Siriwardena, M. (2008) 'Through-life management of built facilities: toward a framework for analysis', in P. Tzortzopoulos-Fazenda and M. Kagioglou (eds), *Proceedings, 16th Annual Conference of the International Group for Lean Construction*, Manchester, University of Salford, UK: 61–71.

Matsumura, S. (2011) 'What can make effective use of vacant buildings happen in the market – new context of Japanese house building industry', *Proceedings: Architecture in the Fourth Dimension, CIB W104*, Boston: Ball State University.

McGrath, T. (1996) *A Structural Profile of the Manufactured Housing Industry in Canada, the United States, Japan and Germany*, Ottawa: Canada Mortgage and Housing Corporation.

Minami, K. (2011) 'The new Japanese housing policy and research and development to promote the longer life of housing', *Proceedings: Architecture in the Fourth Dimension, CIB W104*, Boston: Ball State University.

Ministry of Land, Infrastructure, Transportation and Tourism (2009) *The Report on Reform and Renewal of Buildings*, Tokyo: Ministry of Land, Infrastructure, Transportation and Tourism.

Mont, O. (2008) *Product-service Systems: Panacea or Myth?* VDM Verlag.

Morelli, N. (2002) 'Designing product/service systems: a methodological exploration', *Design Issues* 18(3): 3–17.

Nambiar, A.N. (2009) 'Mass customization: where do we go from here?', *Proceedings of the World Congress on Engineering*, 1, *WCE 2009*, London.

Normann, R. and Ramirez, R. (1993) 'From value chain to value constellation: designing inter-active strategy', *Harvard Business Review,* 71: 65–77.

Sakurai, T. (2011) 'The situation of apartment renovation in Japan', *Proceedings: Architecture in the Fourth Dimension, CIB W104,* Boston: Ball State University.

US Census Bureau (2010) *US Statistical Abstracts of the United States 2010, 129th Edition,* Washington DC: United States Department of Commerce, United States Census Bureau.

USCONDOS (2012) *Three Types of Elements: What Do I Own and What Do We Own?,* available at http://www.uscondos.net/three-elements.html (last accessed 12-12-2012)

van den Thillart, C.C.A.M. (2004) *Customized Industrialization in the Residential Sector: Mass Customization Modeling as a Tool for Benchmarking, Variation and Selection,* Amsterdam: SUN Publishers.

5

Spatial mass customisation: mass-customisable urban spaces and spatial entities

Eric R. P. Farr

ABSTRACT

Mass customisation is a well-known strategy for responding to diverse needs, preferences, and requirements. Its manifestations in the built environment and, more specifically, in urban studies, however, have remained almost untouched. Urban spaces and entities have some potentialities and capacities that make them or their compartments open to the application of mass customisation. Pursuing a systemised approach to mass customisation (MC) in urban studies not only enables the organisation of more resilient types and more responsive modes of urban spaces and entities but also assists managerial and organisational bodies to improve the efficiency, versatility, and flexibility of urban contexts.

This chapter explores why and how MC of urban spaces and entities – what I shall call spatial mass customisation (spatial MC) – can be supported. Defining spatial MC and identifying its means, aspects, and manifestations, the chapter investigates the types of urban spaces that can absorb mass as well as those urban entities with capacities for being customised. It then identifies the customisability of those urban entities that can be used to design, enhance, or modify urban spaces. It explores how mass-customisable aspects of urban spaces and their compartments can be recognised and categorised by providing case examples.

INTRODUCTION

The postmodern era has overarched almost the entire scholarly vision and attitude for at least the last three decades. This has dissuaded the human mind from being dedicated to a single truth, end-state principles, and absolute solutions in both theoretical and practical aspects of almost every discipline and the procedures used within the disciplines. As a result, alternative solutions have been put forward to meet the requirements of such a paradigm shift. In manufacturing and service industries, mass customisation (MC) has been deemed as a strategy and a technology (Kratochvíl and Carson, 2005) for responding to the diversity of the customers' requirements by "treat[ing] different customers differently." Addressing this objective here, I discuss, first, what pursuing the strategy in urban studies means; second, how the strategy is applied to urban spaces and urban entities; and third, what the manifestations are.

More recent extended attempts have brought structured customisation strategies and approaches to architecture and the related disciplines. MC in the production process of building compartments and components (see Piroozfar, 2008; Piroozfar and Popovic-Larsen, 2009) has been pursued to give the maximum profit, flexibility, and variety of choices to designers, manufacturers, and construction managers as well as customers and clients (Kelbaugh and Mccullough, 2008).

Urban planners and designers have implemented mass customisation in its emancipatory sense, taking into consideration the role of citizens in decision and plan making and even co-designing to absorb the mass. However, because of the lack of structured approaches, spatial organisation, for both physical and non-physical features, has a long way to go. Pursuing a systemised approach to mass customisation (MC) in urban studies not only enables the organisation of more resilient types and more responsive modes of urban spaces and entities but it also assists managerial accounts of urban spaces to improve their efficiency.

This chapter investigates how MC of physical aspects of urban spaces or entities – what I shall call spatial mass customisation (spatial MC) – can be supported. First, why should mass customisation be pursued in urban studies, and what types of benefits and implications are imaginable? Defining spatial MC and identifying its means and manifestations, this chapter investigates the types of urban spaces that can absorb mass as well as those urban entities with capacities for being customised. Then it identifies the customisability of those urban entities that can act to reconfigure urban spaces. It explores how mass-customisable aspects of urban spaces and their compartments can be recognised and categorised, by providing case examples.

IMPLICATIONS OF SPATIAL MASS CUSTOMISATION

The urban spaces and environments surrounding us affect their users' expectations, wants, needs, and even habits in many ways. The spaces are also in constant dialogue (and sometimes competition) with each other. They are frequently being compared to, and ranked and preferred over one another based on their contents and *responsiveness* to their users' requirements as well as their cross-connections with their surroundings. In an integrated network of urban spaces, the reciprocal relationship between the spaces (*space–space*) and the vertical integration of users and spaces (*user–space*) should constantly be taken into consideration to maintain the users' satisfaction.

Providing spatial attractiveness – for every kind of space – and improving spatial viability – at every managerial level – are among the general strategies that can serve to enrich the two types of relationships. However, adaptability is the key quality through which responsiveness can be achieved. Adaptability contains other qualities such as vicissitude, dynamicity, flexibility, and resiliency without which the space's lifecycle would shorten and its sustainability could be compromised, at some points. To elaborate on some of the above-mentioned points, spaces should be arranged to perform in adaptable ways and formed to maximise their responsiveness to *space users'* diverse requirements. How can these goals be achieved? A look at the conventional definition of MC reveals that the strategy – with some modifications – can be pursued to implement mass-customisable urban spaces or entities as an approach to responding to the aforementioned question. In other words, the execution of MC in urban spatial cases can be expected to provide customisable spaces:

- to increase the usability and livability of the spaces;
- to provide safer urban contexts with an integral network of urban spaces communicating with each other in a more effective way;
- to boost up space users, to increase the revenue and to cut the maintenance costs;
- to improve the quality of urban spaces and the users' spatial experience; and
- to provide a new understanding of, and approach to, *spatial planning* at all levels.

COMMON MC DEFINITIONS AND DIFFERENTIATIONS FROM SPATIAL MC DEFINITION

Given the structural differences between a space and a manufacturing product that affect their mass customisation means, here we need to examine the prevailing definitions of *mass customisation* briefly in order to arrive at a definition for *spatial MC* in relation to the characteristics of urban spaces.

There is no widely accepted definition for the term MC (Kaplan and Haenlein, 2006). According to Kratochvíl and Carson (2005), early forerunners in Scandinavia frequently referred to such concepts as "custom-tailored mass production." With services excluded, Kaplan and Haenlein (2006) offer three categories of MC: traditional MC – working definition, traditional MC – visionary definition, and e-MC. The shared part of the definitions is that MC is a strategy that creates value by some form of company (producer)–customer (user) inter-action.

Piller defines MC as "customer co-design process of products and services, which meet the needs of each individual customer with regard to certain product features" (2005: 315). Hickman defines mass customisation "as the mass production of objects tailored to individual wants and needs" (2007: 17). Anderson (2003) calls it, rather expressively, "proactive management of variety." And some other definitions of mass customisation used in the literature are "providing products that are created to the consumer's specifications" (Ettlie and Ward, 1997: 54) and "offering unique products in a mass-produced, low-cost, high volume production environment" (Duray, 2002: 314).

When considering the modular components concept, which can be used as a configuration strategy for urban spaces or entities, we should not neglect to mention Pine's (1993) description of the best method for achieving MC by creating modular components that can be configured into a wide variety of end products and services. Also Kumar (2005) suggests that in MC, the consumers began to be viewed as different groups pursuing diverse goals that could be better served with small batches of specialised goods.

For those characteristics of urban spaces that differ from those of manufacturing products, the above definitions do not suffice to define *spatial MC*. This is because, in most spatial cases:

- The space is not a product to be consumed; therefore, there is no consumer–producer relationship.
- There is not a single space to be dealt with as a manufacturing product, to be mass produced and mass customised.
- No user owns the space to be customised to his or her needs. There are only temporal users and ephemeral spaces.
- Instead, a variety of users use the same space at the same or different times.

Hence, the meaning of point of delivery of customisation and the methods are different from those for conventional MCs.

These, then, are the key points of spatial MC: (a) maximising the absorbance of mass, (b) responding to the users' diversity of needs (see the section "Absorbing the Mass") by tailoring to individual or group wants and needs, and (c) fostering the spatial dynamicity to respond interactively to the network of surrounding spaces (see the section "Interactive Urban Spaces").[1] In brief, the spatial MC objectives are to:

- respond to greater mass needs,
- provide spaces with customisable *functions*, and
- accommodate customisable (urban or manufacturing) entities.

Moreover, the low-cost axiom should be substituted with a reasonable or feasible cost of configuration towards customisation. As discussed, while quantifying mass-customised urban spaces, especially those that provide various types of temporal flexibility and functional diversity, is to be seen as an urban strategy, it may also result in cost cuts and increased financial benefits.

In brief, I suggest, therefore, that spatial MC is the strategy that provides spaces/entities sharing, expanding, and configuring their spatial features and services; the spaces/entities that bring interactivity and viability to their contexts by magnifying the mass of spatial users and responding to their spatial needs, with maximum possible flexibility and highly variable components to be custom-ised at reasonable costs.

As was mentioned, at various stages and levels of implementation of this process, the emancipatory role of the spatial user – as a co-designer, co-planner, or co-creator – can be taken into consideration.

ABSORBING THE MASS IN INTEGRAL URBAN SPACES

Trying to absorb the mass of spatial users is a key manifestation of spatial MC. The "mass" concept does not point out merely the quantity of users, which changes based on the size of a specific type of space, but also indicates the variety of the mass absorbed.

The concept of mixed-use development can be enumerated as an effective spatial MC strategy. Mixed-use complexes and urban projects can respond to a wider range of users than can single-purpose projects. In recent years, proven deficiencies of single-use zoning in the American planning environ-ment have made the implementation of mixed-use developments, by acting in an integral way, more prevalent to help establish urban spaces that deal with the mass of spatial users. Maximising the range of user types attracted to specific spaces, *integral urban spaces* contain a range of entities with various functions, including residential, commercial, office, institutional, or any combination of these. The multifunctional nature of such spaces increases the hours during which the spaces are effectively being occupied and used; hence, it enlarges the diversity of the mass of spatial users. Potzdammer Platz in Berlin and Reston city center in Virginia, which have each been successful not only in absorbing a significant variety of mass but also in making the whole place better for living, are two brilliant examples of this class (see Figure 5.1).

SPATIAL CUSTOMISATION

Urban spaces or entities containing temporal functions that are configurative from time to time are mass-customisable spaces. Based on the function of the spaces in their urban contexts, I assign customisable urban spaces to three categories: *adaptive, interactive,* and *versatile*. Adaptive spaces are capable of being switched among some specific functions devised for them. Interactive spaces are modified to interact directly with their surrounding urban functions. And versatile spaces are preplanned specific areas designed to accommodate various types of urban events. However, at one time, some spaces can exhibit, or can be designed to accommodate, more than one of the functions, and the functions are interchangeable or can be shared among the spaces of a spatial network (see Figure 5.1).

Adaptive urban spaces

Adaptive urban spaces have a prevailing function yet are modifiable to be used for at least one other function. This means that a space of this type acts in an adaptive way based on the requirements defined for it. For instance, parts of a wide boulevard like 'Straße des 17. Juni' in Berlin or the parking lot of University Center Plaza in the City of Irvine, California, carries some adaptive spatial aspects. When hosting Saturday markets (flea market or *FlohMarkt* in German), the low-speed lanes of the boulevard and plaza parking lot play adaptive roles in the context, despite their primary defined functions. The adaptive characteristics heavily rely on the spaces' capacities and can be achieved by the application of various strategies or even by the addition of customisable urban entities, like customisable furniture, to the spaces. Under den Linden, another Berlin boulevard, has a green island in the middle that plays an adaptive urban role different from that in the previous example. The space acts flexibly by hosting tourists and regular visitors and by including customisable urban stands (for educating people), advertisement billboards, and seasonal retail stands. Providing adequate and suitable room for various types of urban events and hosting customisable urban entities, these adaptive urban spaces communicate with their users from a variety of backgrounds and with different expectations. The types of spaces that possess potentialities for customisation can be present anywhere in a city. They can appear even in the form of unoccupied urban spaces as *multifunction free spaces*, or what is called *vague terrain*. In addition, pedestrian zones of city centers established to contain a variety of users, retailers, and entertainers are among the devised customisable urban spaces with the capacity to be adaptable (see Figure 5.1).

Interactive urban spaces

Uncomplicated examples of interactive urban spaces include multilane streets whose directions can be changed to accommodate different traffic flow directions, free land that becomes a playground for an adjacent Sunday market, and free land that serves as an extension to a nearby parking lot during busy hours or when the lot hosts a weekly car show platform. Even a parking lot that serves several purposes at various times of a day or a week is a space with interactive characteristics.

Urban spaces that share their spatial services with other spaces and events nearby play interactive spatial roles. The roles are shaped based on the spaces' primary functions and change from time to time. Being associated with other urban spaces, when and where they are required, makes them ready to contribute to customisation premises; hence, they are considered customisable. The pedestrian zone of Manchester city center is an example of this kind. The space performs its primary functions but also contains tables and seats for customers of nearby restaurants and cafes and for other visitors to rest, eat, or socialise (see Figure 5.1).

Versatile urban spaces

Urban spaces designed to provide a versatile stage for a specific function or set of functions can be considered customisable. Such spaces have been devised to accomodate fixed and/or mobile customisable entities. This will be discussed in the next section. Most of these spaces contain the basic infrastructures and stages to cooperate in such a versatile way. The scale and size of such spaces can vary from a large urban space like Chicago's Millennium Park to a very small-scale piece of land used for billboards, flagpoles, and seasonal flowerbeds. Depending upon the size of such spaces, they may also contain various types of adaptive and interactive customisable spaces, as does Millennium Park. Olympic villages in general, and specifically Delhi Olympic Village, which was built primarily to serve the 1982 Asian Games and was later customised to be used as a neighborhood for low-income families, provide significant examples of versatile customisable urban spaces. A similar plan was made for the 2012 Olympic Village in East London, which is to provide higher living standards for the underdeveloped East End once the games are over (see Figure 5.1).

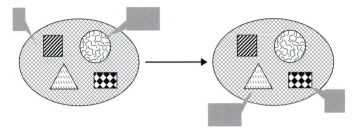

Integral Urban Space (The space containing various functions absorbs various groups of spatial users)

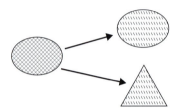

Adaptive Urban Space (The function and feature of such a space can change)

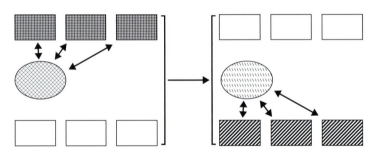

Interactive Urban Space (In interaction with its context, the space can accept various spatial roles)

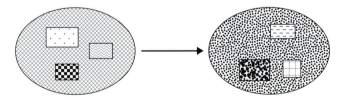

Versatile Urban Space (The spaces and entities of such a space can be modified)

5.1 Schematic overview of different types of customisable urban spaces

CUSTOMISING CHARACTERISTICS AND
CUSTOMISABLE ENTITIES OF URBAN SPACES

The customisation of most aspects of urban spaces that are dependent on the alteration of concrete entities, such as buildings and infrastructures, inevitably incur high costs. Although temporary alterations to, or reconfigurations of, the facades, exterior and interior walls, masonry, and landscaping can be pursued to absorb a bigger mass of spatial users, in most cases, they too can prove costly. They can nevertheless be done for spatial revitalisation purposes with long-term aims and should be recognised as a means of mass customisation. Despite what is typical, some spatial aspects are modifiable at low or reasonable costs, especially when changes are merged with or supported by other purposes. Examples include the wrapping of the Reichstag by environmental artists Christo and Jeanne-Claude while it was undergoing a major refurbishment during 1995; the building reportedly attracted millions of visitors at the time, which rarely happens when similar refurbishment projects are being carried out elsewhere.

Temporary spatial entities that are customisable can be added to a space for a particular period of time and then removed or reconfigured. Those entities assist in giving mass-customisable characteristics to the urban spaces in which they are being embedded. The characteristics vary, as do the entities. The entities can include a variety of options from fixed lighting devices to mobile, seasonal canopies or music devices and stages or, as with the Reichstag, some purely functional element for a particular purpose, to be disposed of when no longer needed.

Besides the natural and environmental customisable aspects of urban spaces, which in some cases can be brought under control (like sunlight or seasonal changes to a landscape), customising aspects and customisable entities can be categorised into five key layers that can be pursed both separately and simultaneously/interactively (see Figure 5.2):

1. (Infra)Structure: fundamental features of an urban space known as structural or infrastructural elements provide some possibilities to modify or adapt that urban space for ephemeral functions, such as fairs or weekend or regional markets, which will benefit from flexible structures, such as multipurpose urban stages or spaces.
2. Compartment: the customisable compartments of concrete construc-tions, such as a restaurant's outdoor tables, chairs, and customisable canopies and shades, can contribute to the customisation of the space. These compartments are mainly attributed to the space second-hand because they are part of one of its structural elements.

3. Element: some urban elements are those tools and elements that belong to an urban space but are easily modifiable, changeable, or removable and are used to customise urban spaces; examples include landscaping and seasonal vegetation, occasional decorations, flags, and exhibition tools and facilities.

4. Furniture: this category includes single- or multifunctional urban furniture that is used differently during various hours of a day or days of a week or on special occasions. Items regarded as furniture are more limited in type and functionality than the elements yet provide greater opportunity for customisation by situation because they are more flexible and manageable and less bound to their specific context. This does not mean that they are necessarily cheaper to provide, maintain, or dispose of.

5. Specification: the specifications of urban spaces can be customised as planned by designers, using what can be seen as nonphysical tools, such as lighting, shade, shadows, sound, music, and so on. Although these things can customise the spaces chiefly in nonphysical ways, their physical requirements (such as lighting devices) should not be overlooked, as they might well have positive or negative contributions to elemental customisation during different time spans (for instance, a light pole, which is not a significant customiser during the night, as opposed to the light pattern it sheds, can, during the day, turn into a crucial element that can contribute to customising the same space in a similar, or utterly different way).

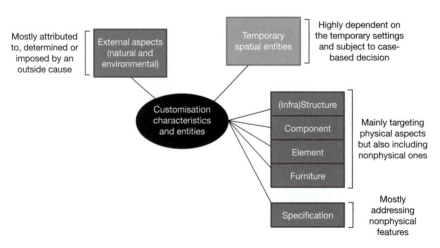

5.2 Overview of spatial mass-customisation components

CONCLUSION

Spatial mass customisation (spatial MC) was introduced in this chapter to study mass customisation and its possible manifestations with special reference to urban spaces. It is pursued to formulate alternative ways to achieve more resilient types of urban spaces. Although bound to traditional MC premises, it holds a more specific definition. The differences between *spatial MC* and *MC's* more established definitions stem both from different focus points and particular features of space. Based on the definition of *spatial MC,* in general, those urban spaces that can be responsive to a mass of users' or consumers' needs or tastes or that can be configured in multiple ways are customisable. In more detail, spatial MC is pursued through three major objectives: absorbing the variety of mass, implementing the customisable spatial aspects and entities in spaces, and benefiting from customisable urban spaces. Having a progressive approach, it can benefit from a variety of MC manifestations from customisable services to customisable manufacturing products. Urban spaces can contain spatial characteristics towards mass customisation and/or customisable spatial aspects and entities.

For further studies, the structural and intellectual differences between space (as a product) and product (of manufacturing) that formulate the spatial MC evaluation method can be articulated and examined.

NOTES

1   The conventional definition of mass customisation can, however, still be applied to spatial entities, such as urban furniture, that have manufacturing characteristics.

REFERENCES

Anderson, D. M. (2003) *Mass Customization, The Proactive Management of Variety.* Available at: http://build-to-order-consulting.com/mc.htm (accessed 20 May 2012)

Duray, R. (2002) 'Mass customization origins: mass or custom manufacturing?', *International Journal of Operations and Production Management,* 22(3): 314–328.

Ettlie, J. and Ward, P. T. (1997) 'US manufacturing in the early 1990s: the chase and challenge', *Business Strategy Review,* 8(4): 53–59.

Hickman, L. A. (2007) *Pragmatism as Post-postmodernism: Lessons from John Dewey,* New York: Fordham University Press.

Kaplan, A. M. and Haenlein, M. (2006) 'Toward a parsimonious definition of traditional and electronic mass customization', *Journal of Product Innovation Management,* 23(2): 168–182.

Kelbaugh, D. and Mccullough, K. K. (2008) *Writing Urbanism: A Design Reader,* The ACSA (Association of Collegiate Schools of Architecture) Architectural Education Series, London and New York: Routledge.

Kratochvíl, M. and Carson, C. (2005) *Growing Modular Mass Customization of Complex Products, Services and Software,* Berlin: Springer.

Kumar, K. (2005) *From Post-industrial to Post-modern society: New Theories of the Contemporary World*, Malden, MA: Blackwell.

Pine, B. J. (1993) *Mass Customization: The New Frontier in Business Competition,* Boston, MA: Harvard Business School Press.

Piller, F. (2005) 'Mass customization: reflections on the state of the concept', *The International Journal of Flexible Manufacturing Systems,* 16(4): 313–334.

Piroozfar, A. E. (2008) 'Mass customization: the application on design, fabrication and implementation (DFI) processes of building envelopes', PhD thesis, University of Sheffield.

Piroozfar, A. E. and Popovic-Larsen, O. (2009) 'Customizing building envelopes: retrospects and prospects of customization in the building industry', in: F. T. Piller and M. M. Tseng (eds) *Handbook of Research in Mass Customization and Personalization*, Singapore: World Scientific Publishing, 925–948.

PART **II**

ENABLING TECHNOLOGIES, DESIGNS, AND BUSINESS MODELS

6

Conceptualising the use of system products and system deliveries in the building industry

Lars Hvam, Niels H. Mortensen,
Christian Thuesen, and Anders Haug

ABSTRACT

This chapter describes the concepts of system products and system deliveries based on the use of product modularisation and product configuration. The concepts are outlined and discussed based on examples from both the construction industry and related industry. The description focuses partly on the product architecture and partly of the setup of the business processes by using, for example, Configure to Order processes and Engineer to Order processes. Furthermore the potential impacts from using system products and system deliveries are discussed based on the examples included.

INTRODUCTION

The concepts of system products and system deliveries are currently being discussed with increasing intensity and interest in the building industry. Many people see system deliveries as a possible solution to a number of problems in the industry and as an important mechanism for increasing the industry's quality, image and productivity. There are a number of companies in the building industry and related sectors which have achieved notable results by using the principles of system deliveries. Schneider Electric LK has increased the turnover of its IHC controls by 30–40 per cent a year, American Power Conversion has reduced the throughput time for delivery of a complete infrastructure system for large data centers from 400 days to 16 days (Hvam 2006), Philips Consumer Electronics has reduced its time to market for new products by a factor of 4. SCANIA has for a number of years been the most profitable company in its sector, and ascribes this to the use of system thinking in both products and business processes (Hvam et al. 2008).

Thus there is much which indicates that there is very considerable potential in using system deliveries. But there are only a few examples, and in most companies it is still a big step to move from discussion to action. A number of players in the building industry have voiced the opinion that the concept of system deliveries is not sufficiently well defined, and that there is a lack of operational methods for actually developing one's company in the direction of using system deliveries. This chapter discusses the use of system deliveries based on examples from industry and theory for use of modules and product configuration.

SCANIA HAS GREAT SUCCESS WITH SYSTEM PRODUCTS

In order to describe the ideas behind system deliveries more closely, we will take as our starting point an example from the automobile industry. The overall aim of introducing system products is, as stated, that this creates greater value for the customer and a larger profit for the participants in the value chain. An example of a company which has had great success in introducing system thinking into both its product range and the company's business processes is SCANIA.

SCANIA is the most profitable company within its sector of industry and ascribes this to the fact that system thinking is being used throughout the value chain. The company has a module-based product range (Meyer and Lehnerd 1997) and a value chain which is based on the manufacture of modules. SCANIA's current module structure is from around 1980, and the stable product structure has made it possible to develop a set of extremely efficient business processes for sales, configuration, production, delivery and after-sales service.

That the current module structure in the product range is from 1980 does not mean that all product development has ceased. On the contrary, the fixed module structure (or product architecture) means that it is considerably easier to carry out development projects related to the development of the individual modules, that SCANIA's products taken as a whole are among the products in that sector of industry which have the largest technology content, and that the company is the leader with respect to the introduction of new technological solutions.

SCANIA's experiences also demonstrate that there is no conflict between the introduction of system thinking and the creation of customer-specific solutions. The use of a module-based product range makes it possible for SCANIA to offer a number of solutions adapted to the individual customer. At the same time, the company has a focused market strategy which means that they say "no" to customers who cannot be dealt with using the available module-based product range.

There are of course a number of differences in relation to the building industry. SCANIA is a very large company which has full control over the complete value chain for production of a truck. The company produces about 60,000 trucks a year, which amongst other things means that it is easier to justify investments in the development of products and business processes.

In relation to the building industry there are also a number of common features. The product is relatively complex, it must be possible to adapt the products to individual requirements, there are a number of external suppliers in the supply chain, the company acts within a market with considerable price pressure, it is essential to be able to deliver on time, and it is vital for one's competitive position to be able to create new, innovative products.

With respect to the building industry, the example from SCANIA can inspire us to think over how one might use a modularised product range in order to reduce the complexity involved in delivering a complex product which is adapted to the customer. The example can also tell us that there is no conflict between delivering a product adapted to the customer and at the same time achieving high efficiency and profitability within the company. In spite of the differences between the building industry and traditional manufacturing industry, it will be possible to achieve the same advantages in the building industry as SCANIA has achieved.

WHAT ARE A SYSTEM PRODUCT AND A SYSTEM DELIVERY?

In order to give a somewhat better idea of what a system delivery and a system product are, we can consider the following list of statements which express different points of view on the concepts of system products and system deliveries in the building industry:

- A system product is a product which can be varied and adapted to current needs – based on a module-based product range and through the use of a product configuration system.
- A system product is a building product which has a complexity and a degree of completeness which means that it can perform several functions.
- System products make it possible to invest resources in developing building systems which have better properties than the corresponding sum of building components which are known today.
- System deliveries denote a change in which the producers of building materials go from delivering components for a building to delivering

complete system products. By the term system products we mean a part of a building which currently has to be put together by using components from different producers of building materials. System deliveries mean that the complete value chain is developed, so that it is possible to deliver and install the system product efficiently and without faults.

- System deliveries mean that the process is altered from the planning of customer-specific solutions to the configuration of system products, based on a well-defined and module-based product range.
- System deliveries mean that, for example, contractors and architects develop solution concepts (such as concepts for wet zones, foundations, facades or roof constructions) which can relatively easily be adapted to a concrete building task.
- The concept of system delivery is a vision of industrial manufacture of finished sub-systems (the system product) for a building project, so that they can be assembled on the building site with a minimum of manpower and materials on the site.
- System deliveries mean that part of the building process is moved into the factory.
- System deliveries mean that resources are invested in developing system products which can be used in a concrete building task, so that configuration, production, delivery and installation can be performed more efficiently, with a higher and more uniform quality, and to a predictable time and price. In other words, system deliveries can be considered as a form of work preparation or industrialisation of the overall building process from drawing/design via the production of materials to erection on the building site.

A system product is a product which is multifunctional and multidisciplinary, and which can be varied in relation to a given need. A system delivery encompasses the system product and the processes which have to be carried out in order to configure, produce, deliver and install/adapt a system product on the building site.

System products are complex and must at the same time be able to be varied. In order to handle this complexity, modules and product configuration systems are used. Put briefly, a module is a delimited part of a product with a well-defined function and a well-defined interface. An example of a system delivery in a building project is bathrooms, where the function is toilet and bathing facilities, while the interfaces are the piping for water, heat and electricity, together with the attachment mechanism. A configuration system is an IT system which contains rules for how modules can be selected, dimensioned and combined in relation to a given requirement.

The examples given here of the development of system products in other sectors have the common feature that a company has initiated, led and organised the entire development – in some cases by making use of suppliers. In the building world, the situation is more complex:

- There have to be system manufacturers who offer products.
- The owners and managers of building projects must adjust their building concept and their building process to be receptive to system products.
- Actors in the building sector must change their roles, tasks and business so as to use system products.

An additional challenge is that many people consider industrialisation as pre-fabrication indoors. This means that they imagine system products with the same technology and materials as are used in the traditional building process. A consequence of this is that it is often too difficult to demonstrate the advantages of pre-fabrication – a contractor can always deliver a cheaper offer for the same solution constructed on the building site. System products must to a greater extent be based on new technologies and materials, which have other values and costs and which cannot be made by artisans on site.

SYSTEM DELIVERIES RELY ON THE USE OF MODULES AND CONFIGURATION SYSTEMS

In order for customer-specific products to be manufactured efficiently, the design of the products is changed so as to use modules (Meyer and Lehnerd 1997, Salvador et al. 2009). That is to say, some product parts (modules) are developed which can be put together in accordance with a set of well-defined rules. Examples of modules could be the engine, clutch and gearbox in an automobile. The engine module is available in a number of different versions, which can for example be described by its fuel type (petrol/diesel), engine size, engine control and engine suspension. The individual variants of the engine module can be combined with a corresponding number of variants of the gearbox and clutch modules according to a set of rules which describe which variants of the modules can be used together.

As the example indicates, the number of variants of the individual modules and their possible combinations in a particular product can quickly become too large for the designer to get a general view of. To handle this complexity, a so-called configuration system is used (Hvam and Pape 2006, Forza and Salvador 2007, Hvam et al. 2008). This is an expert system which can combine modules which individually are described by a number of characteristics. This is done with the help of rules (constraints) that describe which modules are allowed to be combined, and the rules for the components' safety separation etc. The foundation for development of a configuration system is thus that there is a set of well-defined modules with corresponding rules for how these modules can be put together.

Modularisation and configuration are used to an increasing extent in industry. B&O, Grundfos, SCANIA and American Power Conversion are all examples of mass production companies which use modularisation and configuration for efficient creation of customer-specific products.

THE USE OF MODULARISATION AND CONFIGURATION IN THE BUILDING INDUSTRY

We can summarise the basic principles of modularisation and configuration by saying that the aim is to develop modules which have a number of common characteristics in relation to the company's internal work procedures – such as design/customer adaptation, production, assembly and installation – and which at the same time can be varied, so they can fulfill the needs of the customer. In this connection, the big challenge is to develop modules which can be varied in relation to the parameters which the customer thinks especially important and which provide the customer with some value.

If we should try to carry some of the ideas of customisation over to the building industry, we can imagine a "bottom up" process, in which producers of building components, such as electric installations, wall elements, ceiling elements, wet zones, roof constructions etc., develop their products in the direction of more complete system products.

Danfoss, who amongst other things produce valves and thermostats, have over the last 10 years acquired a number of companies who build and assemble so-called district heating units. Such a unit is a system product consisting of valves, thermostats, piping, heat exchangers, hot water tanks etc. A district heating unit takes in heat from a district heating works and distributes heat and hot water to the individual rooms in a building. Danfoss has previously delivered components to the producers of such district heating units, but has now by takeovers moved up in the value chain and is today the world's largest supplier of district heating units. In this way, Danfoss has achieved a size and market position which can justify investment in the development of products and manufacturing processes, which means that Danfoss can supply a district heating unit at a price and quality which makes it economically non-viable for a plumber to shop around and put together his own district heating unit.

The district heating units described above are an example of how a materials supplier can develop system deliveries. This can be looked at as a "bottom up" process, in which producers of building components such as

electric installations, wall elements, ceiling elements, wet zones, roof constructions etc. develop their products in the direction of more complex system
products. Another, or supplementary, possibility is a "top down" process, in
which concepts for types of buildings – for example, office buildings, factory
buildings or particular types of housing – are developed in connection with the
overall planning of buildings.

The two ways of using system deliveries in principle are illustrated in
Figure 6.1. One direction (bottom up) shows the building material producers'
development of system products, while the opposite direction (top down) show
the development of building concepts – or concepts for parts of buildings.

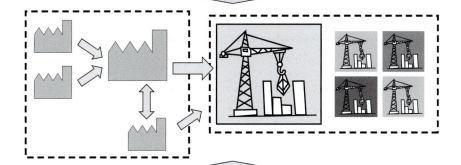

6.1 Use of system products and building concepts

DEVELOPMENT OF SYSTEM PRODUCTS

By developing, marketing and producing a complete system product, such as the district heating units from Danfoss, it becomes easier and quicker to assemble the product and its associated installations on the building site. You get a product with correct production quality, with faster delivery and at lower cost, which possibly gives a lower price for the buyer. In addition there will be fewer actors on the building site – e.g. just one supplier, who delivers a complete district heating unit. The task of coordination and adaptation on the building site is markedly reduced.

The most important challenges in developing system products are to perform a coordinated and coherent development of the system product itself and its components (modules) – including the development of business models and alliances between companies – and also to develop business processes and configuration systems which make it possible to put together (configure) a system product matching the needs of the individual building project. This last in particular is important in the sense that if consortia which deliver system products really have to be competitive, then the products for individual customers must be able to be configured, and not – as is the case today – be developed through a planning process which consumes large numbers of engineer and architect hours, and where there is a risk that the planners introduce special details which do not give the customer any value, but which make the product to be delivered more complicated and more costly.

DEVELOPMENT OF BUILDING CONCEPTS

Figure 6.1 also shows a "top down" approach to the industrialisation of building. This approach is inspired by work on modularisation and configuration which takes place in companies who deliver large plant such as cement factories, spray drying plant or insulin factories. The challenge here is to exploit experience accumulated through many individual customer-oriented projects. This is done partly by developing solutions (modules or building concepts) which can be re-used in several customer-oriented projects, and partly by systematically collecting and storing experience from previous projects in document databases with structured search mechanisms.

For the development of modules or concepts at the building level to be worthwhile, there must be a market for buildings which have so many common features that it will pay to develop a building concept which can be re-used in several customer-oriented projects. "Common features" do not mean that the buildings must be identical, but that there must be some structures and/or elements which appear again and again.

Another essential requirement is that there are some enthusiastic persons in the organisation who can and will take on the task of developing the building concepts. This requires employees with great insight into the relevant company's building know-how and the customers' preferences, and with the ability to think abstractly in terms of building concepts. The management must also focus on the development of building concepts and apportion resources for this development. The development of building concepts is a long-term investment and a tough task which has to be carried out over a number of years.

STRATEGY/BUSINESS PROCESS

Experience from other industries shows that when system deliveries do not always give the expected gains, then one of the explanations is that the business models and strategies have not been made clear. Particularly when system deliveries are developed in a network of companies, then lack of clarity about responsibilities and the distribution of costs and profits is often a source of problems. Thus there is a need for building up competence in the implementation of strategies and business models for networks of companies. Quite basically, it is necessary to build up competence in designing business models and system deliveries which give added value for the customers, compared to supplying components and individual products. A schematic of a business model is shown in Figure 6.2.

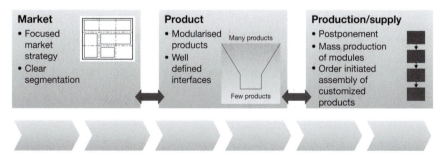

Market
- Focused market strategy
- Clear segmentation

Product
- Modularised products   Many products
- Well defined interfaces
  Few products

Production/supply
- Postponement
- Mass production of modules
- Order initiated assembly of customized products

Clear processes
- Configure to order process [CTO]
- Integrate to order process [ITO]
- Engineer to order process [ETO]

6.2 Example of a business model for system deliveries

This business model contains four components, which are the market, product, production/supply chain and the other business processes, such as sales, engineering, installation and after-sales service. Notable gains can only be achieved if all of these features are addressed. In the example shown, some of the most important decisions in those four components include:

1. *Market:* There exists a clearly focused market strategy that explains which segments and customers the system delivery will service, which product variants go to which market segments, and what are the most important selling points for each market segment.
2. *Product:* In the product range, there is established a clear reference architecture and modules with interfaces which are clearly defined. This means that the product range has a well-defined variation in relation to the market and big family likenesses seen from the company's point of view.
3. *Production/supply chain*: Production is, for example, based on production of modules according to the principles of mass production, possibly in low-wage countries, while final assembly takes place close to the customers. This gives low costs, the ability to react quickly and system deliveries which are adapted to suit the customers.
4. *Processes:* Clear processes have been identified for, for example, sales, planning and installation, which means that these can be executed with great efficiency and predictability (Hvam 2006). Three examples of types of process are shown in Figure 6.2:

   - Configure to Order, in which a product is put together based on known elements/modules.
   - Integrate to Order, in which a product is put together based on known elements, but where products/elements from third party suppliers can also be used.
   - Engineer to Order, in which product parts are developed specifically for the individual order.

Naturally, this model does not suit all types of system deliveries and companies, and it should just be regarded as an example, but the ability to conceptualise and implement business models is a central competence.

The use of system deliveries can be thought of as a systematisation and form of work preparation for both products and business processes. By systematically developing the company's business processes based on a module-based product range and the use of configuration systems, it is possible to develop some business processes for sales, production, installation and after-sales service which have a much higher performance than today with respect to quality, throughput time, productivity and predictability. Sales take place by configuration of known modules/solution concepts into a complete solution adapted to the customer, instead of the current practice of planning from case to case, based on experience from previous projects. In this way it is already possible to create some products/solutions which are well defined in relation to the subsequent processes of production, installation and after-sales service, in the sales phase. This means that much more robust and efficient business processes for production, installation and after-sales service can be developed, based on well-defined and module-based products or solution concepts. Such processes will be better prepared and with a pattern of activity which has been thought through in advance. The challenges associated with this idea are, amongst other things, the low frequency of similar tasks in the building industry, the tradition for "we can do everything ourselves" and the fact that the idea involves different players who often have quite different and contradictory criteria for "the good product" and "the good process".

REFERENCES

Forza, A. and Salvador, F. (2007) *Product Information Management for Mass Customization: Connecting Customer Front-office for Fast and Efficient Customization*, Hampshire: Palgrave Macmillan.

Hvam, L. (2006) 'Mass customization in the electronics industry – based on modular products and product configuration', *International Journal of Mass Customization*, 1(4): 410–426.

Hvam, L. and Pape, S. (2006) 'Improving the quotation process with product configuration', *Computers in Industry*, 57: 607–621.

Hvam, L., Mortensen, N.H. and Riis, J. (2008) *Product Customization*, Berlin and Heidelberg: Springer.

Meyer, M.H. and Lehnerd, A.P. (1997) *The Power of Product Platforms: Building Value and Cost Leadership*, New York: The Free Press.

Salvador, F., de Holan, P.M. and Piller, F. (2009) 'Cracking the code of mass customization', *MIT Sloan Management Review*, 50(3): 70–79.

7
Product and process approaches

Martin Bechthold

ABSTRACT

The demand for the largest possible variety of products, whether architectural, consumer or industrial products, has clearly increased over the past decades. Depending on the product complexity and the need for product variation different production strategies, ranging from craft production to mass production, can be taken. Advances in manufacturing technology combined with the rapid introduction of information technology into the manufacturing world in the 1990s brought about mass customisation as a different business model that claims to resolve the dilemma between variety and high production volumes. The uptake of this new business model has been different in architecture, manufacturing and service industries. This chapter looks at the products and processes of highly deterministic mass production, as the origin of today's industrialised economies. Next, strategies of how to achieve a limited amount of product variety with standard architectural and consumer products are reviewed. Then the product and process view will be extended to mass customisation, where the chapter includes an overview of mass customisation as a business strategy for the future.

INTRODUCTION

The demand for the largest possible variety of products – be they architectural, consumer or industrial products – has clearly increased over the past decades. Products and architectural components can be created in a large variety of ways, depending on the quantities needed, the scale, materials and performance requirements as well as the underlying design concepts. Between the two extreme approaches of individually crafting a one-off artifact and mass-producing a commodity product there are many processes that allow some degree of customisation for intermediate production quantities. Clearly there are obvious differences between buildings and products in terms of function, size, number of units produced, inherent technologies, complexity, methods of construction or manufacturing production, organisation of the design and production team, and so forth.

It is assumed that the reader is familiar with terms such as market-pull, technology-push and platform products as well as user-driven and technology-driven products. Many of these concepts apply more to industrial consumer products than to architectural products. Product complexity, on the other hand, is a useful notion in evaluating the degree to which design and manufacturing have added value to raw materials. There are clear differences between elemental products (e.g. lumber), highly sophisticated ones (e.g. automobiles), and the many products that lie in between. Buildings are generally relatively complex, and many buildings are one-of-a-kind designs. The overall complexity of typical buildings can be achieved largely with standard elements and products that, with minor modifications through simple secondary processes, suit project-specific conditions. The same is true, albeit to a lesser extent, for larger products.

There is an obvious need for product variation, and a great many strategies have been devised to accommodate this demand. The tendency to expect – and be able to obtain – an ever-larger variety of products has been a consistent trend throughout the past decades, and the speed with which new products enter the market is clearly accelerated as companies compete for market share and customers.

There are many strategies to satisfy the demand for product variety, and these strategies impact the design and production processes that this book is primarily dealing with. Most of the broad characterisations in the following sections apply to product design as well as to architecture. There are, however, some significant differences that have to do with issues of scale and the fact that a product is usually pre-fabricated, while buildings typically consist of a mix of ready-made products, pre-fabricated and partially customised components and on-site built elements.

STANDARD PRODUCTS AND VARIATIONS: TRADITIONAL PROCESSES

Standard consumer and architectural products

Standard products are normally associated with high-volume industrialised production on capital-intensive manufacturing and assembly facilities. Set-up and tooling costs of the machines used in high-volume production are typically high, and these mass-production techniques can only operate cost-effectively for large production volumes of identical items. Mass-produced items are present everywhere in our daily lives. Typical assembled products are many consumer electronics, most furniture or light fixtures, but also clothes or shoes, to name just a few. Many buildings are at least partially assembled from mass-produced items such as standard doors and windows, suspended ceilings or raised floors and others.

When designing products that will be produced at high volumes designers obviously have to carefully consider the available manufacturing options: manufacturing techniques with higher tooling and set-up costs might be applicable here that would be impossible to justify for low volume production. Plastic molding techniques, for example, are typically associated with a mass-production mode.

CAD/CAM techniques and parametric design and analysis tools have been extensively embraced to reduce the time-to-market and cut development costs. Standard products are usually guided by a set of well-defined boundary conditions (e.g. standard door and window sizes), and standards and other agreed upon rules can be embedded into digital design environments. Electronic marketplaces are increasingly used to purchase and distribute standard products, and connections between the designer's CAD drawing, the associated bill of quantities, specifications and the databases of available products at online markets may only be a question of time.

Creating variation with standard products

Despite a host of manufacturing strategies such as lean manufacturing or flexible manufacturing cells, mass production remains one of the most cost-effective ways of producing standard products in large volumes. It is less efficient, however, in producing the product variety that end-users and designers expect, because each variety increases the complexity of production through additional set-ups, tools, training and storage, to name just a few. All these factors ultimately increase cost, and there is a strong economic incentive to reduce variety.

User-side configuration

One obvious way to achieve variation while still profiting from mass production is to let the end-user customise the standard product. This approach exists both for consumer products and architectural products, but whereas the consumer product is typically assembled and configured by a lay-person, the architectural product is assembled, configured and installed by an expert (contractor). Design for assembly implications vary accordingly.

Configurations of this type can be as simple as finishing a product in the desired quality or choosing individual installing schemes for shelves or cabinets. In architecture user-side configuration allows the erection of unique buildings with cost-effective, mass-produced elements. North American timber construction techniques are a prime example for site-configuration of standard wood products.

Digital design considerations

Some consumer product companies support online environments that allow users to visualise the possible configurations. Since user-configured architectural products are often quite simple (sheets of plywood, tiles etc.) sophisticated design-development environments are more commonly used for the configuration process itself. Such configuration tools include steel or timber design and detailing software that often interface with CNC machining environments. Other design tools enable layout design and generate bills of quantities (carpets, tiles, suspended ceilings) to facilitate the tedious specification and procurement process. These tools are stand-alone environments largely disconnected from manufacturing and distribution processes. Future directions might include links to online marketplaces or web-based bidding and procurement environments.

Modularity

A modular design approach is an additive design strategy that enables product variety by combining a range of standard physical or functional modules (mass-produced). The term "module" here refers to a self-contained, distinct and identifiable building block for an overall structure. Many modules in product design of modules are primarily functionally defined (e.g. a power module), but some physical shaping and dimensional implications may be present. The physical meaning of the term "module" refers to a standardised unit of size. In its more extreme form, a "modular" design thus generally refers to an overall design based on the use of a pre-specified dimensional array (typically in the form of integral multiples of given dimensions) that serves to define the sizes and locations of all parts and subassemblies (locations of connection or interface points are often predefined as well). In building design, this concept is often associated with pre-fabricated building elements, whereas in electronics it structures components to insert into printed circuit boards with their highly regularised hole spacing. Physical modules are often designed to be replaceable without complete disassembling of the whole configuration; they can be upgraded and extended over time.

In architecture, modular design approaches are normally used in the spatial planning of any building to accommodate commonly available off-the-shelf building components such as standard bathroom or kitchen elements. One departs from these standard dimensions only at great cost. The term "modular housing", for example, has long been associated with an approach wherein whole housing units are built according to standardised dimensions. Standardised units are then aggregated according to certain rules to form a larger development, as can be seen in Moshie Safdie's original Habitat for the 1969 World Fair in Montreal.

Digital design considerations

Parametric design environments are well suited to support modular design activities. Assembly models can be created that allow different modules (part file or subassemblies) to be displayed such that interferences and other design conflicts can be readily detected. The standards inherent in many modular design approaches (e.g. kitchen cabinet modules, masonry blocks) also make specialised design tools for certain systems feasible.

Pre-configured standard products

Leaving the customisation of a standard product to either the end-user (consumer products) or the contractor (architectural products) reduces production complexity and allows for the economy of scale effects of high-volume production. A disadvantage for architectural construction is reduced accuracy and lower productivity for on-site customisation compared to their off-site equivalents. The logical response has long been to pre-configure building products such that on-site activities are limited to pure assembly activities. Timber, steel and concrete design and detailing software supports the design, computer-controlled production and installation of such pre-configured elements.

For consumer products the concept of factory-configured standard products (e.g. versions in different colors) is equally common. Closely related is the notion of the model, a defined product type that is produced in different variations that always maintain the base features. This approach is typical for the apparel or shoe industry, to name just a few. It is a variation of the factory-configured standard product in that a single model – the basic type – is parametrically varied to suit individual needs.

Digital design considerations

Pre-configured standard products are products that truly benefit from digital design and manufacturing techniques, because fabrication processes need to provide for the variations that were traditionally produced on site. There are many advantages to using a parametric modeling tool, since variations of a product are inherently simple to produce by varying the base digital model.

The digital tools employed are high-end parametric design environments such as ProEngineer or SolidWorks for product design, or integrated software solutions for building systems (e.g. BIM-related detailing software).

ARCHITECTURAL CONSTRUCTION AND ONE-OFF PRODUCTION

In many ways parallel to on-site construction is the making of one-off, highly individualised products or construction elements by specialised fabricators. This mode of production remains largely craft-based, but is increasingly supported by the advanced digital design and manufacturing techniques described throughout this book. The challenges of designing and making a unique object, for which little precedent may exist, has in fact been the focus of much of the current discussion on the use of CAD/CAM in architecture. Complexly shaped buildings or intricately patterned facade elements are representatives of this model. For unique elements that are mostly differentiated by their complex shapes, advanced parametric modeling tools have proven useful to represent shapes accurately and support fabrication through CNC control. In extreme examples design and fabrication may be contracted to companies outside the traditional building industry.

MASS CUSTOMISATION

The variations that can be created based on a mass-produced product are inherently limited. Modularity and configuration strategies inevitably lead to a smaller production volume for individual parts and subassemblies, and a lower production volume negatively affects the economy of scale effects that mass production is so dependent on. The relative inflexibility of mass-production techniques not only limits product variety, but production relies on demand predictions that may or may not occur – meaning that the demand for a product can turn out to be below the production volume. Storage costs and the costs of discounts which may have to be granted in order to sell excess quantities can be substantial. Companies have been striving to reduce the risk of pro-duction without markets by reducing the time between demand prediction and bringing the product on the market (time-to-market). Lean manufacturing techniques including just-in-time delivery, and flexible manufacturing cells were introduced mainly to improve flexibility and at the same time lower costs – thus breaking the tradition industrial dilemma whereby per-unit cost advantages were inevitably associated with large production volumes. These advances in manu-facturing technology, when combined with the rapid introduction of information technology into the manufacturing world, brought about a different business model that claims to resolve the dilemma between variety and high production volumes – mass customisation.

The fundamental premise of mass customisation is to no longer manufacture products "blindly" according to a predicted demand, but instead allow production to be directly driven by actual orders. This reduces the cost for storage of unsold items and for costly discounts. Individual customers cannot only order individual quantities: the production processes are devised such that – within the typically modular design of a product – many individual variations can be accommodated. Generating individualised orders in significant quantities is only feasible if the corresponding manufacturing system is actually able to handle this individualisation efficiently, that is without the down-times, set-up times and high tooling costs that would normally occur. Lean manufacturing and flexible manufacturing cells are key components of this process. Since these manufacturing systems are inevitably expensive to set up it is important to point out that the success of mass customisation hinges on large production volumes, but achieves an impressive variety of products.

Mass-customised products can be found on many levels of consumer products as well as in services. Custom clothes and shoes are good examples of mass customisation. Here body scanning techniques in specialised points of sales are usually employed to generate a 3-D model that is stored in the company's database. For subsequent purchases of customised shirts, shoes or suits the customer can simply log onto a website or choose from a variety of models that can be produced in different material qualities and colors (modularity). On submitting an order a cutting pattern is generated automatically and the selected material is cut accordingly. Assembly is often done manually, and custom-made apparel or shoes typically can be delivered after 4–6 weeks from the order. Similar techniques are employed to customise eyeglasses and other products where individualisation may give the advantage of a better fit.

An important aspect of this direct interaction between the customer and the fabricator is referred to as the "learning relationship". As the customer specifies the product variation that best suits his or her needs this information is stored in the company's database and can be retrieved the next time the customer launches an order. The potential time savings for the customer create an incentive to keep purchasing from the same company. Companies can also use this information as a market analysis tool, allowing them to determine what modular variations to offer for future products. These types of customer bonds and learning relationships are more relevant for consumer products or services than for architectural construction products.

The competitive pricing of mass-customised products is what makes this business model so compelling and at the same time challenging to implement.

How can a customised product be sold at a similar price compared to the equivalent mass-produced item? In order to streamline the ordering process it is vital to automate the processing of large numbers of individualised orders. For this purpose customers initially configure their product using a specific system-integrated software or online environment. The choices available in these configuration tools are limited to the variation that a particular company can produce – thus guaranteeing that each individual order can be accommodated efficiently by the given process.

Mass customisation in architecture

Mass customisation is beginning to make an impact on construction products, but compared to mass customisation in consumer products or furniture there are usually few if any direct connections between the product configuration software and the digitally driven manufacturing process. The traditional distribution of responsibilities between the design team and the contractors or fabricators makes any degree of automation between design and production presently a journey into legal no-man's-land.

Shop drawings – electronic or paper-based – exist for many good reasons and cannot easily be eliminated. The need to verify whether an architectural product or component is correctly designed and meets code clearly sets apart all attempts for mass customisation with their counterparts in product design. Consumer products can be modularised in a way that restricts customisation to the technically feasible. Verifying whether an architectural product and components meets code, represents the design intention and can be manufactured is usually a more complex undertaking involving a number of independent parties for design verification. The design software has to communicate with manufacturing facilities at many different companies – an integration that can be extremely difficult to achieve in practice.

Approaches that relate to mass customisation include the custom-manufacturing of large-format masonry blocks by German producer Xella, or the custom design and production of spaceframes with several thousand parts by Mero. In both cases design configuration tools are for proprietary use by producers, with few if any direct connections to software used by design professionals.

The design and manufacturing of custom windows is a related domain of successful mass customisation. Homeowners typically specify a window together with a specialised dealer, using software with an interface particularly suited to individuals with little or no background in construction. Limited choices include frame materials and finishes, different glazing systems and others. The data is sent directly from the dealer to the manufacturer, where

7.1 Research by the Design Robotics Group at the Graduate School of Design at Harvard University. An integrated digital workflow allows for the fabrication of mass-customising ceramic shading lamellas

machine instructions can be generated automatically based on the design submittal. Some producers offer free downloadable configuration software for use by design professionals. These environments offer more design choices, but without direct links to production facilities.

A prototypical system for producing customised ceramic shading lamella is a recent example of mass customisation. Developed at the Graduate School of Design, the system customised an existing software platform. Designers can design and simulate optimal shading lamellas. The same software then creates all needed instructions and code for a novel robotic work-cell that extrudes curved and twisted lamellas from clay-based ceramic material (Figure 7.1).

Case study: e-Skylight.com

This case study describes how a manufacturer of architectural skylights applied principles of mass customisation in the production of small skylights, thus transitioning from a one-off custom production to a mass-customised production within a modular system. E-Skylight's sister company, Architectural Skylight (ASC), originally used an object-oriented design approach to designing and manufacturing custom skylights. This system supplemented AutoCAD with several plug-ins, including third-party software and programs, allowing technicians to import architectural geometry, and generate a complete 3-D model of the skylight or curtain-wall. The same model, after several post-processing steps, was used directly for CNC manufacturing of frame members and custom glass sheets.

With this integrated approach to design and manufacturing well established and proven, ASC sought to expand its market by setting up a system capable of producing smaller skylights for small to medium size commercial and residential construction. An online interface was set up to allow customers to design a custom skylight within the given manufacturing constraints. Within 2.5 years of its implementation architects, glazing contractors and homeowners designed over 65,000 skylights online.

e-Skylight process

The online design interface is structured into a series of simple steps that, at each level, enables either a choice between pre-selected options or the input of dimensions or desired performance values (Figure 7.2).

The design process starts with a selection of the four basic types. In the following steps all other parameters are defined, beginning with the basic dimensions, followed with a selection of frame and glass qualities and finishes. In case the user specifies dimensions that are beyond the range of the supported modularised product line the system prompts an alert and points to the closest possible value. During the design process an image displays a photorealistic rendering of the specific configuration. A quote for the custom skylight is instantly available online based on the 3-D model in the AutoCAD-based

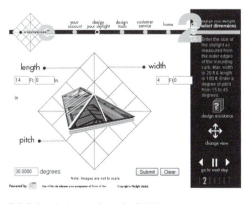
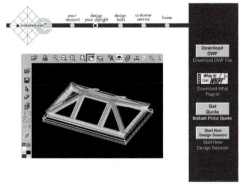

7.2 Online design interface of e-Skylight

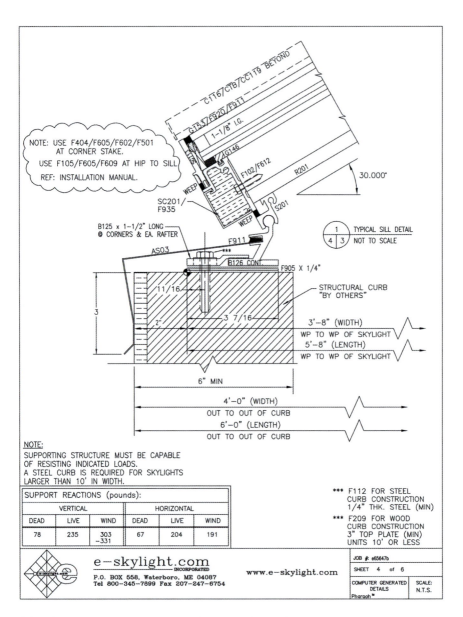

NOTE: USE F404/F605/F602/F501 AT CORNER STAKE.
USE F105/F605/F609 AT HIP TO SILL
REF: INSTALLATION MANUAL.

C167/CTB/CC119 BEYOND
G157/F920/F911
1-1/8" I.G.
G146
F102/F612
R201
30.000°

SC201/
F935
S201
WEEP
WEEP

B125 x 1-1/2" LONG
@ CORNERS & EA. RAFTER
F911
AS03
***
B126 CONT.
F905 X 1/4"

1		TYPICAL SILL DETAIL
4	3	NOT TO SCALE

11/16
3
2"
3 7/16
6" MIN

STRUCTURAL CURB "BY OTHERS"

3'-8" (WIDTH)
WP TO WP OF SKYLIGHT
5'-8" (LENGTH)
WP TO WP OF SKYLIGHT

4'-0" (WIDTH)
OUT TO OUT OF CURB
6'-0" (LENGTH)
OUT TO OUT OF CURB

NOTE:
SUPPORTING STRUCTURE MUST BE CAPABLE
OF RESISTING INDICATED LOADS.
A STEEL CURB IS REQUIRED FOR SKYLIGHTS
LARGER THAN 10' IN WIDTH.

*** F112 FOR STEEL
CURB CONSTRUCTION
1/4" THK. STEEL (MIN)

*** F209 FOR WOOD
CURB CONSTRUCTION
3" TOP PLATE (MIN)
UNITS 10' OR LESS

SUPPORT REACTIONS (pounds):					
VERTICAL			HORIZONTAL		
DEAD	LIVE	WIND	DEAD	LIVE	WIND
78	235	303 -331	67	204	191

e—skylight.com
INCORPORATED
P.O. BOX 558, Waterboro, ME 04087
Tel 800—345—7899 Fax 207—247—6754

www.e—skylight.com

JOB #: e65647b	
SHEET 4 of 6	
COMPUTER GENERATED DETAILS Pharaoh™	SCALE: N.T.S.

7.3A e-Skylight shop drawings are automatically generated from the 3-D design model

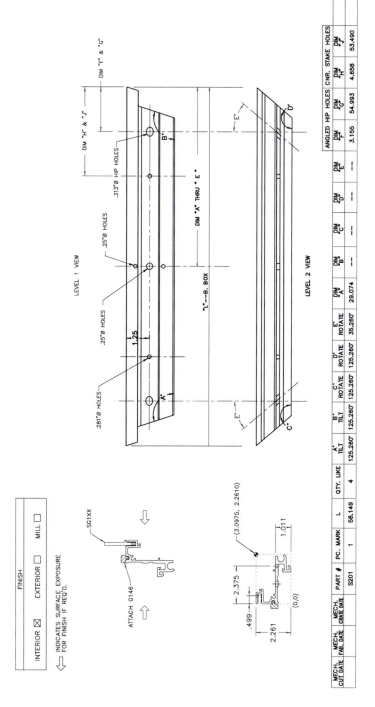

LEVEL 1 VIEW

LEVEL 2 VIEW

.281"Ø HOLES
.25"Ø HOLES
.25"Ø HOLES
.313"Ø HIP HOLES

DIM "H" & "J"
DIM "F" & "G"

DIM "A" THRU "E"

"L"—B. BOX

ATTACH G146
SG1XX

(3.0975, 2.2610)

(0,0)

2.375
.499
2.261
1.011

MECH. CUT DATE	MECH. FAB DATE	MECH. CRATE DATE	PART #	PC. MARK	L	QTY. LIKE	A* TILT	B* TILT	C* ROTATE	D* ROTATE	E* ROTATE	DIM "A"	DIM "B"	DIM "C"	DIM "D"	DIM "E"	ANGLED HIP HOLES DIM "F"	HIP HOLES DIM "G"	CNR. STAKE HOLES DIM "H"	DIM "J"	COMMENTS
			S201	1	58.149	4	125.260°	125.260°	125.260°	125.260°	35.260°	29.074	--	--	--	--	3.155	54.993	4.658	53.490	ATTACH SILL SG'S

7.3B

7.4 CNC machining and assembly of a custom skylight

environment described above. This same model is eventually used to generate machine instructions for fabrication; it is also used to derive the bill of quantities, specifications and all 2-D drawings (Figure 7.3).

Users can download the specifications, overview drawings and construction details – all representing the specific version chosen during the online design session. Once the desired skylight is ordered the glass dimensions are automatically generated from the 3-D model and electronically transmitted to the glass fabricator.

Manufacturing

In order to minimise storage costs e-Skylight outsources the on-demand production of customised aluminum profiles in all available finishes, delivered just in time to e-Skylight for assembly. The software system also creates 2-D shop drawings used for quality control, to guide the assembly and support the installation on site. Aluminum extrusions are CNC cut based on NC code automatically generated from the 3-D model (Figure 7.4).

The programming CAM software includes nesting routines that optimise material use of the customised frame stock. Technicians check the fabricated parts to the 2-D fabrication drawings.

A barcode system tracks parts throughout the manufacturing process. Once all parts have been fabricated units are assembled as far as possible to avoid any errors in the field and maintain a tight quality control. Custom skylights are generally shipped within 4 weeks of the purchase.

Mass customisation – business paradigm of the future?

In the 1990s mass customisation was praised as the business strategy of the future. In the meantime some promising attempts in the building industry have adapted this approach. Consumer product companies embraced mass customisation much earlier, but in the meantime some of the early attempts in mass customisation have failed. Many other companies have switched back to a mode of diversified mass production on flexible and lean manufacturing systems.

One of the main challenges of mass customisation is the need to be cost competitive with equivalent mass-produced items. For customised architectural products or components the industry-specific fragmentation is a major obstacle to mass customisation. Only few companies have successfully transitioned into mass customisation, and with few exceptions those usually had a well-established market position in niche markets or were, such as the large window manufacturers, among the market leaders in their field. Most of the successful mass-customisers also pursue another business model at the same time –

manufacture of standard windows or, in the case of e-Skylight, designing and building high-end custom solutions for large projects. This diversification, and potential of transferring know-how between related production modes, is probably another reason for their success.

NOTE

This chapter is an adapted version of a book chapter written by the author and published in Daniel Schodek *et al.* (eds) *Digital Design and Manufacturing: CAD/CAM Applications in Architecture and Design*, Hoboken, NJ: John Wiley & Sons. It is reprinted with permission of John Wiley & Sons.

8

Customisable architectural systems – emerging types of integrated product deliveries in the building industry

Kasper Sánchez Vibæk

ABSTRACT

Currently two main strategies can be said to dominate the building sector: 'building by pieces' and 'turnkey solutions'. Both strategies share some of the same problems architecturally as well as business-wise.

Through the notion of *system structures* this chapter draws attention towards new more product-based organisational divisions in architecture and construction and discusses the emergence of *integrated product deliveries* (IPDs) as a new different strategy. IPDs are proposed as a means for handling design complexity by integrating design decisions into discrete industrialised products of matter, process and thought that can be configured and customised for a specific delivery and form part of unique construction projects. This can facilitate a more strategically focused design attention and the combination of such discrete subsystems into 'assemblages' can theoretically form complete buildings. This seems in many ways to be an intriguing alternative architecturally, business-wise and even seen from an environmental point of view. However, it also leads to the question whether a future architecture can be seen as more temporary 'assemblages' or configurations of (relatively) independent sub-systems that interface materially and process-wise in the building.

INTRODUCTION

Increased complexity of contemporary buildings as well as the processes of producing them challenge the integrative capacity of architectural practice as, among others, pointed out by Alexander (1964). Bachman (2003) states that 'architecture is perhaps the ultimate profession of integration'. This calls for new and different means to reduce complexity of the architectural design and construction process without impairing the ability to meet the complex requirements of modern societies. It is thus not primarily about reducing the complexity of the outcome but rather about handling it through new products, tools or heuristics that do not force architectural creation into the straitjacket of traditional industrialised mass production.[1] While all construction today is industrialised to some extent, industrialisation can be approached in different ways. The choice of products and systems evidently has significance for the degree of flexibility of the architectural solution space.

Currently two main strategies can be said to dominate the building industry thus partly defining the framework for architectural creation:

1. A strategy based on traditional building techniques and combinations of (industrialised) building materials and components on-site – 'building by pieces', and
2. A strategy of all-encompassing building solutions mostly prefabricated in factory environments and delivered as 'turnkey solutions'.

Both strategies share some of the same problems architecturally as well as business-wise, the latter often 'just' being traditional construction made under roof. Either complexity is high, difficult to control and make profitable or choice is low with standardised solutions leading to poor architectural possibilities (solution space) and too narrow market opportunities.

SYSTEM STRUCTURE AND INTEGRATED PRODUCT DELIVERIES

In the product industry, complex engineered industrially produced design objects as cars, ships and aeroplanes have gradually been decomposed into supply chains of strictly defined subsystems. These are through various tiers joined into larger complex assemblies or chunks that are then put together in the final product. Complex products are often produced and delivered in mass customised versions enabled by controlled variations in the subsystems.

The organisation of subsystems into a product is normally termed the *product architecture* – using the term *architecture* in a slightly different way than architects do, referring to the structural organisation of subsystems and components of the product. In order not to confuse concepts in this chapter such organisation of a building will rather be termed the *system structure*,[2] which then designates the physical and organisational subdivision of a building product or building into several – sometimes (hierarchically) nested – subsystems. System structures represent a particular way of looking at buildings (see Figure 8.1).

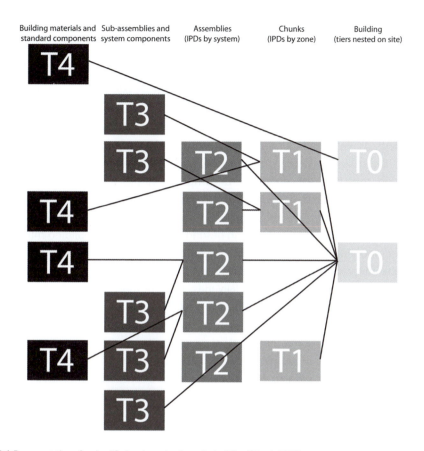

Building materials and Sub-assemblies and   Assemblies   Chunks   Building
standard components   system components   (IPDs by system)   (IPDs by zone)   (tiers nested on site)

8.1 Representation of a simplified system structure of a building (Vibæk 2012)

Any building and its coming into being can be seen as a structural organisation of a number of subsystems of varying complexity levels – any building has a system structure. In traditional building these subsystems would normally correspond directly to the established crafts involved. Hence the brick-layer would together with bricks and mortar constitute a subsystem as well as would the carpenter and the woodwork or historically later specialisations such as plumber/plumbing or electrician/wiring. In modern industrialised products the product architecture tends towards division along lines not necessarily corresponding to any craft. Rather the subsystems here represent multi-technological parts defined by their performance – i.e. the motion of a motor or the information provision of a display. The same phenomenon can be found in construction although still incipient and could constitute a third plausible, though still complementary, strategy in industrialised construction.[3]

The so-called *integrated product deliveries* (IPDs) are normally considered as physical systems that can be configured and customised for a specific delivery in a construction project and help to reduce the complexity of the total process. However, IPDs are not limited to the physical realm alone. Process systems or combinations of process and matter can be seen as equally relevant for development of customisable IPDs in construction.

The IPDs introduce a more nuanced picture of the system structure of a building. As well as a building conceptually can be decomposed into its spaces – i.e. living space, kitchen, entrance – or its architectural elements – wall, opening, roof, floor – it can also be decomposed into its subsystems as they are actually produced and delivered. This has the advantage of better matching the industrialised means of production behind. The IPDs potentially reduce complexity of the design process through nesting and clustering of building materials and components into performance-based entities inserted into the building as discrete integrated or distributed subsystems. Design work is embedded in these systems before they, as specific deliveries, become part of building projects. Using configurable IPDs in architectural design moves the architect's attention towards the interfaces *between* systems rather than the design of systems themselves. An assertion is that a system structure *always* – and even when highly based on IPDs – will be project specific. Every building is depending on systems available, economy, infrastructural issues, project brief, design intentions and a myriad of other factors. This makes it hard to imagine standardised systems structures entirely based on well-established IPDs. Gaps between these will require project specific design attention.

EXAMPLES OF INTEGRATED PRODUCT DELIVERIES

In order to illustrate the broadness of the concept of *integrated product deliveries* (IPDs) in construction this section gives a non-exhaustive overview of some of the different kinds already on the market or on their way.

Bathroom pod

A well-established IPD in construction is the bathroom pod.[4] The bathroom requires a considerable amount of installations – a functionally and spatially well-defined space or utility at the same time representing some of the most expensive square metres of the dwelling. The combination of limited size and many crafts involved in completion often results in long construction time, difficult coordination and a following high risk of errors and deficiencies. This makes the bathroom an obvious target for industrialisation understood as separate prefabrication (Figure 8.2).

Although savings are considerable in larger batches of identical or almost identical bathrooms, factory produced standard deliveries or truly mass customised solutions are still seldom found. Part of the explanation is that market standards never have been established for the bathroom pod as a *product*. Manufacturers generally have only few and loosely defined types (product lines) and no standard measures. In pursuit of flexibly meeting *any* customer's demand, most pods are still mainly delivered as *projects* designed for a specific building. They are not configured based on general design parameters embedded in the system and each delivery still requires considerable design effort.

System for facade renovation

An IPD as defined in this chapter does not necessarily need to be a factory produced clearly physically delimited product. This example is mainly defined by a sequence of well-defined material processes put together in different ways to form a complete delivery – a facade renovation solution.

Although cladded versions of concrete construction are prevalent in modern Danish (large scale) construction, most of the building stock is still dominated by traditional masonry. RBE – a midsized Danish builder – has specialised in facade renovation of these buildings and has engaged in a restructuring of the company and its activities towards a more focused and systematic approach:

> One of the goals has been to decompose a facade renovation into clear and meaningful constituent parts and then to join these again in a whole. A new system for facade renovation!
>
> (RBE, 2009: 32)[5]

The system works with four general types of masonry facades: exposed, smooth finished, plastered or green wall. The different work processes are divided into three main blocks: cleaning, masonry work and finish. By the application of 17 (meaningful) combinations of processes from these blocks the result is either renovation of the existing wall type or conversion into another type (Figure 8.3).

The 17 established methods are estimated to cover the need for facade renovation of approximately 80 per cent of Danish multi-storey apartment blocks built between 1850 and 1950. Hence the system elaboration has also supported the delimitation of a primary business target.

Lighting control system

Both bathroom pod and facade renovation are physically located in specific areas or parts of a building. This system is physically distributed and makes use of

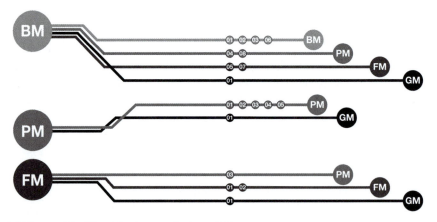

8.3 Diagram of the different facade conversion types, RBE

different technical systems while still delivered integrated as one single system around a specific environmental parameter: the lighting conditions of a room, a dwelling or an entire block or office building.

Artificial lighting constitutes a considerable amount of the energy use in modern living and work environments. Furthermore, solar heating from daylight constitutes an important energy issue in many parts of the world due to the need for ventilation and cooling. These factors interact in many ways but are, however, industry-wise mostly treated as separate physical subsystems with separate suppliers, leaving the architect as the only 'integrator' of the final solution.

Lutron Electronics has specialised in delivery of complete lighting control systems. Using light dimmers as a starting point, the company today delivers a range of different lighting solutions for both residential and commercial settings spanning over – and integrating – dimmers, fixtures, lighting control systems, sensors, window systems and shading devices.[6] Partly due to the distributed character of the system it is widely modularised and easily reconfigurable or extendable making use of existing standard wiring and being compatible with most lighting fixtures and window framings. By connecting all devices to a centralised control unit different lighting conditions can be pre-programmed to support a variety of activities, scheduled work cycles or changing exterior light and weather conditions.

Lutron's system bridges and integrates two different fields of technical expertise that share a common parameter – the lighting conditions in built environment.

User involvement through a process software tool

A software tool – U_build – recently developed for user involvement in construction processes, exemplifies the process as an equally relevant field for development of customisable integrated product deliveries in construction.[7] U_build is meant as a tool for knowledge sharing between more and new players in the process of construction. The tool has been developed from an idea coined by the architectural office Mutopia and enables a controlled user involvement through a semi-automated dialogue between owner/developer and users (defined broadly) applicable for the development of specific building projects and urban planning (Figure 8.4).

The data achieved through the use of U_build can subsequently be applied for qualification of the decision making by owner/developer or consultants through the programming and early design phases.

U_build has been characterised as an 'integrated product delivery spanning across the [traditional] value chain in construction' (Mutopia, 2008:

8.4 A screenshot from a customised version of the U_Build application for Herlev Hospital, Denmark

7). The process is the core whereas the physical outcome itself is not predefined but U_build matches quite well the characteristics of an integrated product delivery: a system supplier delivers a (software) product that is 'configured and customised' for user involvement in a specific project. Content as 3D-model, project material and information and a prepared structure for dialogue and comments is customised for each specific software delivery.

NEW ROLES AMONG STAKEHOLDERS

As mentioned above, traditionally a building was designed and built along the division of the established crafts, hence working as the 'subsystems' expressing the system structure. However, as complexity has increased and specialisation has enhanced the number of stakeholders involved in a building project, the task of controlling these subsystems and their interactions in specific projects on a trade-by-trade basis has become increasingly difficult. The appearance of turnkey contractors as an intermediate actor specialised in providing the client with a singular contract based on an estimate and coordination of all sub-contractors seems, on the one hand, to lock in this traditional division and, on the other hand, to take the control out of the hands of the client and, more important, of the architect who is supposed to specify it. However, incentives to change existing structures for most stakeholders seem small.

Over-specification

Conscious or active use of system structures in construction as a new supplementary design activity could be seen as an integrative phase dealing with many other factors than economy. The architect or other consultants as integrators should be concerned with this issue. But today, for example, the architect is not – or only loosely – in control. Only by specifying to an ever-greater extent can the consultant presently try to control the subcontracting of the turnkey contractor. This can, however, easily result in over-specification on a relatively uninformed basis where the focus becomes specific solutions instead of their performance. The result can again be that the contractor is locked in an inappropriate system structure with an incoherent result – this time forced by the architect or consultant who does not have direct access to the suppliers, thus specifying on the basis of deficient knowledge.

Configuration of embedded knowledge

An alternative – and more industrialised – scenario could be new kinds of project specific trade-by-trade contracts based on a design process that from the beginning draw on integrated products rather than on the traditional crafts. What if architectural design to a wider degree entailed configuration and orchestration of *assemblages* of integrated product deliveries in a total system structure? This is seen as opposed to the chaotic translation of form into a coordination of crafts along divisions that no longer match the processes and components of the construction industry. Considerable design knowledge could be embedded in these systems rather than – as traditionally – in the crafts and could reduce the complexity of the particular project-based design task – again without necessarily reducing the complexity of the physical result itself. Such a strategy would, however, require a direct link between manufacturers and specifying consultants and early involvement of the former. Current available contractual models obstruct this kind of organisation which is only found in extremely specialised high end technical solutions as, for example, high performance facade solutions that integrate teams of designers, planners, engineers, consultants and technical specialists around specific projects – not products.

In the scenario sketched above the architect can still be seen as a central, though by no means *exclusive*, creator of a building. However, in order to make architectural creation possible today it is here argued that architects and other specifying consultants *need* to rely on knowledge embedded in industrialised systems – as they equally relied on knowledge in the crafts. A future industrialised architecture based on assemblages or configurations of discrete integrated product deliveries could represent an opportunity of getting out of the work overload of over-specification and (again) rather concentrate on architectural wholes.

Robust combinations of different integration levels

It is important to point out that it is not an either/or; contemporary architecture and construction already use more integrated products than mere building materials and components while not necessarily ending up in closed all-encompassing systems. The use of a combination of products on different integration levels will probably always be necessary – and desirable from an architectural point of view!

By designing hierarchies or (supply) chains of nested products on various integration levels, ideally leading through IPDs to be inserted in a building, the complexity to be handled on each level is considerably reduced. This would equally concern the integrative design work to be performed by the architect and other consultants. If nested products can be independently replaced on various system levels (e.g. according to life span or changed requirements) the result could be a very robust architectural design also stressing an environmental point of view led by equal flexibility of design, conversion and maintenance.

FUTURE PERSPECTIVES

A question is whether a new specific industrialised product-by-product structure of the built environment can be drawn to replace the fading traditional trade-by-trade structure of the crafts. Earlier we took the standpoint that any building project has its particular system structure due to contextual factors. Buildings will never meet a 'one-fits-all' structure. Seen from the industry the most rational would be fixed conventions on interfaces between clearly defined integrated products. This could create the basis for well-structured markets of IPDs as subassemblies. In the car industry almost every car consists of the same basic structure of main components: chassis, body, engine, doors, 4 wheels, windshield etc. Specific versions of these components can be produced by one manufacturer and used across many different car brands. This makes it somehow easier to design and produce a new car as it does not really question what a car IS! This is different in architectural creation. Although architects do not necessarily have to 'reinvent the wheel' in every project, there are considerable differences due to the much larger web of contextual interactions and dependencies (physical, organisational, cultural, economic etc.). Although technically complex, a car deals basically with the question of moving you from a to b. However behavioural, cultural, environmental and material issues are either universal or relatively simple for a car when compared to the built environment.

Industrialised architecture

What is proposed here is that a system structure seen as a flexible project specific *pattern* potentially could represent a systemic way of creating a better overview of the complex context specific coupling of materials, components and an increasing number of IPDs appearing on the market. The IPDs can, as nested or embedded systems, potentially contribute to complexity reduction on different integration levels – in the supply chain as well as in the architectural design process. The gain could be more commoditised but still integrated architectural wholes: a new combination of economies of scale and economies of scope. We have shown how some of these new products span across markets and how they can integrate elements of both matter and process.

To make this new *architecture* possible it is, however, necessary that these new products are flexible in their internal structure and function as well as in their interfaces with the surroundings and other adjacent product deliveries on varying integration levels. There is a risk that industrially produced systems will tend towards a limited solution space of standardised products in order to attain economies of scale rather than the architecturally far more appealing economies of scope that rather draw on standardised operations or processes. The first industrialisation wave of construction in the 1960–1970s resulted in such inflexible systems. Although present computer technology with superior processing and information storing capacity does constitute a different basis for production based on economies of scope, it is still difficult to see whether the economic incentive is present in the building industry. Many legislative, contractual and organisational issues still seem constraining. If the subsystems, i.e. IPDs, are inflexible most probably so will be the solution space of the assembled result.

Whether IPDs will become primary elements of a new architectural practice only time will show. Apart from many obstacles it can also be discussed whether it is a desirable scenario seen from an architectural point of view. What is certain is, however, that producing architecture in a predominantly intuitive way has become more problematic as design issues today are far more complex and the number of stakeholders involved in the creation of a building is increasing. This has created problems with lack of coherence in our built environment. More systematic approaches seem indispensable at least as supplementary or design supportive activities. Faced with real world conditions, the new combination of economies of scale of the IPDs and the economies of scope of their assembly into particular buildings points towards the assumption that the use of sufficiently customisable IPDs will enhance design flexibility compared to both the 'building-by-pieces' and the 'turnkey solution' strategies. Further conceptualisation, investigation and development of new proactive supporting tools will, however, be necessary to explore and exploit their potential.

NOTES

1   For an explanation of *heuristics* see e.g. Maier and Rechtin (2009: 5).

2   Ulrich and Eppinger (2008: 15) use the similar term *system level design* for products as e.g. printers, photocopiers and scooters. For an elaborated introduction to the concept of *system structure* see Vibæk (2012).

3   See also Beim et al. (2010)

4   Partly taken from Beim et al. (2010: 90).

5   Includes author's own translations from RBE (2009).

6   http://www.lutron.com/ (accessed September 30 2010).

7   Partly taken from Vibæk (2009).

BIBLIOGRAPHY

Alexander, C. (1964) *Notes on the Synthesis of Form,* Cambridge: Harvard University Press.

Bachman, L. R. (2003) *Integrated Buildings – The Systems Basis of Architecture,* Hoboken, NJ: John Wiley & Sons.

Beim, A., Nielsen J. and Vibæk K. S. (2010) *Three Ways of Assembling a House,* Copenhagen: Royal Danish Academy of Fine Arts, School of Architecture.

Maier, M. W. and Rechtin E. (2009) *The Art of Systems Architecting,* 3rd edn, Boca Raton: CRC Press.

Mutopia (2008) *U_build – Fremtidens proces og dialogværkktøj,* Copenhagen: Mutopia.

RBE (2009) *Facadeguiden – Rundt om facaden,* Ringsted: RBE.

Ulrich, K. T. and Eppinger S. D. (2008) *Product Design and Development,* 4th edn, New York: McGraw-Hill.

Vibæk, K. S. (2009) 'User involvement as a configurable integrated product delivery', in F. T. Piller and M. M. Tseng (eds) *Proceedings of MCPC2009 – Mass Customization and Personalization Conference,* Helsinki: University of Art & Design.

Vibæk, K. S. (2010) 'System level design and nested systems in industrialised architectural design' (unpublished), Royal Danish Academy of Fine Arts, School of Architecture.

Vibæk, K. S. (2012) *System Structures in Architecture – Constituent Elements of a Contemporary Industrialised Architecture,* Royal Danish Academy of Fine Arts, School of Architecture.

9

Design and construction of three-dimensional lightweight timber grid structures explored through a mass-customised approach

Olga Popovic Larsen

ABSTRACT

Mass customisation has successfully been applied in the product industries and in recent years is also finding application in the built environment. Examples of how to enhance the building processes and architectural practice by applying mass-customisation principles are becoming more evident. We are starting to see architectural examples where facade elements have been mass-customised and as a result we have solutions that are constructed to a higher specification within comparable budgets. Also this method offers possibilities of a more integrated design/build approach with possibilities for better and more appropriate use of materials, construction methods and processes. Sustainable design/production processes become more easily applied without compromising the architectural qualities. However, as a result of the manually operated and craft nature of the building industry, mass customisation within the built environment is still only applicable in some cases where industrialised approaches to design/production have been used. This chapter discusses the architectural potential and design/construction opportunities that lightweight timber grid load-bearing roof structures can offer. A case study with two lightweight timber structures involving the construction of two full-scale physical models – a gridshell and a multiple reciprocal frame structure – is presented in the context of mass customisation.

LIGHTWEIGHT GRID STRUCTURES – POTENTIAL FOR MASS CUSTOMISATION

Typically lightweight grid structures offer efficient structural solutions. In the case of both single and double layered grid structures the optimal three-dimensional form is used which typically results in greater structural efficiency. Most efficient structural grids are *form-active* grids, which typically are double-curved where the structure works by achieving shell action. These structures are similar to surface shells, only the surface of the shell is formed by a three-dimensional grid. Single-curved (vaulted structures) and flat grids in comparison are not as efficient as double-curved forms. Still, one can argue that they are lighter than more solid structures and as a result the dead-weight of the structure is reduced.

In cases of structural grids there is often a great degree of repetition and as a result off-site fabrication methods can be used. This is common practice when uniform materials such as steel or aluminium members are used for the grid structure. Good examples are space grids, perhaps the Biome Structures at the Eden Project by Grimshaw and Partners and Anthony Hunt Associates (AHA-SKM) are some of the largest ever built (Pearman and Whalley 2003).

In cases where the steel members that are not identical are used to form the structure, present CAD-CAM production methods also allow for off-site production methods. Good examples are steel gridshell structures consisting of a great number of small members all different in length and connected by customised connections. A recent and well-known example is the Great Court roof gridshell by Norman Foster and Buro Happold.

Similarly to the steel and aluminium examples, in the case of timber grid structures there also is a potential for mass-customising the structure. The customisation allows for creating timber structures where the form of the structure is customised to the particular architectural/spatial requirements whilst fulfilling the technical requirements for structural safety and serviceability. All these are also done within a viable budget. The case study presents an exploration with full-scale physical modelling of two innovative timber grid structures: a multiple reciprocal frame grid structure and a timber gridshell. This chapter discusses the architectural opportunities of these two structural types and the potential for their mass customisation.

THE CONTEXT OF THE CASE STUDY

Two full-scale models were built as part of the *Organic Structures* specialist course that was run for the first time during 2009/2010 at the Royal Danish Academy of Fine Arts, School of Architecture (KA). It was aimed at third year students and the main topic of study was nature-inspired load-bearing structures and their application in architecture. Special emphasis was put on the 1:1 hands-on modelling workshops, one on gridshells and the other one on multiple reciprocal frames.

RECIPROCAL FRAMES AND MULTIPLE RECIPROCAL GRIDS

Reciprocal frame (RF) structure is a form of a three-dimensional grillage structure. In their simplest configuration they are formed by placing beams in a closed circuit in which each beam is supported by the preceding beam at the inner end, and by an external wall or ring beam on the outer end. In their more complex configurations gridshell-like structures with a double curvature can be formed. Although RFs have been used in many countries throughout history and are known under different names – Serlio-type ceiling; Reciprocal frames, Svastica structures, Nexorades, Lever-arch structures etc. – they are not widely known and as a result have not been used often in buildings.

It is likely that the contemporary reciprocal frame structure originates from a form of a traditional Japanese layered structure which has evolved in its present form (Popovic Larsen 2007). Only writings about the historic Japanese RFs exist and unfortunately none of the original structures have survived time. It is not surprising though that the most beautiful contemporary examples have been built in Japan (Popovic Larsen 2009). The work of architects Kazuhiro Ishii and Yasufumi Kijima, as well as structural engineer Yoichi Kan, show the potential of RFs for creating imaginative architectural and structural forms. All of the few built examples use traditional carpentry methods and although there is a lot of repetition mass customisation has not been a consideration (Figure 9.1).

For the organic structures specialist course run at KA the multiple reciprocal grid that was constructed was based on a four member single RF unit. The overall structure formed a closed loop with the two bands of the structure crossing each other. It was decided to model in full scale the part where the two RF wings crossed each other presented in Figure 9.2. To do this before the construction took place 200 one-metre square section pine timber pieces of (sectional dimension 25 mm by 25mm) were cut to length. Three holes of diameter 5mm were pre-drilled at a distance of 33 cm from each end to enable the members to be connected together. The simple connection was chosen for speed of construction.

The 7 metres full-scale multiple reciprocal grid full-scale model took about 5 hours to construct by a group of 10 students. This was clearly a temporary and experimental structure but had the project been for a more permanent use similar design/construction principles could have been used. In such a case the timber elements with a customised joint for a specific cladding system could be pre-made off-site.

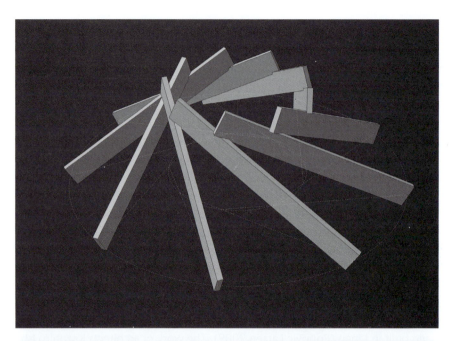

9.1A AND B A single RF unit and the multiple RF roof – courtesy Kazuhiro Ishii

9.2 The multiple RF structure – nearing completion

This particular example was not clad. The grid was left open and the shell suggested space without really enclosing a space. To clad the structure it would be best to design a simple secondary structure supported by the double curved main grid. Another possibility would be to use fabric cladding or ETFE panels.

To avoid vertical supports in this particular example, cables were used that were tensioned between the two symmetrical wings of the grid. These together with the points of the grid which were supported directly on the ground created a stable and safe structure. One could of course consider other ways of supporting the grid – this was the simplest and most elegant in this particular case.

An unexplored mass-customisation potential of multiple RF grids is the possibility of using different single RF units to create three-dimensional complex doubly curved grids. If one combines units that have different number of beams in the single units the overall grid structure will have a different overall geometry and appearance. Also this will have implications on the structural behaviour. An on-going research project by the author of this chapter currently investigates the potential of multiple RF grids, looking at the geometrical definition, architectural potential and structural behaviour. Mass customisation as a design/construction approach will also be explored further as part of the project.

GRIDSHELL STRUCTURES

The second workshop part of the same course on organic structures was on gridshells. Gridshells are a three-dimensional structural system in which short members are combined to form a load-bearing grid structure. Due to the achieved shell action the members in the grid work mainly in compression which makes the system structurally efficient. In addition the three-dimensional forms of the structure create a distinct architectural aesthetic and a possibility for creating a new language of expression.

Timber gridshells have not been used widely in architecture, yet they have so much to offer. If constructed out of timber they offer a great opportunity for material saving. This is due to the fact that the clear span grids are formed by using short and small section pieces of timber joined together to form long flexible laths, which are assembled into a three-dimensional system of mutually supporting load-bearing structure. At a time when sustainable approaches in design are becoming increasingly important, the opportunity to save material by using an efficient structural system is essential. In addition, similar to multiple RF grids, gridshells offer the opportunity of creating distinct three-dimensional architectural forms. This three-dimensionality of gridshells as a structural system has an architectural/spatial implication. The structural/technical and the architectural/aesthetic aspects are inseparable in the gridshell design process.

Examples of timber gridshell buildings include: The Mannheim Multihalle, 1975, by Carlfried Mutschler, Frei Otto and Ove Arup & Partners (engineers); roof canopies, Expo 2000, Hanover, by Thomas Herzog and Bois Consult Natterer (engineers); The Downland Gridshell, near Chichester, 2002, by Edward Cullinan Architects and Buro Happold (engineers); The Savill Building, Windsor (2008) by Glenn Howells Architects and Buro Happold (engineers).

During the organic structures workshop a 7 metre bamboo gridshell was constructed. The design process involved testing the structure through sketches and small-scale models. The design that was chosen for scaling up was constructed by using bamboo sticks that were connected to form the correct length of members. There were only two members with the same length and some of the longest members exceeded 10 metres in length. The two assemblies of the fan-like structures were interwoven and connected. The overall construction of the gridshell took about 5 hours (Figure 9.3).

Although the described gridshell was only an experimental and temporary open structure (with no cladding) it showed that by pre-making the members the construction process could be finished in a very short time. In the construction of timber gridshells one has to take into account the bending of the timber laths which if too fast can cause permanent damage and breaking of the members. This was not an issue when building with bamboo due to the

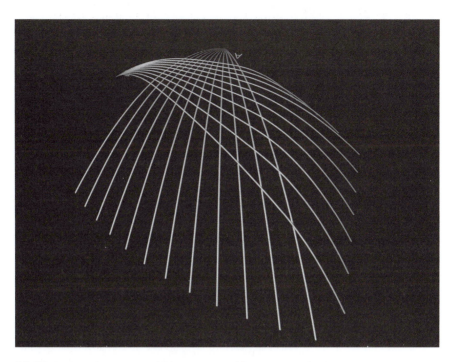

9.3 CAD drawings of the constructed 7 metre bamboo gridshell – courtesy D. Lee

great flexibility of the material. Perhaps materials that flex more easily and are more elastic would be something to explore as a possibility for constructing gridshells in a faster way. Figure 9.4 shows the completed bamboo gridshell.

The customisation aspect in the second example is in the opportunity for creating mass-customised doubly curved forms. Present design tools as well production tools using CAD/CAM techniques and digital crafting methods allow for relatively easy and fast form definition and production. In simple words – the design/production tools at present are at a level to produce an endless spectrum of mass-customised gridshell forms. Not surprisingly, and probably as a result, there is a whole new family of customised gridshell structures – known as *free-form shells*. Free-form shells clearly offer a great space generation opportunity and an even greater opportunity for creating novel architectural expressions. However, one should not forget that the three-dimensional shape of a form active structure (such as a gridshell) will influence the structural efficiency of the structure. Although the structural efficiency of a load-bearing structure is not always the leading factor when deciding on the structural form, it is a very important factor and one that cannot be overlooked.

9.4 The completed bamboo gridshell

CONCLUSION

The chapter presented two examples of lightweight roof structures and investigated their architectural potential. Also it examined if mass customisation can be used as an approach to design/construction of these systems. Both structures showed a great potential for creating distinct and interesting architectural forms. Also the construction of the full-scale experimental physical models showed that mass customisation would be an appropriate approach for constructing these structures. However, for mass customisation to be fully applicable more research into production techniques would need to be carried out.

ACKNOWLEDGEMENTS

The course was initiated and organised by the author of the paper, supported by Professor Tony Hunt, visiting Velux Professor at KA, founder of Anthony Hunt Associates (now SKM AHA), Tom Hay, Associate Director Buro Happold Copenhagen and Consultant to KA, Gabriel Tang, Senior Lecturer at Sheffield Hallam School of Architecture and Biagio de Carlo, Architect from Italy.

BIBLIOGRAPHY

http://en.wikipedia.org/wiki/Eden_Project (accessed 14 May 2012).

http://www.fosterandpartners.com/projects/0828/default.aspx (accessed 14 May 2012).

Interview with Glenn Howells, 10 June 2009 by O. Popovic Larsen and G. Tang.

Pearman, H. and Whalley, A. (2003) *The Architecture of Eden*, London: Eden Project Books.

Popovic Larsen, O. (2007) *Reciprocal Frame Architecture*, London: Elsevier.

Popovic Larsen, O. (2009) 'Reciprocal Frames in Japan', *Proceedings IASS 2009*, Valencia.

Popovic Larsen, O. and Tyas, A. (2003) *Conceptual Structural Design: Bridging the Gap between Architects and Engineers*, London: Thomas Telford.

10

Robot oriented construction management

Thomas Bock and Thomas Linner

ABSTRACT

The construction industry has a low productivity rate of raw material input and about 40–50 per cent of global raw materials are used for the construction of our environment. Construction waste represents the largest waste fraction even in highly industrialised countries and buildings are among the most expensive goods that we produce. Although we have achieved high effiency in the production of complex high-tech products as cars and computers, we have not brought the production of simple low-tech products such as buildings to a comparable level. An alternative method to conventional construction is the large-scale deployment of industrialisation, enabled by applying automation and robotics based processes and technologies throughout all phases of the life cycle of built environments. The present chapter first analyses best-practice industrialisation/automation and building production projects, which have been tested or applied successfully in larger scales during the last decades. Furthermore, the chapter derives from that analysis a framework for combined on/off-site building production as an approach for managing sustainable and resource efficient construction processes. Strategies from the presented framework are currently applied by the authors of this chapter to various projects around the world.

INTRODUCTION

The paradigm of sustainability gradually pervades all industrial sectors, all levels of value creation and all aspects of daily life, leading to a new twenty-first-century industrial revolution (Hawken *et al.*, 1999) where the importance of environmental and social factors is merely equated with pure economic efficiency. Legal frameworks, financial incentives and market/price developments urge more and more industries to change their processes and to shift from economic growth to sustainable development. This change affects the value system as well as multiple enterprise levels and reaches from organisation, new product structures, new processes and technologies, microelectronic devices, ICT structures, flexible automation, robotics and knowledge based logistics to life cycle performance, reuse and remanufacturing. Industrialised structures are deployed in nearly all industrial sectors and form a solid basis for steady advance and gradual development towards a more sustainable economy. However, in construction industry industrialised structures are merely developed and advanced devices, which are state-of-the-art technology in other producing industries, are still rejected. The construction industry has the lowest productivity rate of raw material input and about 40–50 per cent of global raw materials are used for the construction of our environment. Construction waste represents the largest waste fraction even in highly industrialised countries and the capability of that waste to be recycled with low environmental impact is rather low (OECD, 2008). Moreover, the working conditions for construction workers in highly industrialised countries as well as in the emerging construction industries of India and China are challenging. Furthermore, buildings are among the most expensive goods that we produce, and although we have achieved complex high-tech products such as cars and computers being relatively affordable for everybody, we have not brought simple low-tech products as buildings to a comparable level.

State of the art in automation and robotics

An alternative method to conventional construction, which is labour intensive, consumes tremendous amounts of energy and material, causes large amounts of waste, provides unsatisfactory working conditions and, moreover, is not able to supply more affordable buildings, is the large-scale deployment of industrial-isation: prefabrication, automation, advanced logistics, Enterprise Resource Planning (ERP), flexible automation, robotics and other smart assistance devices. Toyota Home prefabricates customised and highly modular housing units "to order" while it relies on adapted principles of Toyota's lean and demand oriented production system. Flexible machinery, "Kanban", "Kaizen" and "Just-in-time Just-in-sequence" minimise the input of workforce, resources and energy, meanwhile the only products fabricated are those that are demanded (Linner and Bock, 2009). Other prefab companies in Japan operate their business in a similar manner. The total output of Japan's prefabrication industry is about 150,000 buildings per annum. Finkelzeller (2003) suggests that Radio-frequency Identification (RFID) enabled construction logistics systems are being developed and tested in Europe in order to upgrade conventional construction logistics

(Helmus *et al.*, 2009). Those RFID logistics are currently developed further for integration with ERP systems. The automation of high-rise construction and on-site factories have been realised in Japan by several of the leading construction companies (Shimizu, Obayasi, Kajima, Takenaka) since the 1980s. There, the construction process has not only been partly automated, but logistics are organised strictly and the construction progress is displayed and controlled in real time (Ikeda and Harada, 2006). Today those systems are also able to erect not-rectangular and individually designed buildings with reduced workforce and optimised resource performance (Bock, 2009). Autonomous mobile and modular site robots for finishing and refurbishing tasks have been developed and used since the 1990s in Japan and Germany (Bock and Linner, 2010a). Recent R&D in Korea, supported by the authors of this chapter, is now focusing on human–machine cooperative systems (Lee *et al.*, 2007), power-assistance devices, wearable robots and new types of automated construction sites (Bock *et al.*, 2009). The goal of Korean research is to integrate the workers' skills and intelligence and the power of the machines and robots. Furthermore, the digital data gathered throughout planning and construction can be used for the operation of mobile servicing robots, such as examples from Japan (Kajima, Taisei) and France (Louvre Glass Cleaning Robot) demonstrated by Bock and Linner (2010a). Finally, systemised and partially automated systems (Kajima) for controlled deconstruction allow a recycling rate of up to 93 per cent (Bock, 2009) and Japan's prefab makers try to build up reverse logistics and remanufacturing systems (Sekisui Heim, 2009).

BEST-PRACTICE INDUSTRIALISATION PROJECTS

Industrialisation projects are organised and presented in accordance with the value-added steps in order to show that all projects, processes and technologies in combination would represent the whole value chain. This book chapter derives from that analysis a framework for integrated on/off-site industrialisation technologies as an approach for managing sustainable construction processes through closing the value chain. Finally, the findings are summarised in the conclusion.

Conveyor belt based off-site fabrication in Japan

Customised fabrication has a long history in Japan. After the Second World War, Toyota Motor Corporation searched for a way to improve its productivity by a factor of ten (Ohno, 1988). At that time, the Japanese market was changing fast and demand was for an extremely small series of cars. Toyota researchers at that time also visited the factories of Ford and GM and concluded that a fabrication strategy based on mass production strategies and "economies of scale" would not be efficient and successful in the Japanese socio-economic system. This strongly demand oriented thinking in industrial fabrication made it easy for Japanese companies to later deploy industrialised structures in the fabrication of houses as well. Nowadays, the production systems of Toyota Home (85 per cent factory completion), Sekisui Heim (80 per cent factory production) and Sekisui House (50 per cent factory completion) are highly advanced and automated. Toyota Home (Skeleton and Infill) and Sekisui Heim (Unit Method) have based their systems on cubical metal frames specially designed for customised and demand oriented factory production of buildings (Bock and Linner, 2010a) on the conveyor belt.

Advanced logistics and ERP solutions

Complex projects are characterised by a high number of operators, activities and logical links. Therefore, in all advanced industries with a high diffusion rate of automation and robotics technology (i.e. automotive industry, aircraft industry and ship industry), real-time ERP communication systems are used to coordinate highly modularised organisational structures. Modularisation offers the possibility to react to changes fast and dynamically. Nowadays, modularity is not only limited to the product itself, but cuts across all enterprise levels: management, design and product engineering, logistics, supply and production (Moum, 2006). Sekisui Heim, famous for its legendary "Unit-Method", introduced its HAPPS (Heim Automated Parts Pickup System) in the 1970s (Furuse and Katano, 2006), and started to deliver industrialised houses with individual floor plans. HAPPS was one of the first ERP solutions enabling continuous workflow management for industrialised production of individual buildings.

On-site/off-site combined fabrication

From 2002 to 2005 NCC (Nordic Construction Company) Sweden worked on developing an industrialised concept for multi-storey residential buildings and for which they ran a test project called "NCC Komplett" from 2005 to 2007 (Thuesen and Jonsson, 2009). This was a manufacturing system combining factory prefabrication with a mobile on-site assembly hall. In the off-site factory, concrete walls were customised according to customer demands and architect plans. Most of the fit-out work, i.e. installation of electrical cables and appliances, sub-components, windows, doors, radiators and fixed furniture modules for bath and kitchen, was performed in the factory. Only four assembly workers and one assembly foreman were needed per average building, since the flow of materials, components and resources was highly controlled through advanced logistics systems and the combination of controlled off-site and on-site processes.

Modular and flexible on-site automation

Since 1990, about 25 automated high-rise sites (Bock, 2007) have been operated by various Japanese companies (Taisei, Takenaka, Kajima, Shimizu, Maeda, Kumagai, Ohbayashi). An automated high-rise construction site can be defined as a vertically moving factory (Figure 10.1) combining semi- and fully automated storage systems with transport and assembly equipment and/or robots to erect a building almost completely automatically. The high rate of defined processes reduces material and resource consumption, and construction waste

10.1 Shimizu's vertically moving "SMART" factory in operation

10.2 Skanska's prototype of an automated building construction system

is nearly completely avoided. Moreover, on-site factories provide an appropriate and safe working environment. Automated Building Construction Systems can be designed to be highly modular and flexible. Today, European construction firms have also adopted flexible site-automation systems (e.g. Skanska, Figure 10.2).

Flexible on-site robots

Early on-site construction robots were introduced in the civil engineering sector, because of repetitive working tasks such as road construction, tower and bridge building, dam construction, nuclear power plant construction and tunneling. Major Japanese construction companies have been researching and developing robotised construction processes since the beginnings of the 1980s. Initially, individual robots and remote controlled manipulators were developed for specific processes on building sites. This included robots for delivering and handling concrete, applying fireproofing to steel constructions, handling and positioning large components, and facade inspection or painting robots (Figure 10.3). In Japan over 400 different robots were developed in total which were used on building sites. In Germany since the 1990s various robots have been implemented for supporting interior finishing and refurbishing work in order to increase productivity of building stock modernisation.

10.3 Wall and facade painting robot capable of multilayered painting, Japan

10.4 Kajima has developed several robotic systems for supporting automated construction and deconstruction tasks

Systemised deconstruction

Within 11 months, three high-rise buildings in the center of Tokyo were recently deconstructed by a semi-automated deconstruction system (Kajima). The process of deconstruction was reversed and re-engineered. It starts with the dismantling of the ground floor. While dismantling the ground floor, the upper part of the building was held by IT-coordinated hydraulics. With this method, floor by floor was dropped down subsequently and disassembled at the ground floor level. As the deconstruction was highly coordinated and could conveniently be conducted on the ground floor level, 93 per cent of the building components could be recycled (recycling rate of conventional demolition: 55 per cent). This example shows that the consequent deployment of advanced on-site technologies could be crucial for sustainability in construction/deconstruction in the future. Kajima has developed several robotic systems for supporting automated construction and deconstruction tasks (Figure 10.4).

Off-site building re-customisation

All obsolete building modules of Sekisui Heim can be accepted as trade-in values for a new Sekisui Heim building. Therefore, the deconstruction process is a reversed and modified version of the construction process which is based on subsequent unit factory completion of modular units on the conveyor belt as described before. For deconstruction, joints between steel frame units are initially eased, and then the house is transported to a special dismantling factory unit by unit. There, the outdated finishes are dismantled and fed into advanced reuse cycles established around factories. The bare steel frame units are further inspected and renovated, and are finally equipped with new finishes, specified by a customer who has chosen to buy a remanufactured house. On a web-platform for "Reuse System Houses", Sekisui organises a gathering of people who want to sell their modular house for reuse, and people willing to buy a remanufactured home. The newly outfitted units are then assembled on a new foundation in the new site.

INTEGRATION ALONG THE VALUE CHAIN BY ROBOT ORIENTED MANAGEMENT

Information can be seen as a common element of development, planning, production and (building) product. Based on the knowledge about a prospective customer, information is embedded in a product through design and production. T. Fujimoto, famous for his research on the Toyota Production Systems, goes even one step further and claims that consumers consume not goods or services but information: "what he or she consumes is essentially a bundle of information delivered through the car rather than the car as physical entity" (1999). Similarly, Piller (2006) describes production as a process where physical materials are transformed through machinery, organisation and information into products. From this information point of view, it is necessary to see all steps of the value creation process as a set of complementary subsystems which is jointly embedding information and transforming physical materials through information in order to create value. For the integration of processes along the value chain in construction, advanced production technology, advanced product structure, advanced management and organisation, and advanced philosophies have to be synchronised and applied as a complete and co-adapted set of strategies (Figure 10.5).

Advanced production technology

Automation and robotics

Fully automated and semi-automated on-site factories reduce labor requirements by around 30 per cent, and in the future they are expected to achieve a labor saving of more than 50 per cent. Today semi-automated high-rise construction systems are even capable of creating individual and not explicitly rectangular

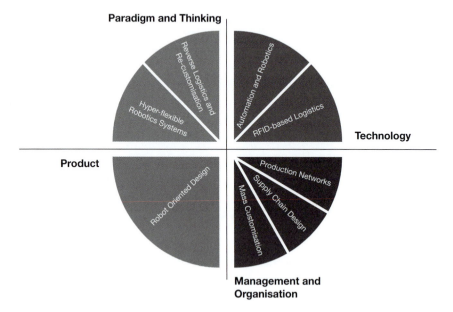

10.5 For the integration of processes along the value chain in construction, advanced production technology, advanced product structure, advanced management and organisation, and advanced philosophies have to be synchronised and applied as a complete and co-adapted set of strategies

buildings. The high rate of defined processes reduces material and resource consumption and construction waste is nearly completely avoided. Moreover, on-site factories provide an appropriate and safe working environment. Automated Building Construction Systems can be designed in a highly modular and flexible way.

RFID based logistics

Through tagging goods and products with RFID, logistics within a network or within a company can be traced and controlled in real time. Thus the physical location of products and the state of the network can be displayed in a digital and alphanumerical way supporting advanced use of this data. RFID logistics can be integrated with ERP and expert systems thus allowing for optimised coordination and just-in-time just-in-sequence production flows. Thus, RFID used in logistics allows the representation of the physical condition of a logistics/production flow in an informative way – again information, its transmission and transformation are the key to efficiency. Even in construction, RFID supported site logistics have been tested and advanced in recent research projects in order to improve organisation and material flow on construction sites.

Advanced product structure

Robot oriented design

In integrated industrialised construction, the product structure is the most crucial and most complex item of the whole process chain. Yet construction products are still inflexible, showing a highly interdependent component structure in contrast to what, for example, Baldwin and Clark (2000) consider as industry and innovation supporting modularity. Systemised and modularised building structures have to be developed in close cooperation with the needs of fabrication, logistics, customisation and robotic and cooperative applications (Bock, 1988). Furthermore, greater agreements and standards on those systemised building structures should be deployed in the industry's legal framework, to foster the exchange and substitution of materials, sub-components and components among the industry's players.

Advanced management and organisation

Supply chain design

For integration along the value chain, supply chain design is an important tool for setting up the flow of information and physical goods within a value creation network of firms. Fastening innovation cycles and increasingly dynamic economic environments demand that those networks are flexible and can rearrange and adjust quickly and on demand the amounts of goods and information transferred between them. Thus, new concepts such as information sharing in supply chains and IT tools for collaborative planning and managing of supply chains evolve in the field of supply chain design, in order to improve the integration along the value chain and thus the ability to respond quickly as a total system to market changes.

Mass customisation

Conventional construction today is heavily reliant on human power. It delivers individual products, yet at high costs and nearly without relying on high-tech solution. Robotics and advanced equipment are not in the focus of architecture and construction. Industrialisation in architecture and construction for a long time has not been considered as being able to deliver individual buildings adjusted to locations and people's need (Bock and Linner, 2010b). With mass customisation (Piller, 2006), construction industry gets a strong new tool: based on integrating organisational structures over the whole value chain corresponding with information flows between enterprise, product, machinery, robots, customers and all complementary sub-processes.

Production networks

Prefabrication of components, modules or completed units, logistics, ERP, automated on-site construction, construction robotics, robotic co-workers, systemised deconstruction and other new technologies and processes could be seen as complementary elements, forming an ecology of factories, devices, equipment, processes, resources and human beings.

Advanced paradigm and philosophy

Hyper flexible robotic systems

The next generation of robots will work in the direct operating range of human workers in order to achieve optimum flexibility, which is a basic requirement for customisation and flexible individual product fabrication by industrialised methods. Robotic systems of the next generation will be "assistants" (EUROP, 2009), helping human workers to perform complex tasks, rather than fully autonomous systems. New interaction concepts, interfaces, concepts for lightweight robots, integrated force-torque sensors and teaching systems, are therefore now developed by researchers around the world. The strategy of "Human-Robot-Cooperative-Manipulation" (Lee et al., 2007) integrates the advantages of both robots and human beings, and creates highly flexible cooperative systems that are predestinated for complex tasks in factories or on construction sites.

Reverse logistics and re-customisation

Eco-factories are factories that produce at high efficiency and in accordance with environmental needs: carbon neutral, powered by renewable energy, zero-waste (Business and Economy Trends in Japan, 2011). An essential economic and ecologic factor in most industries today is the implementation of factories with low or even no environmental impact. Factories are increasingly able to manage the closed-loop circulation of all resources and materials efficiently. Additionally, disassembled components can be reused or recycled with high efficiency through the dismantling process taking place in a controlled factory environment, feeding them again into new industrial transformation circles.

CONCLUSION

New organisational structures, new processes and technologies, microelectronic systems, ICT, flexible automation, robotics, human–machine cooperative systems, tagged equipment, modular building components and knowledge based logistics are enablers of a shift towards sustainable economic construction, when they are designed as complementary parts of a total system. Industrialised structures provide the basic foundation for a gradual development towards a more sustainable construction industry. Therefore, in this chapter, examples have been given which outline best practices in sustainable industrialised construction. Moreover, a framework for future industrialisation and robot oriented management has been presented, which suggests the combination and integration of processes and technologies to an advanced ecology of factories, devices, equipment, resources and human beings.

BIBLIOGRAPHY

Baldwin, Y. C. and Clark, K. B. (2000) *Design Rules – The Power of Modularity*, Cambridge, MA: The MIT Press.

Bock, T. (1988) *Robot Oriented Design*, Tokyo: Shokokusha.

Bock, T. (2007) 'Construction robotics', *Autonomous Robots*, 22(3): 201–209.

Bock, T. (2009) 'Daruma-otoshi skyscraper deconstruction: The roof is constructed first and the ground floor is deconstructed first' (Das Dach wird zuerst gebaut -und das Erdgeschoss zuerst rückgebaut), *Bauingenieur*, 2: 47–55.

Bock, T. and Linner, T. (2010a) 'Automation and robotics in on-site production and urban mining', in G. Girmscheid and F. Scheublin (eds) *New Perspective in Industrialization in Construction – A State-of-the-Art Report*, CIB-Publication, 281–298.

Bock, T. and Linner, T. (2010b) 'Individualization of design variation in construction', *27th International Symposium on Automation and Robotics in Construction (ISARC)*, Bratislava, June 2010.

Bock, T., Linner, T. and Lee, S. (2009) 'Integrated industrialization approach for lean on-/off-site building production and resource circulation', *7th Global Conference on Sustainable Manufacturing*, India, December 2009.

Business and Economy Trends in Japan (2011) *Japan Business and Economy National Statistical Data* (in Japanese). Available at: http://www.stat.go.jp (last accessed on 14-12-2012).

EUROP (2009) 'Strategic research agenda for robotics', *Robotic Visions to 2020 and Beyond*, July 2009.

Finkelzeller, K. (2003) *The RFID Handbook*, 2nd edn, Chichester: John Wiley & Sons.

Fujimoto, T. (ed.) (1999) *The Evolution of a Manufacturing System at Toyota*, New York/Oxford: Oxford University Press,

Furuse, J. and Katano, M. (2006) 'Structuring of Sekisui Heim automated parts pickup system (HAPPS) to process individual floor plans', *ISARC 2006 International Symposium on Automation and Robotics in Construction*, Japan, June 2006.

Hawken, P., Lovins, A. and Lovins, L. H. (1999) *Natural Capitalism: Creating the Next Industrial Revolution*, London: Earthscan.

Helmus, M., Meins-Becker, A. and Laußart, L. (2009) *RFID in der Baulogistik- integriertes Wertschöpfungsmodell*, Deutschland: Vierweg + Teubner.

Ikeda, Y. and Harada, T. (2006) 'Application of the Automated Building Construction System using the conventional construction method together', *ISARC 2006 International Symposium on Automation and Robotics in Construction*, Japan.

Lee, S. Y., Lee, Y. K., Lee, H. S., Kim, J. W. and Han, C. S. (2007) 'Human–robot cooperation control for installing heavy construction materials', *Autonomous Robots,* 22(3): 305–319.

Linner, T. and Bock, T. (2009) 'Smart customization in architecture: towards customizable intelligent buildings', in F. T. Piller and M. M. Tseng (eds) *Proceedings of MCPC2009 – Mass Customization and Personalization Conference*, Helsinki: University of Art & Design.

Moum, A. (2006) 'A framework for exploring the ICT impact on the architectural design process', *ITCon Special Issue: The Effects of CAD on Building Form and Design Quality*, 11: 409–425. Available at: http://www.itcon.org/cgi-bin/works/Show?2006_30 (accessed on 24-05-2012).

OECD (2008) *Measuring Material Flows and Resource Productivity*, Synthesis Reports, Paris, France.

Ohno, T. (1988) *Toyota Production System – Beyond Large-scale Production*, Massachusetts: Massachusetts Productivity Press.

Piller, F. T. (2006) *Mass Customization*, Wiesbaden: Deutscher Universitätsverlag.

Sekisui Heim (2009) *System Reuse House*. Available at: http://www.sekisuichemical.com/about/division/housing/reuse.html (accessed on 24-05-2012).

Thuesen, C. and Jonsson, C. C. (2009) 'The long tail and innovation of new construction practices – learning point from two case studies', *Open Building Manufacturing, Key Technologies, Applications, and Industrial Cases,* Manubuild 2009, 51–64.

11

Economic analysis of customised apartments

Guohua Tang and Mitchell M. Tseng

ABSTRACT

Customisation of living space is intrinsically valuable and has been supported by the increasingly wider application of customised housing. With customised housing, customers have wider choices beyond the monolithic decision in traditional housing. Given the additional choices for customers, developers are facing new challenges in deciding different business alternatives, such as what is the right mix of customisable attributes offered to customers, range of choices etc. This chapter addresses this challenge from the economic perspective by developing a decision framework based on discounted cash flows. To simplify the problem, Customised Apartment (CA) is selected to neutralise the geographic location factor. This chapter presents a framework for developers to evaluate the economic feasibility of CA with considerations of different customisation schemes within a unified framework. Thus developers can provide choices not only catered to customer needs, but also avoid complexity and redundancy. Furthermore, a case study of high-rise apartments is presented to discuss the operating window of CA in a specific business environment by demonstrating how some critical factors can be incorporated into the framework.

INTRODUCTION

With ever-increasing urbanisation and improved quality of life, demand for high quality housing has also been increasing significantly. As the ultimate criterion for high quality, customer satisfaction depends heavily on individual tastes, preferences and lifestyles. Moreover, given every house has its own location, views, sunlight and other factors, customisation is essential to achieve better energy conservation and environmental sustainability. Therefore, customers' increasing demand for housing variety leads to the fact that customised housing has been widely recognised as a prominent trend in the housing industry (Naim and Barlow 2003, Leishman and Warren 2006). Evidence in the US, Japan, the UK and some EU countries demonstrates that numerous homebuilders are exploring ways to deliver higher levels of customisation in housing design (Hofman *et al.* 2006). In practice, customers are offered with the flexibility to configure their unique houses by making choices in a vast number of options such as location, exterior finish, floor layout etc.

However, most of the so-called successful cases are low-rise houses. This chapter particularly addresses high-rise apartment buildings because they are not only important for the areas where land cost is high, but also the factor of localisation could be neutralised in the economic analysis. That means geographical preferences are neutralised in their choice decision-making. In order to build the common ground for discussion, Customised Apartment (CA) is defined as follows: a customised apartment is a type of apartment that is designed and built according to customers' specific preferences and ultimately sold or leased to them.

Nevertheless, CA brings new challenges in making rational decisions to customers and developers in respect that both of them are exposed to a substantial number of choices for each option, which engenders decision-making complexity for both. From the developers' perspective, questions like how to provide the right mix of customisable attributes and the right range of customisation are the starting point of CA. In other words, this is to manage the trade-off between increased product variety and efficiency loss due to customisation, since unlimited choices are obviously unaffordable for developers, and may not be favored by customers either. But eventually developers need to make it economically profitable and sustainable, since otherwise developers will have no incentive to deviate from the standard and adopt the CA strategy model if they will suffer relative profit losses. Thus economic analysis of CA becomes imperative.

The purpose of this chapter is to present a framework in which CA developers can address salient questions like:

- How to decide which attributes to customise for customers and within what range?
- Do added values outweigh additional costs? How should a CA project be evaluated?
- What are the operational and strategic implications for the CA development life cycle?

The rest of this chapter is structured as follows. First, common challenges facing CA developers are addressed, since meeting those challenges may impact decisions of product offerings and the profitability of a CA project. This is followed by a theoretical model to capture the trade-off in product offering decision and economic evaluation. Finally an empirical case of CA is presented to discuss the operating window of CA in a specific business environment by demonstrating how some critical factors can be incorporated into the framework.

CA CHALLENGES

Promising to offer flexibility and thus a wide range of products, CA contradicts traditional practices for high-rise apartment development in many ways, which poses great challenges to the developers. This section discusses some challenges, which are by no means exhaustive, and their cost implications in implementation.

Structure system design

Compared with low-rise custom houses, one prominent challenge emerging in CA is the structure issue. In residential buildings, a shear wall system is usually adopted due to its better effectiveness in resisting lateral (wind and seismic) loading than a column frame system. However, a shear wall system imposes partitioning restraints onto the unit's internal layout. In general, to increase the cost effectiveness and structural efficiency in residential buildings, some of the internal partition walls are designed as structural reinforced concrete walls. Allocation of those internal structure walls limits the room layout flexibility. Therefore, to suit different customer needs, a structural system that allows flexible partition layout is needed. However, it may incur additional costs in design and construction, as well as impacts on net usable spaces, which requires careful evaluation.

Sales and marketing

Challenges in sales and marketing are strongly linked to the diversity of customers and frontline sales duties. First, defining the range of customisation could be a challenge. Initially, all attributes pertaining to a flat are candidates for customisation. However, there are several factors restricting the feasibility of offering numerous options. From the sales and marketing point of view, overfull options tend to confuse customers and undermine economic feasibility. A complex set of product offerings is also likely to lengthen the configuration process and require a larger sales force. Second, verbal communication may not suffice customers' full understanding of their selections. Sales thus need to apply new tools to enhance a customer's view of their home configurations. Other sales and marketing challenges, like pricing strategy and sales contract related issues, may also arise because of laws and regulations, which vary from case to case.

Project management

In CA customers must be involved in defining design specifications, thus confirmed customer order information will only be available after the sales contract is signed with the design finalised. This is likely to cause project delays, since the contractors require the details of customer orders to proceed with construction and internal installations. Therefore developers will face a major challenge in limiting this delay due to the business nature of requiring high capital turnover, and at the same time customer orders can be finalised at least before the construction work for the particular units start. In this sense, the efficiency of CA projects largely depends on the effectiveness of customer order management. Making CA more challenging, customer orders for different units in a building will arrive randomly. This is the same case for traditional apartment construction, but it has no adverse impact on the construction progress since the units are almost predefined. Therefore, it is not difficult for contractors to maintain construction efficiency because the sales and construction processes are essentially decoupled. However, sales and construction are intertwined in CA, which challenges developers to maintain the efficiency. Additional costs can be substantial if sales and construction are not synchronised well.

ECONOMIC MODEL FOR CA

Compared with traditional practice of developing apartments, CA poses various challenges and requires introducing new approaches to meet those challenges, which may incur additional costs. Nevertheless, as with many other customised products, CA developers can enjoy a premium in selling price and thus higher revenue. Moreover, this trade-off is associated with the complexity of product offerings. To this end, it is pivotal to develop an economic model to address the relationship between different sets of product offerings and profitability so that CA developers can decide on the right mix and right range of customisable attributes.

Mathematical model

Considerations from multiple aspects need to be analysed in an integrated manner to decide the right mix and right range of customisable attributes for

CA. We adopt a comprehensive framework for developing the model. With the objective to maximise profit when different sets of choices can be generated, the CA developer has to consider how the market will respond to different product offerings. The relationship is typically built upon utility function (Jiao and Zhang 2005). Like other typical mass customisation systems, CA necessitates a product platform, a process platform and a supply platform, where cost drivers need to be identified.

To characterise the problem rigorously, we introduce the following notations. Given a set of product attributes $A \equiv \{\alpha_k \mid k = 1,...,K\}$ with each attribute holding some levels $A_k \equiv \{\alpha_{kl} \mid l = 1,...,L_k\}$, we will have a set of potential products $Z \equiv \{z_j \mid j = 1,...,J\}$, where each product is represented by $z_j = [\alpha_{kli}]_K$. Thus, a customisation scheme, Λ, can be defined as a subset of Z, i.e. $\Lambda \equiv \{z_j \mid j = 1,...,J^*\} \subseteq Z, \exists J^* \in \{1,...J\}$. Therefore, the problem is to find the optimal customisation scheme, namely a set of CA products, which will yield the best profit for the developer.

Furthermore, we also assume multiple market segments, which are denoted by $S \equiv \{s_i \mid i = 1,...,I\}$. Each segment has relatively homogeneous customers with a market size of Q_i. Because market segments can frequently be differentiated along one or some vertical attributes, thus it is reasonable to assume that they can be ordered from low end to high end. Therefore, we assume segment s_i is higher end and segment $s_{i'}$ is lower end, if $i > i'$.

Therefore, the objective function of maximising a CA developer's profit can be formulated as follows.

$$\max \sum_{i=1}^{I} \sum_{j=1}^{J} \left[\left(p_j - C_j^V \right) P_{ij} Q_i - C_j^F \right] y_j \tag{1}$$

Where p_j is the price of product z_j, C_j^V and C_j^F indicate the variable cost and fixed cost allocated to product z_j respectively. Moreover, the customer choice is represented by P_{ij}, which means the probability that a customer in segment s_i will purchase product z_j with unit price of p_j. Also y_j is a binary indicator such that:

$$y_j = \begin{cases} 1 & \text{if the developer decides to offer product } z_i \\ 0 & \text{otherwise} \end{cases}$$

In particular, we model customer choice probability based on discrete choice models, because discrete choice models are best suited to estimate customer preferences directly from choice data (Green and Krieger 1996). Given a total choice set (Ω) with N products, probability that a customer under segment s_i will choose product z_j with the price p_j is

$$P_{ij} \mid \Omega = \frac{\exp\left(\eta U_{ij} - p_j\right)}{\displaystyle\sum_{n=1}^{N} \exp\left(\eta U_{in} - p_n\right)} \tag{2}$$

where U_{ij} is the utility of segment s_i for product z_j. Typically, we derive U_{ij} from conjoint analysis, which essentially captures product inherent utility. While in customisation, the utility that a customer perceived from a customised product does not only rely on the product itself, but also on the process of configuration and delivery. There are no exceptions to CA. The total utility a customer receives may be substantially jeopardised if he has to go through a lengthy process before finalising the design of his ideal home. It may also be true when too many choices are presented to him, which leads to mass confusion. Consequently, we extend the traditional approach by taking account of the impact of degree of customisation and delivery time as follows.

$$U_{ij} = \left[\sum_{k=1}^{K}\sum_{l=1}^{L}\left(w_{jk} u_{ikl} x_{jkl} + \pi_j\right) + \epsilon_{ij}\right] + \alpha \cdot u\left[DC\left(\Lambda\right)\right] + \beta \cdot u\left[T_w\left(\Lambda\right)\right] \tag{3}$$

The first part is the product inherent utility that derived from part-worth approach (Jiao and Zhang 2005), where u_{ikl} is the part-worth utility of segment s_i for the lth level of attribute α_k (that is α_k^*); w_{jk} is the utility weights for attributes, $\{\alpha_k \mid k = 1,\ldots,K\}$, in product z_j. x_{jkl} is a binary indicator such that:

$$x_{jkl} = \begin{cases} 1 & \text{if the } l\text{th level of attribute } \alpha_k \text{ is in product } z_j \\ 0 & \text{otherwise} \end{cases}$$

Also in (3), π_j is a constant when the composite utility from part-worth utilities is derived for product z_j. ϵ_{ij} is a pair-wise error term for segment s_i to product z_j.

The second part represents the disutility from increased degree of customisation $DC(\Lambda)$. This is the dissatisfaction a customer gained from the complexity of configuration, which is positively associated with the scope of product offerings. Therefore, for every customisation scheme that specifies the mix of products, a metric to represent the degree of customisation can be quantified between 0 and 1 (Tang 2010). However, the disutility is sensitive to the effectiveness of the configuration system (α). If the configuration system is better designed and more efficient, it is believed to be able to handle a larger scope of product offerings.

The third part represents the disutility from lengthened product delivery lead time $T_w(\Lambda)$ and the disutility is proportional to customers' sensitivity to the delivery delay (β). Indeed, home buyers may be more tolerant to the delivery delay, compared with common consumer products. That means β is small in

CA, even negligible. Moreover, delivery time of commercial housing, such as apartments, is frequently regulated by the government.

However, the objective function is subject to following constraints.

$$U_{ij} - p_j \geq U_{ij'} - p_{j'}$$

$$U_{ij'} - p_{j'} \geq U_{ij} - p_j$$ (4)

$$U_{ij} - p_j \geq 0$$

$$U_{ij'} - p_{j'} \geq 0$$

$$\forall i, i' \in \{1..., I\}, \ \forall j, j' \in \{1..., J\}, \ i > i', \ j > j'$$

$$\sum_{l=1}^{L_k} x_{jkl} = 1, \ \forall j \in \{1..., J\}, \ \forall k \in \{1..., K\}$$ (5)

$$\sum_{k=1}^{K} \sum_{l=1}^{L_k} \left| x_{jkl} - x_{j'kl} \right| > 0, \ \forall j, j' \in \{1..., J\}, \ j \neq j'$$ (6)

$$\sum_{j=1}^{J} y_j \leq j^*, \ \forall j^* \in \{1..., J\}$$ (7)

$$x_{jkl}, y_j \in \{0,1\}, \ \forall j \in \{1..., J\}, \ \forall k \in \{1..., K\}, \ \forall l \in \{1..., L_K\}$$ (8)

Constraint 4 is to avoid product cannibalisation so that high end customers will buy high end products only and low end customers will buy low end products only. Constraint 5 is an exclusion condition that guarantees exactly one and only one attribute level can be selected for a product. Constraint 6 is a divergence condition, indicating that the offered products must be pair-wise different in at least one attribute level. Constraint 7 is the capacity condition to limit the maximum number of products that can be offered, while constraint 8 is trivial binary restrictions.

Combining all the equations, we derive a cohesive model to facilitate choice determination with economic justification for CA. Additionally, with this model, opportunities to improve the product platform, process platform and supply platform exist as well.

Discussion

The above model combines important considerations from multiple aspects with the decision to determine the optimal customisation scheme, which can be represented by the decision variables of x_{jkl} and y_j. A general search-based approach can be adopted to solve the optimisation problem, although discussion on the solution approaches is beyond the scope of this research. In general, various customisation schemes can be generated with given sets of attributes and attribute levels. By iteration of evaluating different customisation schemes, the optimal one can be identified. However, the bottleneck to find the optimal customisation scheme lies in the evaluation step because the cost and benefits parameters in the objective function are not easy to estimate. Therefore, the industry case is discussed in the next section to demonstrate some practical techniques to simplify the problem.

CASE STUDY

The theoretical model provides a rigid approach to deciding the right mix and right range of customisable attributes in CA, i.e. the right set of product offerings. However, the optimisation problem can become so complicated that searching for the optimal solution is computationally prohibitive, given a sizable number of attributes in an apartment and a considerable set of levels for each attribute. To this end, efforts to make it pragmatic in industry application are worthwhile. This section introduces a real case to illustrate how the theoretical model can be adapted to help the developer make sound decisions.

Background

Shui On Land (SOL, http://www.shuionland.com), headquartered in Shanghai, China, is well established as one of the Chinese Mainland's most visionary and innovative property developers. Observing numerous successful cases of customised housing developments and considering the scarcity of land and resources in China, SOL sees the potential of developing customised apartments to offer substantial benefits for customers, developers and the public at large. Therefore, CA is adopted to create additional value by allowing customers to customise the layout, fittings and finishing of their newly purchased home according to their individual needs, preferences and lifestyles. Figure 11.1 shows the outlook of the building that SOL decided to introduce CA. However, before implementing this innovative idea, a thorough study to find a set of feasible solutions to operating the CA business model and its economic justification is needed.

Model in practice

According to the initial market survey, hundreds of product attributes are qualified to be options provided to customers. Even after several rounds of narrowing down the scope by managerial decisions, 48 customisable attributes

11.1 Perspective view of SOL CA building (Courtesy of Shui On Land)

remained and most of them with at least three attribute levels. Typical attributes are kitchen and bathroom partition layout, paint in the rooms, flooring in the rooms, kitchen cabinet, and so on. Facing numerous possible product offerings, we built a practical spreadsheet-based economic model to help decide the right product mix by enabling sensitivity analysis of key factors. As depicted in Figure 11.2, the economic evaluation model is based on discounted cash flow (DCF).

Focusing on a particular project, the theoretical model can be simplified substantially. Instead of quantifying every single cash flow to calculate the net present value of CA, we concentrate on comparing the differences between CA and non-CA. Besides, market demand and customer choices can be boiled down to the sales rate simulation based on historic market data. Therefore, different product offerings will generate different revenue and costs. By quantifying all

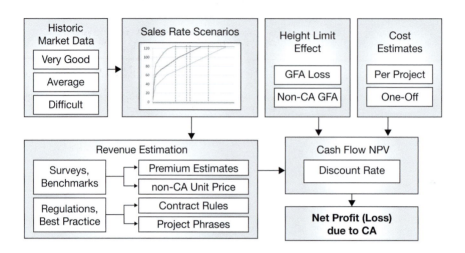

11.2 DCF-based economic evaluation model

	Sales Stages			
Sales commencement or RC carcase completion	I	II	III	IV (time)
Kitchen and bathroom partition layout	✓	✗	✗	✗
Kitchen and bathroom wall and floor tiles	✓	✗	✗	✗
Bedroom and living room partition layout	✓	✓	✗	✗
Kitchen cabinets and desktop	✓	✓	✗	✗
Bathroom sanitary appliance	✓	✓	✗	✗
Bathroom cabinets	✓	✓	✗	✗
Wardrobe	✓	✓	✗	✗
Internal doors	✓	✓	✗	✗
Bedroom and living room floor finishing	✓	✓	✗	✗
Paint color, wallpaper	✓	✓	✓	✗
bathroom water tap	✓	✓	✓	✗
Kitchen electrical appliances	✓	✓	✓	✗
Air-conditioners	✓	✓	✓	✗

11.3 Stage-based planning for customisation scope reduction

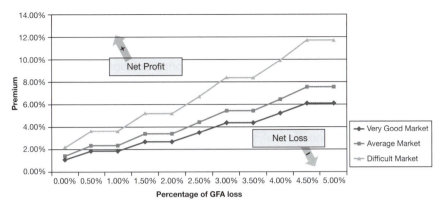

11.4 Sensitivity analysis of CA price premium and percentage of GFA loss

the cash flow differences between CA and non-CA, net profit or loss due to CA can be calculated. Thus fine-tuning some key parameters by sensitivity analysis leads to better CA solutions. Figure 11.3 illustrates a stage-based coordination between construction and sales, which reduces the customisation scope that customers can enjoy as sales proceed. This coordination approach clearly shows how CA developers can strike a balance between avoiding project delay and providing as much flexibility to customers as possible. Facing a wide latitude of customisable options, compromise has to be made to maintain construction efficiency and meanwhile a cohesive set of option system with packages can be developed to reduce the operation complexity.

Gross floor area (GFA) loss is an interesting problem pertaining to the SOL CA project. On one hand, local government imposes height limits for high-rise residential buildings. On the other hand, the floor slab thickness has to be increased to support the new architecture design so that partition layout is flexible in the rooms. Consequently, a certain percentage of GFA is lost due to CA, which varies from different architecture designs. Based on the economic model, price premium of CA and percentage of GFA loss are two key factors that impact project return. Assuming other factors are static, different combinations of premium and percentage of GFA loss that yield break-even for the project according to different market situations can be plotted as Figure 11.4. This provides strategic insights for the developer that it is pivotal to provide increased customer value with implementation efficiency and cost control.

CONCLUSION

Customised apartment has been recognised as a strategy that attracts the interest of property developers. As a disruptive business strategy to the traditional

12

Emerging trends and concepts of mass customisation in Taiwan's housing industry

Kung-Jen Tu and Hao-Yang Wei

ABSTRACT

This chapter intends to present the emerging trends and concepts of mass customisation observed in the building delivery process in Taiwan's housing industry, and identify the supply chain strategies underlying these mass customisation concepts and systems. It has been found that during the planning and design phase of housing projects, there is a trend of applying 'open building' concepts to supply 'support-only' apartment products to the market, which is considered a 'segmented standardisation' supply chain strategy. During the construction phase, the unique 'pre-sale' and housing customisation system allows homebuyers to start real estate transactions earlier in the construction phase and gain an early opportunity to customise the 'basic infill parts' of their units, which is also regarded as a 'segmented standardisation' supply chain strategy. During the sale and occupancy phase, householders turn to the housing remodeling sub-industry, where modular and integrated infill systems (cabinet, floor, partition) are emerging, for interior furnishing services, which is considered a 'tailored customisation' supply chain strategy. In conclusion, we found that the two housing sub-industries in Taiwan are moving towards mass customisation strategies: the new apartment building sub-industry is moving from 'pure standardisation' towards 'segmented standardisation'; and the housing remodeling sub-industry is moving from 'pure customisation' towards 'tailored customisation'. Both sub-industries subscribe to the 'support' and 'infill' open building framework, which manifests an emerging industry evolution of adopting the 'open building' principle towards mass customisation.

INTRODUCTION

Mass customisation (MC), a concept that emerged in the late 1980s (Davis, 1989), relates to the ability to provide customised products or services through flexible processes in high volumes and at reasonably low costs. It has been a holy grail for the manufacturing industry for many years (Tseng and Jiao, 2001). In the building construction field, limited studies have been conducted to explore issues involved in adopting MC strategies in the construction industry. For example, Japan's factory-based housing industry, where firms supply customised homes which are pre-assembled from standardised components or modular systems, has been investigated and several MC supply chain strategies identified (Barlow *et al.*, 2003). On the other hand, the UK's speculative housing industry, often criticised for failing to meet customers' needs, has been urged to move towards customisation by developing customer-focused strategies (Roy and Cochrane, 1999), exploring the possible use of lean and agile production (Naim and Barlow, 2003), and re-engineering the building process (Roy *et al.*, 2003). Despite these research efforts, it remains a great challenge for the speculative housing industry to adopt MC strategies.

The housing industry in Taiwan is also considered speculative and has problems similar to those of the UK industry. The industry is fragmented and lacks large factory-based housing developers as there are in Japan. Nonetheless, the key research questions remain: Can 'mass customisation' be achieved in the speculative housing industry? What can be done to achieve such a goal? This chapter argues that any conventional pure standardisation strategy adopted by the speculative housing industry no longer satisfies customers with diverse needs. There must be a motivating force from customers pulling the industry towards customisation. As expected, emerging trends and concepts of mass customisation in Taiwan's housing industry have been observed. This chapter intends to present these emerging MC trends and concepts, and identify the supply chain strategies underlying these concepts and systems.

CHARACTERISTICS OF THE HOUSING PRODUCTS AND INDUSTRY IN TAIWAN

Characteristics of apartment products

'Row houses' and 'apartments' are the two major types of housing products supplied in the housing market in Taiwan (Lin and Liang, 2006). The 'apartment' will be the research subject of this chapter, since it accounts for 32.2 per cent of total dwelling units in Taiwan and represents the primary product supplied by the housing market in major cities. Roughly 70 per cent of the total dwelling

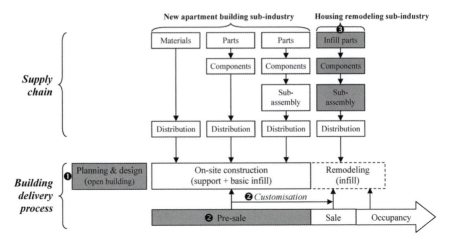

12.1 The conventional building delivery process and supply chain model observed in the housing industry in Taiwan

units built in Taipei metropolitan area were 'apartment' products and the annual 'apartment' housing market size accounts for 35 per cent of the total housing market size in Taiwan (Tu and Wei, 2007). In Taiwan, a typical apartment unit is usually configured to have a living room, a dining room, a kitchen, one or two bathrooms, and several bedrooms. The average size of 'apartment' units is 114m^2 with an average of 3.1 bedrooms (Lin and Liang, 2006).

Conventional building delivery process of apartment products

The conventional building delivery process in supplying apartment products to the housing market in Taiwan can be divided into three phases: planning and design, construction, as well as sale and occupancy (Figure 12.1). Most developers in Taiwan tend to adopt a 'pure standardisation' strategy, i.e. developing standardised apartment products with limited level of customer choice and taking the lowest cost approach to maximise profits. Such products are less likely to satisfy homebuyers with diverse needs. By examining the supply chain models in each phase of the building delivery process (Figure 12.1), several emerging mass customisation concepts or systems are identified and described in the following sections.

PLANNING AND DESIGN PHASE: THE 'OPEN BUILDING' APPROACH

The 'open building' concept

'Open building' is a design concept and approach aiming to deliver buildings with maximal capacity for accommodating the diverse needs of different house-holders over time. To achieve such goals, the followings have to be retained:

1. The making of a building is divided into two stages: the 'support' of a building (base building elements with longer lives and which remain unchanged, such as structure, envelope, etc.) and the 'infill' (fit-out elements with shorter lives and which change more often, such as partitions, floors, equipment, service pipelines, cabinets, etc.).
2. The 'support' of a building is designed to form a flexible and open architecture to accommodate diverse 'infill' parts. Systematic design methods, such as the SAR method devised by Habraken (1976), may be applied in the design of the 'support'.
3. An 'infill' industry is formed to supply diverse 'infill' systems and parts that are highly integrated or interconnected, and can be independently installed or upgraded within an open architecture (support) for each householder.

'Open building' has been implemented worldwide in the making of residential open buildings (Kendall and Teicher, 2000). It represents a design approach that could lead to the 'mass customisation' of housing products. 'Open building' was first introduced to Taiwan in the mid 1990s. But it is still considered a relatively new approach to be explored in delivering building products by today's housing industry (see part (1) of Figure 12.1).

Designing 'support-only' apartment buildings

A complete new 'apartment' product sold in Taiwan usually includes two parts: the 'support' part and the 'basic infill' parts (interior partitions, finish ceilings and floors, equipment and cabinets in kitchen and bathrooms, pipelines and wires, switches, and power outlets). Other 'infill' parts such as furniture, closets, beds, curtains, air conditioners, light fixtures, washers and dryers are usually excluded and furnished by homebuyers.

However, such standardised products have a few disadvantages. First of all, they may not fully meet the needs of individual homebuyers. Besides, the homebuyers are likely to tear down the existing 'basic infill' parts and have them customised, resulting in extra demolition costs which seem avoidable.

To solve these problems, some developers have adopted the 'open building' approaches to supply 'support-only' apartment products to the market. Only the 'support', but not the 'basic infill' parts, of apartment units are constructed and sold to homebuyers. The 'support', such as the vertical shafts and horizontal pipelines, are carefully placed and distributed, and the slabs of wet space areas (bathrooms) are sunk by 5cm, awaiting the homebuyer's subsequent customisation.

The 'support-only' apartment products have several advantages. First, by excluding the 'basic infill' parts, the price of an apartment unit should be lower than the conventional counterpart, which is more appealing to homebuyers. Second, after purchasing the 'support-only' apartment units, homebuyers can proceed to work with an interior architect to customise their units without incurring unnecessary extra costs.

Developing design method of 'support'

Wei *et al.* (2007) have developed the Integrated Façade System (IFS) by applying the theories, concepts, and technologies of open building, systems integration, and double façade, to meet residents' needs in spatial flexibility, climatic control, security, and functionality. The core of the IFS is a design method for flexible 'support'. Open building design principles such as RC frame structures with modular spans, as well as externalised and accessible 'vertical shafts' and 'trench floors' for piping distribution have been presented (Figure 12.2a). These principles allow wet spaces (kitchen and bathroom) to be placed flexibly around the building perimeter, free up the rest of the space, and therefore increase the spatial flexibility of the apartment unit (Figure 12.2b).

CONSTRUCTION PHASE: 'PRE-SALE' SYSTEM AND HOUSING CUSTOMISATION

'Pre-sale' system

In Taiwan, the 'pre-sale' system is a unique real estate transaction mechanism that allows developers and homebuyers to start the transactions during the construction phase of a residential property. The 'pre-sale' period may begin as soon as the construction permit for a property is obtained, and continue throughout the whole building construction phase (see part (2), Figure 12.1). During this phase, the developer and homebuyers have an extended period to complete real estate transactions, and the homebuyers are given opportunities to customise their apartment units.

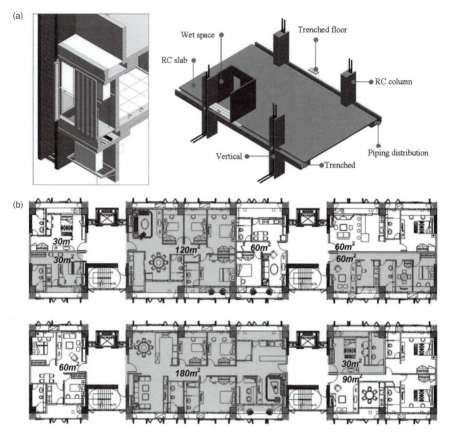

12.2 (a) The IFS is employed at the perimeter of conventional RC structures to ensure spatial flexibility, climatic control, security, appearance, and functionality; (b) various floor plans of a typical linear-shape apartment building showing great flexibility at the 'floor' level (producing units of five different sizes) and 'apartment unit' level (allowing flexible configurations and diverse layouts) (Wei *et al.*, 2007)

After the planning and design of a residential property is finalised, the developer would hire advertising, and a sale agent for the marketing and sale of the property (Figures 12.3a and 12.3b). Once a homebuyer decides to purchase a particular apartment unit and sign a real estate contract, he will be asked to pay 15–30 per cent of the sale price in several installments, usually over the pre-sale period, and be allowed to consult with the developer to customise his apartment unit.

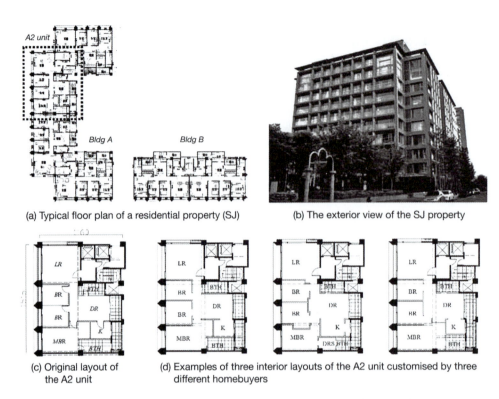

(a) Typical floor plan of a residential property (SJ)

(b) The exterior view of the SJ property

(c) Original layout of the A2 unit

(d) Examples of three interior layouts of the A2 unit customised by three different homebuyers

12.3 The typical floor plan, exterior view, and customised layouts of a particular unit of the SJ residential property

Housing customisation

Homebuyers can only customise the 'basic infill' parts of their units, such as reconfiguring interior layouts and partitions (Figures 12.3c and 12.3d), redistributing pipelines and wires, relocating power outlets and light fixture switches, selecting the materials of interior finishes and type of kitchen equipment. Homebuyers usually are not allowed to relocate bathrooms (minor reconfiguration allowed). For each homebuyer, the customisation plan has to be finalised by the time the construction of the building's basement is complete; the associated construction cost will be re-estimated, which may incur extra payment or reimbursement. The developer and contractors will construct the individual unit according to the finalised customisation plan, and transfer the ownership of the unit to the homebuyer after the building is completely constructed. The homebuyer can choose to perform further interior furnishing (adding closets, curtains, furniture, etc.) on his apartment unit afterwards.

SALE AND OCCUPANCY PHASE: MODULAR AND INTEGRATED 'INFILL SYSTEMS'

During this phase, homebuyers may shop around and choose from the un-sold apartment units in certain properties. Once the homebuyers acquire the ownership of their units, they then have to turn to the domestic housing remodeling sub-industry to seek remodeling products and professional services for further furnishing or upgrading the 'basic infill' parts of their units.

In contrast to the conventional housing remodeling practice which is considered a 'pure customisation' supply chain strategy, several modular and integrated 'infill systems', adopting other supply chain strategy, have been developed in the housing remodeling sub-industry to meet householders' furnishing needs in the sale and occupancy phase (see part (3), Figure 12.1).

Panelised cabinet system (PCS)

The panelised cabinet systems usually consist of two types of parts: modular panels and hardware. The modular panels are manufactured in imported engineered wood and surface finished products (120cm × 240cm in size, and 1.8cm or 2.5cm thick). Panels in two different thicknesses and different surface colors and patterns are available for selection. The hardware includes different types of hinge parts, door knob parts, rail parts, etc. These panels and hardware are combined to make diverse closets, cabinets, furniture (table, bed) designs. The suppliers usually have a factory mass producing various panel products.

When a customer asks a panelised cabinet system supplier for a housing furnishing service, the supplier will first take interior measurements of the unit and provide interior design services (design of layout and closets, selection of panels and hardware). The order for panels and hardware will be placed. The supplier will then cut the panels into designated sizes in the factory, package and ship the panels with the hardware, and finally assemble them on site. Compared to the conventional pure customisation approach (woodwork on site), the panelised cabinet system is considered more precise (industrialised) and more efficient (quick assembly on site), but less diverse in design.

Integrated open building remodeling system (IOBRS)

The IOBRS was designed to meet the diverse furnishing or remodeling needs of any householder in any phase of apartment building life (Lin *et al.*, 2009). The IOBRS intends to achieve maximum ceiling height and spatial flexibility, minimum material consumption and construction waste, and integration for wire

and pipe management in interior furnishing or remodeling projects. The IOBRS consists of four major elements:

1. Coordination system: A 30cm grid line system is used within an apartment unit to coordinate the construction dimensions of all subsystem components and existing building structure.
2. Trenched floor (Figure 12.4a): It is configured around the perimeter of the unit for distributing wires (power, cable, network) and plumbing pipelines.
3. Floor subsystem (Figure 12.4b): A composite subsystem (10cm thick), consisting of wood flooring, cement board, concrete blocks, softwood bed, and waterproof membrane (under wet spaces).
4. Partition subsystem (Figure 12.4b): A composite subsystem (10cm thick; 45cm or 90cm wide; 210–300cm tall), consisting of light gauge steel C-channel, calcium silicate board, and fiberglass. Where a partition intersects a trenched floor, the pipes and wires will rise into the bottom of the partition and are redistributed to certain equipment or outlets.

In a remodeling project employing the IOBRS, the supplier will take orders for all the required subsystem components from the customer once his interior layout is finalised (Figure 12.4c). The modular partition structures (light gauge steel C-channel), with different widths and heights, will be mass produced in the factory. The ordered partition structures and all other components will then be shipped and assembled on site. The IOBRS offers a high level of spatial flexibility to cope with diverse customers' needs over time. In a case study of an apartment remodeling project (75m²), the first cost of the IOBRS may be 50 per cent higher than the conventional counterpart, but it offers a potential 30 per cent cost saving in each subsequent remodeling (Lin *et al.*, 2009).

SUPPLY CHAIN STRATEGIES

The generic supply chain strategies classifications and criteria proposed by Barlow *et al.* (2003) are used to determine the supply chain strategies underlying the aforementioned MC concepts and systems observed in different phases of the building delivery process in Taiwan's housing industry. Supplier's concerns such as cost as well as homebuyer's concerns such as lead time, cost, and level of choice among all MC concepts and systems are tabulated and summarised in Table 12.1.

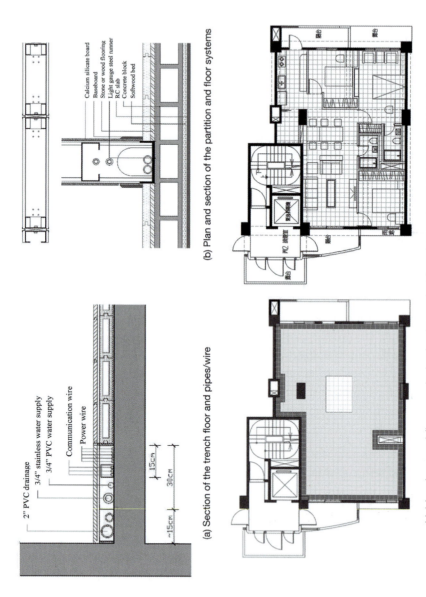

2" PVC drainage
3/4" stainless water supply
3/4" PVC water supply
Communication wire
Power wire

15cm
30cm
~15cm

(a) Section of the trench floor and pipes/wire

Calcium silicate board
Baseboard
Stone or wood flooring
Light gauge steel runner
RC slab
Concrete block
Softwood bed

(b) Plan and section of the partition and floor systems

(c) A housing remodeling example showing the trenched floor along perimeter and the resulting layout

12.4 The IOBRS: Components and applications (Lin et al., 2009)

TABLE 12.1 Supply chain strategy analyses of the mass customisation concepts observed in different phases of the building delivery process in Taiwan's housing industry

Bldg delivery process	Planning & Design Phase		Construction (Pre-sale) Phase		Sale and Occupancy Phase	
MC concepts & systems	Open bldg support-only	OB design method	Pre-sale system	Housing customisation	Modular PCS	Integrated OBRS
Supplier's concerns						
Cost	Lower construction cost (no customisation personnel, infill costs)		Extra personnel cost Extra infill construction cost Early capital collection		Lower cost (manufacture + personnel + assembly)	Higher first cost (infill material)
Homebuyer's concerns						
Lead time	Same as conventional one (1–3 months)		Longer (1–2 years)		Shorter (several weeks)	
Cost	Lower construction cost (no infill demolition cost)		Lower furnishing cost (no infill demolition cost)		Slightly lower (quick assembly)	Higher infill cost Lower LC cost
Level of choice	Limited product choice but layout customisable		Limited product choices but layout customisable		Many product choices (limited only by panels)	
Supply chain strategy						
	Segmented standardisation		Segmented standardisation		Tailored customisation	

CONCLUSIONS

This chapter presented the emerging trends and concepts of MC observed in the building delivery process in Taiwan's housing industry, and identified the supply chain strategies underlying these mass customisation concepts and systems.

It is found that during the planning and design phase of apartment projects, there is an emerging trend for the developers to apply 'open building' concepts to supply 'support-only' apartment products (with lower construction cost) to the market. Homebuyers are provided with apartment products featuring lower cost, limited product choice, and open layouts for easy customisation. This is considered a 'segmented standardisation' supply chain strategy.

During the construction phase, developers construct and supply conventional apartment building products (with 'support' and 'basic infill' parts) to the market. The unique 'pre-sale' and housing customisation system allows homebuyers to start real estate transactions earlier in the construction phase and gain a 'time-window' to customise the 'basic infill' parts of their units. Housing customisation may incur extra personnel and infill construction costs for the developers, but allows early capital collection from homebuyers. Homebuyers are provided with apartment products featuring longer lead time, lower furnishing cost, limited product choice, and customisation services. This is also considered a 'segmented standardisation' supply chain strategy.

During the sale and occupancy phase, householders turn to the housing remodeling sub-industry, where modular and integrated infill systems (cabinet, floor, partition) are emerging, for interior furnishing services. The suppliers of modular and integrated infill systems manufacture modular parts in large numbers to achieve economies of scale. The householders may seek these suppliers for interior design services, choose from the modular and integrated parts available, then have them made in manufacturers and assembled on site. Homebuyers are provided with infill products featuring high levels of customer choice (although not as high as pure customisation) and shorter lead time. This is considered a 'tailored customisation' supply chain strategy.

In conclusion, there are trends moving towards MC strategies in both sub-industries: the new apartment building sub-industry is moving from 'pure standardisation' towards 'segmented standardisation' to offer higher levels of customer choice to homebuyers; whereas the housing remodeling sub-industry is moving from 'pure customisation' towards 'tailored customisation' to offer lower cost products at the expense of the level of customer choice. Both sub-industries tend to cater to homebuyers' needs at different times, and subscribe to the 'support' and 'infill' open building framework, manifesting an emerging industry evolution of adopting 'open building' principles towards MC.

BIBLIOGRAPHY

Barlow, J., Childerhouse, P., Gann, D., Hong-Minh, S., Naim, M. and Ozaki, R. (2003) 'Choice and delivery in housebuilding: Lessons from Japan for UK housebuilders', *Building Research & Information*, 13(2): 134–145.

Davis, S. (1989) 'From future perfect: Mass customizing', *Planning Review*, 17(2): 16–21.

Habraken, N. J. (1976) *Variations: The Systematic Design of Supports*, Cambridge, MA: MIT Press.

Kendall, S. and Teicher, J. (2000) *Residential Open Building*, New York: E&FN Spon.

Lin, J. H., Wei, H. Y. and Tu, K. J. (2009) *Development of an Integrated Open Building Remodeling System for Residential Buildings*, *Research Project Report*, Taiwan: Architectural and Building Research Institute.

Lin, Y. H. and Liang, H. W. (2006) 'Report on the housing status survey', *Research Project Report*, Taiwan: Construction and Planning Agency.

Naim, M. and Barlow, J. (2003) 'An innovative supply chain strategy for customized housing', *Construction Management and Economics*, 21(6): 593–602.

Roy, R. and Cochrane, S. P. (1999) 'Development of a customer focused strategy in speculative house building', *Construction Management and Economics*, 17(6): 777–787.

Roy, R., Brown, J. and Gaze, C. (2003) 'Re-engineering the construction process in the speculative house-building sector', *Construction Management and Economics*, 21(2): 137–146.

Tseng, M. M. and Jiao, J. (2001) 'Mass Customization', in G. Salvendy (ed.) *Handbook of Industrial Engineering, Technology and Operation Management*, 3rd edn, New York: John Wiley & Sons.

Tu, K. J. and Wei, H. Y. (2007) Mass customization and residential open building system development, Research Project Report, Taiwan: Architectural and Building Research Institute.

Wei, H. Y., Tu, K. J. and Lee, W. W. (2007) 'Development of an adaptable integrated façade system for housing in Taiwan', in *Conference Proceedings of CIB World Building Congress: Construction for Development,* Cape Town, South Africa: 1561–1574.

13

Automation, robotics, services: evolution of large-scale mass customisation in the Japanese building industry

Thomas Linner and Thomas Bock

ABSTRACT

Japanese prefabrication and construction automation are often presented as genius and advanced strategies that were developed by companies, innovators and governmental institutions in the 1970s, 1980s and 1990s. Often it is also discussed why large-scale industrialisation and automated construction have only been successfully applied in Japan, and why innovators in other locations and environments cannot manage to build up similar structures. One helpful contribution to these discussions and questions can be given by an evolutionary view on the subject. Just as Takahiro Fujimoto describes today's performance of the Toyota Production System as a consequence of evolution (Fujimoto, 1999), the existence of large-scale and highly automated prefabrication of individual buildings in the Japanese housing industry can be described as the outcome of a long-term learning and development process. Japan's advanced prefabrication industry has been formed by a combination of continuous incremental and disruptive innovations and a unique socio-economic and socio-cultural environment (desire for new, fast changing markets; earthquakes; reduced human resources; service attitude) stepwise over time.

INTRODUCTION

Organisational culture in Japan is traditionally based on collective, non-hierarchical and informal decision-making ("ringi seido"), bringing information from customers and production directly to management and product design, allowing thus the company's organisation to evolve and adapt over time.

Although in Japan the term "Mass Customisation" is not used, Japanese prefabrication companies are among the strongest performers in the production of small batches of both consumer goods and individual customer-oriented and value added buildings by industrialised, highly flexible and automated production systems. Mass customisation is a method which is historically deeply woven into Japanese organisational culture and service thinking. It has been developed so naturally out of history, mentality and culture, that it is even difficult to find an explicit expression for this strategy in Japanese science.

FROM JAPAN'S TRADITIONAL ORGANISATIONAL CULTURE TOWARDS TPS AND TOYOTA HOME

Since prefabrication has been deeply connected to Japanese architectural culture and tradition, Japanese timber construction can be considered as an early example of high-level prefabrication in the building industry. Additionally, Japanese tradition is closely related to a strong favour for order, standardisation and systematisation. An important activator for early prefabrication can be found in the famous Ken, a 1:2 relation proportion and measurement system. Furthermore, Tatami mats, the traditional Japanese floor finishing, principally follow strict grids and order systems (Osamu, 1994). Having usually an edge length of 85/170 cm Tatami mats can be combined in a lot of variations in order to shape the room's dimension, which will end up always in an exact number of mats, a necessity since the mats had continuously been changed between the rooms, according to their current usage. Two layouts became common. The Syugijiki layout always has two Tatami mats in its centre, surrounded by a number of additional mats, whereas the Fusyugijiki layout places several mats parallel in a strict orientation.

Today it is still usual that a room size is expressed with the number of Tatami mats instead of meter squared. Contemporary Japanese architects are at the same time familiar with these rules and measurement systems, and standardisation often results in a particular multilevel grid, which can be found not only in the building's footprint but also as the underlying rhythm in its elevations as well as its decorative and built-in parts, such as religious corners, wardrobes or shoji-screens (traditional Japanese sliding doors), allowing an easy combination or reconfiguration of rooms. Even some urban master plans follow these incremental measures since each building unit is related to a multiplication of Tatami mats. This very Japanese favour for standardisation and measurement systems generated a supportive environment for prefabrication centuries ago, and up to today, engineers and architects have managed to keep this culture alive and advanced its state of the art.

First approaches to mass production: PREMOS Home

The ignition for large-scale factory-based mass production of buildings was Kunio Maekawa in the late 1930s with his PREMOS Home (Reynolds, 2001). He can be considered as the pioneer of modern Japanese prefabrication. Maekawa pointed out that a contemporary home should not just accommodate its inhabitants resting, eating and sleeping, but it should also facilitate cooking and cleaning, adequate light, ventilation and heat. New American houses often included those facilities. With their electric ranges, washing machines, refrigerators, flush toilets, heating and insulation, Maekawa also acknowledged that Japan was still a poor country and couldn't yet afford all these conveniences, but he hoped that mass production would soon bring them into Japanese homes.

Like many modernists, Maekawa believed that the building industry could emulate the automobile industry. He believed that "in the face of the current shortage of four million houses in our country, industrialisation is the only far-reaching solution". The name of the project "PREMOS" was an acronym: "pre" for "prefabrication", "M" for Maekawa, "O" for Kaoru Ono, his structural engineer and professor at Tokyo University, and finally "S" for Sani'in Manufacturing Company. The project was a collaborative effort (joint venture). The first two PREMOS units were completed in 1946. The earliest full-scale version was known as "model #7". While maintaining the living unit of the Tatami mat as the basis for these minimal 52 m² units, Maekawa incorporated a system of self-supporting honeycomb panels covered by plywood sheeting and shallow wood trusses to support the roof. Until 1952 the joint venture produced more than 1,000 units in several variations but all based on the major ideas of "model #7" (Matsukuma *et al.*, 2006; Reynolds, 2001).

Influences of local and cultural specifics

Kunio Maekawa established a technical basis for modern Japanese prefabrication. Nevertheless, a number of local characteristics had an additional impact on the development of prefabrication in Japan. Important for the wide acceptance of prefabrication was also the ability of this culture to transform itself. A number of historical Japanese cities experienced dramatic changes during their (often rapid) evolution, e.g. by natural disasters like fires or earthquakes. Another habit characteristic of Japan was to also change the capital with the introduction of a new emperor. Entire cities were quickly moved and relocated, requiring strong and effective systems of measurements and sophisticated prefabricated frames in order to allow rapid and affordable transformation and relocation processes. Thus, major governmental and religious buildings were prefabricated using standardised and industrialised construction methods.

In contrast to European cultures where a transformation of historical buildings is generally connected with a loss of local spirits (*genius loci*), Japanese culture has developed a spirit of continuous renewal. A major gash in Japan's history took place in 1867, when its stability was harshly tested. After centuries of international isolation, the country opened its gateways to the outside world. This was followed by a rapid transformation into a modern industrial nation in order to maintain its power as an independent state. However, this was not to be the last challenge. It was at the end of the Second World War when almost 30 per cent of Japan's housing had been destroyed. Due to the dramatic housing shortage, the immediate and rapid deployment of shelter was required, initially prefabricated and characterised by poor quality. These uncomfortable living conditions dominated Japan in the post-war era. After covering that demand, people gradually started to increase their standards by asking for safe and durable high-quality houses. Again, one of the answers was prefabrication, where the industry managed to transform itself shifting from delivering prefabricated homes with poor quality to a premium class strategy of delivering individual, earthquake-resistant and service-accompanied homes.

Sekisui Heim M1: design for production

Kazuhiko Ono developed in 1968, as part of his doctoral thesis at Tokyo University, the legendary M1 system of Sekisui Heim. This three-dimensional modular kit was famous for the genius of its simplicity. It could reduce the complexity in order to allow industrial line-based production. The M1 was a prototype for merging multiple qualities, design and production aspects. The "units" based on steel frames were perfectly suited to industrial production, and the low number of components could generate a variety of possible solutions for the customer. In the 1970s, the M1 reached a steady production of more than 3,000 units per annum allowing the investment in advanced automation.

Toyota Production System and Toyota Home

A further milestone in the evolution of mass customised building production has been set up by Toyota and the application of the legendary Toyota Production System (TPS) (Monden, 1983) to manufacturing of space units. After the Second World War, the Toyota Motor Corporation was initially seeking methods to increase its productivity rapidly. During several visits to the factories of Ford and General Motors, managers of Toyota came to the conclusion that a production concept based on mass and variation production would never work successfully and efficiently, especially under Japanese conditions (Ohno, 1988). In their eyes, the ability of a fast adjustment to the frequent change of market needs in Japan was essential for a new production system. Under these circumstances Toyota started to invent its own market-based production system, tailored to Japanese requirements: the Toyota Production System. The revolution was the extension of conventional material and information flows ("push production"), into a new concept, based on current demands ("pull production").

In a pulling production, the assembly line delivers only products which were demanded, to avoid stocks and overproduction. An integrated communication system called "Kanban" was developed to support the new information and material flow. The important aspect is that this process is basically triggered through the demand by a customer. Thus the factories' output is "pulled" by customers, instead of the former "pushing", when the output was defined by the factory management and storage capacities. The complete synchronisation of production and customer demand also requires a strict synchronisation between factory and suppliers, since previous work steps are only being executed on the request of subsequent steps, in combination and full coordination with 'just-in-time' and 'just-in-sequence' production strategies.

Another achievement of Taichi Ohno was the application of a "zero-wastage policy". Since Japan got only limited economic support after the Second World War, he was requested to find an efficient way to work with existing resources. Therefore, he disclosed seven major waste producers in his concept. The most common waste producer according to Ohno was overproduction: a product is being delivered without a customer's demand. Finally in the 1970s, Toyota started to develop its housing business with Toyota Home, and started to produce prefabricated houses, transferring thus the Toyota Production System from its automotive section to the industrialised and production line-based manufacturing of buildings. During the following decades, all the other main players of the prefabrication industry followed this newly set trend, installing the basic ideas of TPS in their plants, products and organisations.

Automated and robotised production as sales argument

In this section it has to be mentioned that Japanese people in general have a very positive attitude towards automation, robotics and technology. Several historical occurrences have shaped a unique view on advanced technologies. For example, in the sixteenth century the Japanese developed their own types of timepieces, i.e. "Wadokei" (Yoshida et al., 2005), which allowed people to adjust time measurement to their individual rhythm of work. Later on, the "Ningio Karakuri", which can be considered as the predecessors of modern automation and robotics in Japan, had been popularised as mechanised toys for entertainment (Wißnet, 2007). Automation and robotics in Japan gradually gained the image of being designed to serve people, and not the other way around. Furthermore, during times of extensive automation in the twentieth century, companies shifted people into their service and development sections, rather than laying them off.

Furthermore, when faced with upcoming challenges as the demographic changes and population declines in Japan, again robotics (Service Robotics) and personal assistance technologies are widely accepted today as a potential solution. In Japan, the fact that a house is fabricated by using automation, robotics and other advanced technologies has an extremely positive influence on the image of the producing companies and their products. Moreover, the steady success and increased automation of the main prefabrication companies, like Sekisui House, Daiwa House, Sekisui Heim and Toyota, has been followed by a visible increase of their quality. So after decades of reliable products and services, the Japanese have developed a strong trust in their prefabrication companies.

Sekisui Heim – ERP Systems and BIM

After the successful application of the Toyota Production System (TPS) in the fields of building manufacturing, Sekisui Heim followed Toyota and adapted and refined TPS. However, in the 1980s Sekisui came up with another essential innovation: the parent company Sekisui Chemical developed an innovative computer-based Enterprise Resource Planning (ERP) system for controlling the production and logistic flow. This ERP system was subsequently transferred to the Sekisui Chemical's subsections.

In the housing section, this ERP system laid the foundation for HAPPS (Heim Automated Parts Pickup System) (Furuse & Katano, 2006). The system translates floor plan and design requirements of architects and customers directly into production plans and data needed to operate automated production. It can also be used today to develop new platforms, components and solution spaces. It assures complete communication between suppliers, work steps on different sections, timing and feeding of the 400-meter assembly line. Therefore, HAPPS chooses for one building approximately 30,000 parts out of 300,000 listed items, arranging them just-in-time and just-in-sequence for production. Nowadays, Sekisui has one of the world's most advanced BIM systems, allowing more than 90 per cent of all design and parts-related information to be directly translated into production and assembly operations. Further, Sekisui already uses BIM to manage delivered building products over time: customer relations, maintenance, upgrade offers, rearrangement and deconstruction.

JAPAN'S PREFABRICATION INDUSTRY TODAY

Japan's housing industry is among the strongest worldwide. However, it has undergone a steady change and decline since the 1990s. A maximum production peak was reached in 1994 with 573,173 newly constructed owner-occupied housing units (see Table 13.1). Later in 2000 about 450,000 units were constructed and in 2009 the construction went down to just 318,000 units (see Table 13.2). During the peak times, the percentage of prefabricated houses, those being entirely prefabricated, was about 18–19 per cent. Today's quota has decreased depending on the region to just 13–15 per cent. However, a high amount of prefabricated elements are also being used in conventional construction, which increases the actual percentage of prefabrication in the whole building industry, although it is hard to express this phenomenon in numbers. The prefabrication of entire buildings could be broken down into about 80 per cent steel-based building kits, 15 per cent wood-based building kits and 5 per cent concrete-based building kits.

Sekisui House, which is still the main player in Japan's prefabrication industry, reached its peak in 1994 with a production of 78,275 housing units, when its share of the total building construction market reached 5.3 per cent (see Table 13.1). It is interesting to see that both Sekisui House and Daiwa House, the second largest player in Japan's prefabrication industry, try to counter the decline in the market by going into a developer position. Houses and apartments are developed, planned and constructed, in order to rent them later to customers. These houses and apartments are also based on mass customisable housing kits and ensure that the capacities of expensive automated production facilities are utilised to a maximum. Figures 13.1–13.4 are recent pictures from today's factories of the described main players, showing various scenes from the highly automated production processes that those companies have deployed, in order to produce enormous amounts of highly customised buildings.

TABLE 13.1 Housing maximum production peaks of main players of the prefabrication industry

	Sekisui House	Daiwa House	Sekisui Heim	Toyota Home
Units/year (peaks)	78,275 (1994)	44,500 (2007)	34,560 (1997)	5,024 (2006)

Source: Yearly Financial Reports of Companies

13.1 Similar to the automotive industry the production process starts with the processing of steel coils (Sekisui House)

13.2 Robots position various steel components automatically onto a laying table for frame elements. The laying table then carries the frame into the automatic welding station. Thus every 3–5 minutes a new basic frame element is generated (Sekisui House)

13.3 Interior view of one of the two supply sides which flank the production line. The components and materials are supplied from the left side just in time and just in sequence to a small "preparation" area which can be seen on the right side. The preparation area is located next to the production line (Sekisui Heim)

13.4 On the 400m production lines, the steel frame chassis passes several workstations. There components and workers wait to complete the chassis just in time and just in sequence. A factory completes about 150 units (= 10–15 houses) per day. The maximum speed of production is one unit every 1.5 minutes (Sekisui Heim)

TABLE 13.2 Housing production of main players in 2009

	Sekisui House	Daiwa House	Sekisui Heim	Toyota Home
Detached houses (sold to customers)	17,389	8,586	10,300	4,302
Apartment houses (sold to customers)	5,699	3,511	4,250	
Houses and apartment units (built and rented to customers)	32,000	29,021		
Houses sold with other brand names (subdivisions)		1,729		
Total	55,088	42,847	14,550	4,302

Source: Yearly Financial Reports of Companies

TOWARDS ADVANCED SERVICE SYSTEMS

To manage the decrease in demand and to build up new ways of value creation, all main players are focusing more and more on the buildings' utilisation phase, building performance and advanced Building Information Modelling (BIM), for managing the building life-cycle services. Sekisui House is working on modular upgrade packages for older model lines, allowing their owners to easily and continuously upgrade both building design and performance. Daiwa House cooperates with companies like Cyberdyne (HAL) and Toto (Intelligent Heath Toilet), in order to develop assistive technologies and advanced health care services related to residential applications. Sekisui Heim is trying to gain a leading position in matters of sustainable low energy houses and is building up a system for reverse logistics and building re-customisation with its Reuse House System. Furthermore, Sekisui Heim has built up together with its suppliers a BIM-based information management system, which allows dynamic data management of the building, components, customers, maintenance and services. Toyota Home is gradually improving its graded warranty and service models, with the intention of a long-term building maintenance and facility management. If Japan's prefabrication industry continues towards a successful implementation of the mentioned life cycle services, and connects them to approved mass customisation structures and customer integration strategies, a new prototype of construction industry based on the fusion of mass customisation and building/ household-related services will be introduced. The focus will not be on material, resource and labour input exclusively, but rather on long-term customer relations and product-service systems.

BIBLIOGRAPHY

Fujimoto, T. (ed.) (1999) *The Evolution of a Manufacturing System at Toyota*, New York/Oxford: Oxford University Press.

Furuse, J. and Katano, M. (2006) 'Structuring of Sekisui Heim automated parts pickup system (HAPPS) to process individual floor plans', *ISARC 2006 International Symposium on Automation and Robotics in Construction*, Japan, June 2006.

Linner, T. and Bock, T. (2009) 'Smart customization in architecture: towards customizable intelligent buildings', in F.T. Piller and M.M. Tseng (eds) *Proceedings of MCPC2009 – Mass Customization and Personalization Conference*, Helsinki: University of Art & Design.

Linner, T. and Bock, T. (2010) 'Mass customization in a knowledge-based construction industry for sustainable high-performance building production', paper presented at CIB World Congress, Salford, May 2010

Linner, T. and Bock, T. (2012) 'Evolution of large-scale industrialisation and service innovation in Japanese prefabrication industry', *Journal of Construction Innovation: Information, Process, Management,* 12(2): 156–178.

Matsukuma, H., Inada, T., Yuzuhana, A., Tani, T., Matsuzawa, H. and Ichida, T. (2006) *'Kuino Mayekawa Retrospective'*, Exhibition Catalogue, The Japan Institute of Architecture.

Monden, Y. (1983) *Toyota Production System*, Atlanta, GA: Institute of Industrial Engineers.

Ohno, T. (1988) *Toyota Production System – Beyond Large Scale Production*, Massachusetts: Massachusetts Productivity Press.

Osamu, S. (1994) 'A history of Tatami', *Chanoyu Quarterly, 77*.

Reynolds, M.J. (2001) *Maekawa Kuino and the Emergence of Japanese Modernist Architecture*, Berkeley, CA: University of California Press.

Wißnet, A. (2007) *Robots in Japan – Backgrounds of a Phenomenon (Roboter in Japan–Ursachen und Hintergründe eines Phänomens)*, München: Indicium Verlag GmbH.

Yoshida, M., Kubota, Y. and Yokota, Y. (2005) 'Mechanism of the Man-Nen Dokei; A historic perpetual chronometer; Part 1: Wadokei, a Japanese traditional clock', *Journal of Nihon Kikai Gakkai Nenji Taikai Koen Ronbunshu*, 5: 51–52

14

Commercialisation principles for low-carbon mass customised housing delivery in Japan

Masa Noguchi

ABSTRACT

Japanese housing manufacturers have been at the forefront of the commercialisation of mass-customisable homes which correspond with today's market needs for low to zero operational carbon dioxide (CO_2) emissions, as well as demands for the affordability and design customisability. Nonetheless, there is no collective knowledge of the principles of their design, production and marketing approaches and strategies to which the industry and academia particularly outside Japan can refer. Accordingly, in order to scrutinise their overall business operations, technical study visits to Japanese housing manufacturers' state-of-the-art production and sales facilities were initiated and organised in 2006, 2007, 2008 and 2010. In total, 71 international delegates attended the knowledge transfer educational events (which were later called 'ZEMCH Mission to Japan') and contributed to solidifying their diverse individual experiences into some universal knowledge of the housing manufacturers' design, production and marketing principles. Based on the mission outcomes, as well as literature reviews, this chapter will systematise the manufacturers' commercialisation principles being practised for their sustainable delivery of low CO_2 emission mass custom homes in Japan.

ZEMCH MISSION TO JAPAN

Global warming is a serious concern in our society and the emissions of greenhouse gases including carbon dioxide (CO_2) need to be controlled strictly. The International Energy Agency (IEA) Solar Heating and Cooling (SHC) Task 40 and Energy Conservation in Buildings and Community Systems (ECBCS) Annex 52 joint programme claims that 'Energy use in buildings worldwide accounts for over 40% of primary energy use and 24% of greenhouse gas emissions' (IEA 2010). In the UK, the housing sector is responsible for 27 per cent of the total carbon footprint (Boardman 2007). There is a clear need for sustainable supply and operation of low to zero CO_2 emission homes that help alleviate global warming issues arising today.

Generally, homebuilders tend to restrict their information search to the programmed decision since the search for information for non-programmed decisions takes too much time, money and effort (Noguchi 2008). A 'programmed' decision reflects a habitual (or routine) purchase, and it may lead almost immediately to a purchase, whilst a 'non-programmed' decision may require more time (which can also be considered as a cost relating to the search) for the acquisition and processing of information on a product to be purchased.Therefore, in order to open the gate for conventional house-building stakeholders to consider their future production of low to zero carbon homes, technical study visits were initiated and coordinated by the author (Noguchi 2011). In 2005, CANMET Energy Technology Centre (called 'CanmetENERGY' today), Varennes, Natural Resources Canada, appointed Masa Noguchi and Roger-Bruno Richard as coordinators of the 'Japan Solar Photovoltaic Manufactured Housing Technical Mission 2006.' The educational event was held from 20 to 23 February, 2006, with the aim to provide Canadian homebuilders, housing manufacturers, building component suppliers, architects, academics and government officers with opportunities to explore not only the state-of-the-art production facilities of the then four leading net zero-energy-cost housing manufacturers in Japan, i.e., Sekisui Chemical Co. Ltd, Misawa Homes Co. Ltd, PanaHome Corp. and SANYO Homes Corp., but also a sales centre that displays a variety of Japanese manufacturers' housing prototypes (Richard and Noguchi 2006). Based on past experience, from 3–5 September 2007 the educational event was reorganised by the Mackintosh School of Architecture, The Glasgow School of Art, in collaboration with the Centre for the Built Environment in the UK. Then, it was renamed 'Zero-carbon Mass Custom Home Mission to Japan' and a visit was added to Sekisui House Ltd which was committed to the development of a zero carbon emission house. In 2008, the title was again changed to 'Zero-energy Mass Custom Home Mission to Japan' (or 'ZEMCH Mission to Japan') and it was held from 10 to 12 September. In 2010, the mission was executed as part of the Renewable Energy 2010 International Conference's related educational events, held successfully from 23 to 25 June. In addition to the company visits, a post-mission strategic 'Zero-energy Housing' workshop was also held within the conference programme in which 20 delegates from Australia, Brazil, Canada, Italy, Korea, Portugal, Sweden, the UK and the USA were invited to serve as the panellists who would report the mission's overall outcomes so as to solidify the delegates' individual experiences and diverse observations into some universal knowledge of Japanese housing manufacturers' design, production and marketing principles that support their delivery of low to zero carbon homes which are replicable and marketable.

The following sections detail Japanese housing manufacturers' quality-oriented mass custom design and production approaches, and high cost-performance marketing strategy, which articulate the uniqueness of their business operations as a whole.

MASS CUSTOM DESIGN AND PRODUCTION

In Japan, a total of 813,126 houses were newly built in 2010 and among them, 126,671 homes, or 15.6 per cent, were estimated to be prefabricated (JPA 2012). Today, most of the prefabricated homes in Japan are mass customised and built in response to homebuyers' individual requirements, desires and expecta-tions (Noguchi 2003). In Japan, 'mass customisation' is far from new, having been applied not only to the production of industrialised housing units but also that of automobiles and electric appliances with the aim to accommodate today's diverse needs and demands of individuals and society (Davis 1987; Pine 1993). One of the successful mass-customisation approaches being applied to the Japanese homebuilding industry is the standardisation and/or modularisation of housing components. In 2002, the mass custom design system model was initially introduced and tailored to the quantification of possible ordered pairs (or combination) of given standard housing components (Noguchi and Friedman 2002). Afterwards, the mass customisation (MC) model applied to housing design became generalised, having been expressed simply using a conceptual analogue model as follows: $MC = f(PS)$. In this model, the service sub-system (S) concerns communication platforms that invite users to participate in customising their design output, while the product sub-system (P) covers production techniques that aim to encourage the standardisation of housing components for mass production and dissemination (Noguchi and Hadjri 2010).

Standardisation of building components seems to be a limited hindrance to design customisation if communication platforms are well systematised. Design-consulting staff and an appropriate communication interface are required to facilitate user choice of standard design components. These fundamental design service factors can also be integrated into a comprehensive model: $S = f(l, p, t)$. In this model, the service sub-system (S) is supported by the existence of the location (l), personnel (p) and tool (t) factors and they are necessarily interrelated. Basically, building components can be divided into three categories: volume, exterior and interior. They are the main elements of the product sub-system (P) which can be explained by the following conceptual model: $P = f(v, e, i, o)$. The volume (v) components are used to configure the building's internal space that determines the size and location of each room while the interior (i) and exterior (e) components serve to co-ordinate decorative and functional elements that customise a building. In addition, 'o' denotes other optional features such as housing amenity and security systems, inclusive design components and renewable energy technologies. Generally, fabric and ventilation heat losses are associated with building volume and envelope exposures while thermal transmittance links up with materials applied to exterior and interior components. Energy monitors may fall into the category of optional features.

Today, most of the net zero-utility-cost housing manufacturers in Japan have begun to install a number of renewable energy technologies as standard features rather than options (Noguchi and Collins 2008). Seemingly, the increase of installing standard features in the houses is based on the manufacturers' high cost-performance marketing strategy which usually leads to continuous improvement of product quality rather than mere reduction of selling prices.

HIGH COST-PERFORMANCE MARKETING STRATEGY

The high cost-performance marketing strategy has been applied to a variety of end user products around the globe. For instance, although today's automobiles can be produced with lower production costs than those in the past, their selling price does not seem to be affected dramatically by higher productivity. New cars are still generally regarded as expensive; nevertheless, the list of items now offered as standard in new cars, such as air conditioning, a stereo set, airbags, remote-control keys, power steering, power windows and adjustable mirrors, were offered only as expensive options in older models. Clearly, the quality of newer models is much higher than that of older models. The same is true for the pre-fabricated housing industry in Japan (Noguchi 2003). The manufacturers' quality-oriented production may hardly be secured without being based on such strategy. Japanese housing manufacturers usually acquire ISO 9000 and 14000 accreditations that certify the quality control of their products, as well as the companies themselves. They set higher standards than ordinary building regulations, maintaining uniform product quality by strict control over their products. In particular, most Japanese manufacturers establish their own quality standards in order to improve structural resistance, durability and amenities, as well as to produce net zero-utility-cost housing today whose operational CO_2 emissions can be either low or zero with the support of the installation of renewable energy technologies such as photovoltaic (PV) solar power generating systems (Ishida 2008).

Between 1994 and 2003, Japan's housing industry experienced the drastic increase of domestic PV installations from 539 to 52,863 houses (Table 14.1). In order to alleviate the eccentric appearance of solar panels, Japanese housing manufacturers tend to neatly integrate PV cells into building envelopes (Figure 14.1).

TABLE 14.1 Number of residential PV installations in Japan: 1994–2003
(Ikki and Tanaka 2003)

Year	Annual number of houses equipped with PV systems	Annual installed capacity (MW)
1994	539	1.9
1995	1,065	3.9
1996	1,986	7.5
1997	5,654	19.5
1998	6,352	24.1
1999	15,879	57.7
2000	20,877	74.4
2001	25,151	91.0
2002	38,262	141.4
2003	52,863	201.4
Total	**168,628**	**622.8**

14.1 PV mass custom home by Sanyo Homes

Sekisui Chemical Co. Ltd, one of the largest solar PV housing manu-facturers in Japan, reported that the production of energy-efficient houses contributed to the growth in sales and orders, and between 2002 and 2003 the company increased the delivery of their PV solar homes from 32 per cent of the total housing sales to 46 per cent (Sekisui Chemical Co. Ltd 2004). Since the early 2000s, the manufacturer has installed a solar electric system as a standard feature rather than an option, and today the total sales of their factory-built homes equipped with 'built-in' PV systems are estimated at over 80,000 units (Sekisui Chemical Co. Ltd 2010).

Japanese housing manufacturers' quality-oriented production aims to contribute towards the delivery of high cost-performance housing in which high-tech modern conveniences that are installed as options in conventional homes are available as standard equipment (Se). In this context, the product sub-system (P) can further be modified into the following conceptual model: $P = f(v, e, i, o) + Se$. In fact, Japanese housing manufacturers today are mass-producing low-carbon customisable homes in which a variety of housing amenities and renewable energy technologies are installed as standard features. Despite the reduction of equipment choices, volumetric, exterior and interior design components still remain substantial options from which the users can choose so as to customise the end product. The high cost-performance market-ing strategy being applied to housing delivery in Japan aims to increase overall product quality while helping to lessen operational CO_2 emissions that contribute to global warming. Sekisui Chemical Co. (2003) demonstrated that by installing their typical 3kW PV system on the rooftop of a house, the annual energy cost can be reduced by 33 per cent and CO_2 emissions by 36 per cent (Table 14.2).

TABLE 14.2 The impact of built-in PV applications on annual CO_2 emissions and utility costs (Sekisui Chemical Co. Ltd 2003)

Housing type *	Housing without PV	Housing with 3kW PV	Housing with 3kW PV and thermal
Electricity consumption (kWh/year)	5,814	5,814	5,814
Electricity generation (kWh/year)	0	3,125	3,125
Net electricity cost (A) (JPY/year)	143,712	72,247	72,247
Natural gas consumption (m³/year)	527	527	317
Natural gas cost (B) (JPY/year)	70,790	70,790	47,050
Annual CO_2 emission (kg/year)	1,036	661	526
Total energy cost (A+B) (JPY/year)	214,502	143,037	119,297

* Typical prefabricated housing model equipped with HVAC systems, Tokyo: 158 m² in total floor area

Furthermore, the company also introduced a PV hybrid system that generates not only electricity but also thermal energy that can be fed into water heating. In this option, the annual energy cost can further be reduced by 44 per cent and CO_2 emissions by 49 per cent.

HOUSING USER-MANUFACTURER COMMUNICATION

Japanese housing manufacturers' communication approaches derived from their cultural context in which 'customer satisfaction' is of utmost concern. Prior to entering into a contract with their clients, the manufacturers supply an extensive amount of information in order to motivate consumers to learn more about the company's products and services during the buying decision-making process. In order to enhance clients' motivation for purchase of high cost-performance housing, the manufacturers have been practising three principal communication approaches to dealing with potential homebuyers: (1) advertisement, (2) education and (3) value assurance. Their communication approaches applied to each stage of their marketing efforts are proven to be influential in the enhancement of customer satisfaction. The JPA (2012) unveiled an annual survey of consumer preferences in the purchase of industrialised housing in Japan. The survey indicates that the perceived high quality of industrialised housing was the utmost significant factor that attracts potential buyers (Table 14.3).

In fact, 22 per cent of the 1,000 respondents who purchased pre-fabricated homes indicated that the primary factor influencing their buying decision was the reliability of the large-scale housing company which somewhat reflects the brand name effect on the sales. Eighteen per cent of the buyers preferred to live in an industrialised house due to the higher levels of housing performance. Ranking next to them, 17 per cent of the homeowners responded that they purchased an industrialised house because it was designed to be earthquake-resistant. Fifteen per cent of the buyers preferred the factory-built home since they were well convinced of the sales staff's explanation as to the product features and the company's services offered to their clients before and after occupancy. These results suggest that homebuyers in Japan tend to consider the quality of housing to be the top priority while the selling price is less of a consideration. In fact, only 2 per cent of the buyers regarded the total price of industrialised housing as relatively low. In Japan, consumers venture to purchase an innovative industrialised house whose price is approximately 8 per cent higher than the site-built one if convinced of the superior housing quality (Noguchi 2003).

TABLE 14.3 Buyers' motivation to purchase industrialised housing in Japan (JPA 2012)

Motivation factors selected	Year 2008 (%)
Reliability of the large-scale company	22
Superior product quality and performance	18
Earthquake resistance	17
Convinced by the sales persons' explanation	15
Good post-purchase services	2
Good design	4
Customisation according to needs and demands	5
Reliable safety measures	0
Short construction time	2
Wide variety of equipment selections	1
Confirmed by visiting housing exhibitions	1
Consideration of environmental issues	1
Recommendation from acquaintance	3
Relatively low price	2

CONCLUSIONS

Japanese housing manufacturers produce marketable and reproducible low-carbon mass custom homes that meet the wants and needs of individual users as well as society. The mass custom design approach applied widely by the manufacturers in Japan helps achieve a high level of standardisation of housing components that homebuyers can directly select in planning their new home. On the other hand, the user choices of the mass-producible standard components paradoxically increase a level of design customisability. Therefore, it contributes to reducing design and production costs by achieving the economies of scope while helping to customise a house in consideration of the buyer's economic constraint. Nonetheless, Japanese housing manufacturers implement quality-oriented production that focuses more on enhancement of product quality than reduction of selling prices. The manufacturers seem to be investing the money saved from lowering design and production costs through mass customisation for rigging their prefab homes with luxurious standard equipment; thus, this, in turn, upgrades housing quality and distinguishes their products from conventionally built houses. Today, based on the high cost-performance marketing strategy, the manufacturers tend to install a variety of housing amenities and renewable energy technologies as standard features rather than options and emphasise that they have been producing better-quality homes for about the same price as conventional ones with limited amenities.

In order to deliver marketable and reproducible low-carbon mass custom homes, the strategic balance between the optional and standard features seems to be critical. The optional features may be provided with the aim to enhance design quality (or customisability) that helps contribute to satisfying desires and expectations of individual stakeholders. The standard equipment, on the other hand, may need to be installed in buildings as it aims to exceed product quality whose levels can be adjusted in conjunction with societal demands and requirements.

ACKNOWLEDGEMENTS

The author would like to express his sincere gratitude to Sekisui Chemical Co. Ltd, Misawa Homes Co. Ltd, PanaHome Corp., SANYO Homes Corp., Sekisui House Ltd, and INAX Corp. for their collaboration on the execution of the Zero-energy Mass Custom Home Mission to Japan, as well as for their generous provision of catalogues and photographs that well capture their business operations.

BIBLIOGRAPHY

Boardman, B. (2007) *Home Truths: A Low-Carbon Strategy to Reduce UK Housing Emissions By 80% By 2050*, Oxford: Environmental Change Institute, University of Oxford.

Davis, S. M. (1987) *Future Perfect*, New York: Addison-Wesley.

IEA SHC /ECBCS Task 40 / Annex 52 (2010) *Towards Net Zero Energy Solar Buildings IEA SHC /ECBCS Project Factsheet*, Paris, IEA: 1.

Ikki, O. and Tanaka, Y. (2003) *National Survey Report of PV Power Applications in Japan*, Paris: International Energy Agency.

Ishida, K. (2008) 'The global warming prevention strategy for housing in Japan', *Open House International*, 33(3): 38–47.

Japan Prefabricated Construction and Suppliers and Manufacturers Association (JPA) (2012) *Prefab Club*. Online. Available at: http://www.purekyo.or.jp/3-1.html (accessed 6 January 2012).

Noguchi, M. (2003) 'The effect of the quality-oriented production approach for the delivery of prefabricated housing in Japan', *Journal of Housing and the Built Environment*, 18(4): 353–364.

Noguchi, M. (2008) 'A choice model for mass customisation', *International Journal of Mass Customization*, 2(3/4): 264–281.

Noguchi, M. (2011) 'Enhancement of industry initiative through the Zero-energy Mass Custom Home Mission to Japan experience towards commercialisation', *International Journal of Mass Customisation*, 4(1/2): 106–121.

Noguchi, M. and Collins, D. (2008) 'Commercialisation strategies for net zero-energy-cost housing in Japan', *Open House International*, 33(3): 96–104.

Noguchi, M. and Friedman, A. (2002) 'A mass custom design model for the delivery of quality homes, learning from Japan's prefabricated housing industry', *in Proceedings of the CIB W060-096 Joint Conference, 6–8 May, Hong Kong*, 229–243.

Noguchi, M. and Hadjri, K. (2010) 'Mass custom design for sustainable housing development', in: F. T. Piller and M. M. Tseng, *Handbook of Research in Mass Customization and Personalization*, Hackensack: World Scientific Publishing.

Pine, B. J. (1993) *Mass Customization: The New Frontier in Business Competition*, Boston: Harvard Business School Press.

Richard, R. B. and Noguchi, M. (2006) *The Japan Solar Photovoltaic Manufactured Housing Technical Mission 2006*, Varennes: CanmetENERGY, Natural Resources Canada.

Sekisui Chemical Co. Ltd (2003) *Unit Technology*, Tokyo: Sekisui Chemical Co. Ltd.

Sekisui Chemical Co. Ltd (2004) *On the Right Track with Cutting-Edge Chemical and Environmental Technologies: Sekisui Chemical Co., Ltd.,* Annual Report 2004, Tokyo: Sekisui Chemical Co., Ltd.

Sekisui Chemical Co. Ltd (2010) *Building Momentum for Growth: Sekisui Chemical Co., Ltd.,* Annual Report 2010, Tokyo: Sekisui Chemical Co., Ltd.

15

Mass customised structures for relief: physical production with digital fabrication

Lawrence Sass and Daniel Smithwick

ABSTRACT

Presented here is a novel exploration of a computational system used to physically produce mass customised building designs. This design system, *Materialisation,* supports an interactive working process between building design, manufacture, and assembly of small structures. Implicit in the work described here is the proposal that the process may be applied to any environment in need of new structures. For this study, the focus is on the design production of temporary relief shelters (or 'housing') for the population in need in post-Katrina New Orleans. This chapter provides a theoretical overview of a rule-based system used to convert a 3D digital design model into easy-to-assemble, interlocking wooden components.

INTRODUCTION

Shortages in housing and disaster relief replacement structures are an on-going, worldwide problem. The limitations in building production are greatest for communities whose infrastructure has been destroyed by natural disaster. Victims of natural disasters are typically housed in tent structures while they wait for planning and development of longer-term housing solutions. Tents work well for immediate relief from the elements after a disaster: they are low cost, easy to transport, and rapidly assembled. Unfortunately, tents are commonly used as interim shelters expected to serve communities far beyond product lifespan, in some cases up to three years. Alternatively, North American relief agencies have made use of trailers as an interim solution, e.g. the New Orleans' Katrina FEMA trailers. These are factory made structures equipped with basic functional utilities needed to support individuals and small families. They are socially unpopular generic structures that perform the technical duties of housing while ignoring the more important social, cultural, and symbolic needs of a community. In this chapter, specific needs considered relate to the stylistic elements associated with place. As a secondary focus, the research shows that regardless of design intricacy and complexity, all home construction (temporary or permanent) can reflect local culture and individual tastes. The idea of design style as a consideration in home production after a disaster has been considered by others (Knight and Sass 2010). For many cultural and technical reasons new technologies are slow to market for housing. This research asserts it is possible to produce hundreds and thousands of units of housing at low cost and of varying styles by using new, digitally based, computer-aided design and manufacturing technologies (CAD/CAM) coupled with the process of Materialisation.

The motivation to consider style as a design constraint in addition to function for relief housing is based on a need to address social issues related to FEMA trailers in post-Katrina New Orleans (Aldrich and Crook 2008). While indeed providing a low-cost solution, the social failure of trailers has increased interests in acceptable interim buildings with integrated technologies (Lee et al. 2008). Flexible design and manufacturing tools are needed to service the production of variation of all types from form to size. Considered here are digital fabrication technologies as the dominant system for such production. Unlike prefabricated housing which primarily uses traditional construction methods, albeit in a controlled indoor environment, digital fabrication works seamlessly between CAD software and Computer Numerically Controlled (CNC) machines, thus enabling low-cost production of mass customised artefacts. By directly coupling the digital design model with the physical manufacturing, costly processes of translating traditional construction drawings into buildable forms are eliminated.

In theory Materialisation can be used to manufacture housing units with 5- to 15-year lifespans. Although it is theoretically possible to produce permanent buildings with digital fabrication, interim housing solves problems found in tents and trailers for post-disaster solutions. These buildings are expected to be replaced by permanent buildings as part of a well-planned community design. These types of shelters can be assembled by members of the community within weeks or days following a natural or man-made disaster. Rapid assembly is possible because attachment features are embedded into each component. The nature of CNC manufacturing and digital design tooling means that mechanical systems such as electric, plumbing, and heating can be embedded into the building production. Prototype examples of digitally fabricated structures have been documented (Sass 2006; Bergdoll and Christensen 2008; Smithwick 2009).

Initial investigations into the concept of mass customised housing have been documented by Noguchi et al. (Noguchi and Friedman 2002; Noguchi and Hernández 2005). However, his work is missing a system of production describing how houses can be fabricated; it can be assumed that traditional manual methods of construction will support the concept. Building production with traditional methods vary in quality, price, and delivery time. Such methods also require expertise in building construction, the production of paper drawings, and many types of hand-powered tools. The alternative is 50-year-old prefabricated construction methods where houses are manufactured in large factories and shipped to construction sites on flat-bed tractor trailers. Prefabricated housing requires cranes, experienced set crews and skilled craftsmen: it is a high-energy building production system greatly limiting building customisation.

At the center of the mass customisation production system described in this chapter is digital fabrication. It can be used to produce thousands of building components of varying shape at scales of efficiency previously only achieved through mass production systems. Generation of each component in CAD is guided by a rule-based system defined here as a Materialisation. The resulting 3D digital model is similar in representation to the models found in building information modelling (BIM) where most components are virtually represented (Eastman et al. 2008). Unlike methods found in BIM, however, Materialisation is focused on manufacturing every element of the model with computer controlled machinery similar to methods found in aircraft manufacturing (Harik et al. 2008). Design examples in this study embody a range of facade styles found in New Orleans' shotgun houses (Figure 15.1). This work shows how digital fabrication and Materialisation can allow for mass customisation both at small scale, such as with the ornamental design of facade details, and at large scale, for structural components such as walls, roofs, and columns.

DIGITAL FABRICATION

The grand challenge is to be able to rapidly produce hundreds of housing structures of varying styles ready for assembly with integrated electrical and plumbing systems. This concept has been addressed before, first by Sears and Roebuck in the 1920s. Sears developed a kit-of-parts house catalogue from which customers could customise their house by selecting and combining various mass-produced components, e.g. window frames, doors, stairways, trim, etc. Later, in the 1950s other US companies such as the Lustron House Corporation and the General Panel Company created a mass production manufacturing system which limited the amount of customisation but increased the potential production output (Gropius 1956; Wachsmann 1961). For a more in-depth discussion of early twentieth-century housing companies, see Smithwick (2009).

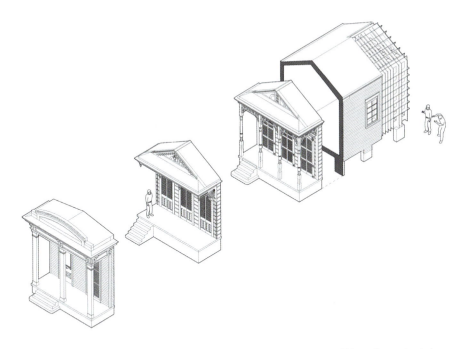

15.1 Mass customisation strategy: three example unique facade design options which can be constructed with a standardised cabin

More recently there have been two emerging theories on the potential impact and application of digital design and fabrication technologies for mass customisation in housing production. The first is an integrated manufacturing, delivery, and assembly system whereby sheet material such as plywood is cut by CNC machines into interlocking components and assembled by hand to form a rigid substructure with attached sheathing (Sass and Botha 2005). A second conceptual example is layered manufacturing with concrete sections, as described in a process known as Contour Crafting (Khoshnevis 2002). As a theoretical approach to physical artefact production Contour Crafting follows similar methods found in layered manufacturing (rapid prototyping) (Gebhardt 2003). Both methods are controlled by computer-based tools that subdivide the 3D shape of the design geometry into discrete 2D layers which are later translated into tool paths for automated CNC manufacturing. Contour Crafting has not solved issues related to complex geometry such as overhanging structure above doorways or openings as part of its layer-defining process. In contrast, the approach originally developed by Sass and Botha (2005) and later refined by Smithwick (2009) is limited by time-consuming hand assembly of interlocking components in contrast to the automated assembly of layers made possible in Contour Crafting. In addition, both methods of digital fabrication are limited to production of the substructure and do not address how to integrate and manufacture systems such as electrical, plumbing, and insulation into their structures. Both cases, however, allow for mass customised manufacturing of large-scale artefacts such as housing from initial CAD data.

GENERATING A DESIGN

Many questions related to the speed of production, variation in quality, and system flexibility arise from the goal to customise each building. The field of shape grammars is one of the first areas of design research to address these problems. It is a highly flexible method of design production that has illustrated ways to generate architectural designs as drawings and 3D models (Stiny 2006). One important advantage of shape grammars is in the pictorial representation of rules, and opportunities to generate new shapes without writing new rule sets. Shape grammars have been used to successfully generate floor plan drawings in the style of Andrea Palladio (Stiny and Mitchell 1978). Three-dimensional examples of shape grammar production were seen first in *The Queen Anne Grammar* developed by Flemming (1987) as a way to produce a specific design style from floor plan drawings to 3D models. The drawings that resulted from *The Queen Anne Grammar* were used to produce designs for a pattern book as part of Pittsburgh's redevelopment initiative in the 1980s (Flemming et al. 1986). More recently, *The Siza Grammar* was also a 3D shape grammar developed as a comprehensive method of shape generation with detailed rules sets used to create houses in the style of Álvaro Siza (Benros and Duarte 2009). Duarte describes a method to design mass customised houses using shape grammars which generates a design model in CAD using rules that guide design production. Evaluation of the resulting designs demonstrates that Benros and Duarte's and Flemming's grammars generate design models of consistent styles in three dimensions. Missing from design research is exploration into methods of physical production (manufacturing and assembly) from generated designs.

MATERIALISING A DESIGN

Materialisation is defined here as a production system that translates a design shape into a CNC machine tool path for automated manufacturing. This system combines machine production (digital fabrication) with generative design methods (shape grammars) to work as a flexible system of rapid building production. It is flexible enough to satisfy a need for the generation of hundreds of style and functional variations from commercial storefronts to water pumping stations and soup kitchens. The interest in a complete system of design and physical production is similar to the development of automated design in electronics in the early 1980s. Today electronics industries have developed tools and techniques for automated CAD tools that generate designs, test for design behaviour and drive tools for manufacturing (Jansen 2006). Electrical components, such as PCBs (Printed Circuit Boards), are directly manufactured with CAD/CAM technologies resulting in low cost production and efficient integration of other systems. Materialisation is one of many possible methods of building production using digital fabrication and rule-based systems. To maintain the spirit of automation in design and manufacturing Materialisation expects that every component in a building will be manufactured by digital fabrication machinery. A production system of this type requires a change in product architecture from standardised dimensional lumber to customised components for ease of assembly. Materialisation is computation of a design model for manufacturing similar to slicing algorithms found in rapid prototyping where a scan line is generated from the 3D design model then manufactured by a machine (Gibson 2002). Contrary to the automated process used in layered manufacturing, full-scale building construction means that component reduction cannot be completely automated. Rules sets are needed to control the subdivision of the building components in order to evaluate structural integrity and order of assembly.

COMPUTING A DIGITAL DESIGN
FOR MANUFACTURING

An example illustrating the Materialisation process is shown in Figure 15.2 beginning with the initial 3D design shape of the entire building, ending with 2D CNC machine tool paths (Figures 15.2A–C). Before the shape can be subdivided it must be approved for structural loading and functional building programming. The shape model (Figure 15.2A), which can be created using a wide variety of 3D digital modelling software such as AutoCAD, Rhino, or even free software such as Google SketchUp, is used to generate the object model which is composed of interlocking 2D components represented in 3D space (Figure 15.2B). The size, shape, and complexity of the components generated are primarily determined by properties of the materials from which they will be cut, the speed of manufacturing needed, and ease of hand assembly. These constraints are interrelated and together form the rule sets for generating components from the initial design model. For example, while it is both more time and material efficient to generate larger components when considering the cutting speed of the CNC machine, if components are too large, they become very difficult to lift and assemble by hand. Currently such rules must be determined from the designer's experience; however, they can be integrated and automated in future digital design tools. Lastly, the components are re-arranged

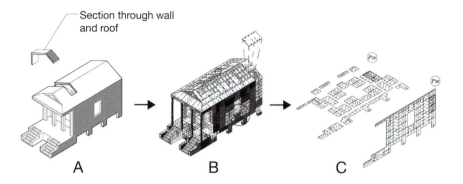

Section through wall
and roof

A   B   C

15.2 Materialisation process: A) shape model; B) object model showing 2D components in 3D space; and C) components organised for CNC milling

into 2D space and converted into tool paths ready for CNC manufacturing (Figure 15.2C). Additional rules can easily be integrated into the Materialisation process for reducing time, cost, and energy required. For example, rules may determine efficient nesting of components for greater material utilisation; flat packaging for efficient shipping; and component assembly order for efficient hand assembly and site management.

CONCLUSION

A built example of a structure designed and manufactured via Materialisation is shown in Figures 15.3 and 15.4, a structure in the style of a New Orleans' Shotgun house and exhibited at the Museum of Modern Art in New York City (Bergdoll and Christensen 2008). Secondary systems such as plumbing and electrical were not included in this prototype. The structure is assembled entirely out of CNC-cut wood and plastic sheet material and assembles quickly as there is little need for mechanical fasteners such as screws or nails. Instead, the assembly is sustained by frictional forces between the interlocking components (Figure 15.3). Shaping, subdivision, and interlocking connections between components are determined by rule statements as described earlier. The process of generating geometry by rules enables other types of grammars to be considered as part of the design process. For example, a grammar that generates electrical components or circuits can be used in conjunction with a grammar to design water movement through the building. There is also the possibility that new tools can aid local participation in the design and manufacturing of their own homes and other structures.

As a method of production, Materialisation has its limitations in the time consumed to produce component geometry and the logistics of physical

15.3 Clockwise from left: Researcher Dennis Michaud assembling wall 'panel' components; detail of interlocking floor 'rib' components; New Orleans shotgun house design beginning to take shape

15.4 Digitally fabricated house for New Orleans on exhibit at 'Home delivery: fabricating the modern dwelling', Museum of Modern Art, NYC, 2008

component delivery. The construction industry expects its operations to be dominated by manual labour for some time to come, making a quick adoption of mass customisation via digital fabrication into the industry questionable. Digitally fabricated products do not lend themselves well to integration of manually manufactured components, as the system works best when defined as a complete structure produced by digital machines. Lastly, there are limited CAD tools that can support generative design of the type illustrated here. Materialisation requires expertise in areas of design and computer science outside of traditional architectural design training such as structural modelling, manufacturing technologies, design of product architecture, and logistical management.

New CAD tools and the evolution of the construction industry will allow for a more mass customised process of digital modelling by communities of designers and engineers with common interests and skill in CAD and CAM tools. These new tools and changes will enable a more efficient and more customised disaster relief housing design, manufacturing, and delivery system. Through Materialisation, residents whose homes have been destroyed in disasters can have mass customised interim housing solutions. They will have their local design aesthetics met, and they will have the capability for local, on-site manufacturing and assembly of their homes.

BIBLIOGRAPHY

Aldrich, D. and Crook, K. (2008) 'Strong civil society as a double-edge sword: Sitting trailers in post-Katrina New Orleans', *Political Research Quarterly*, 61: 379–389.

Benros, D. and Duarte, J. P. (2009) 'An integrated system for providing mass customized housing', *Automation in Construction*, 18: 310–320.

Bergdoll, B. and Christensen, P. (2008) *Home Delivery: Fabricating the Modern Dwelling*, New York: Museum of Modern Art.

Eastman, C., Teicholz, P., Sacks R. and Liston, K. (2008) *BIM Handbook: A Guide to Building Information Modeling for Owners, Managers, Designers, Engineers and Contractors*, New York: John Wiley & Sons.

Flemming, U. (1987) 'More than the sum of parts: The grammar of Queen Anne houses', *Environment and Planning B*, 14: 323–350.

Flemming, U., Coyne, R., Pithavadian, S. and Gindroz, R. (1986) *A Pattern Book for Shadyside: Technical Report*, Department of Architecture, Pittsburgh, PA: Carnegie-Mellon University.

Gebhardt, A. (2003) *Rapid Prototyping*, Munich: Hanser.

Gibson, I. (2002) *Software Solutions for Rapid Prototyping*, London: Professional Engineering Publishing.

Gropius, W. (1956) *The New Architecture and the Bauhaus*, Boston, MA: Charles T. Branford Company.

Harik, R., Derigent, W. and Ris, G. (2008) 'Computer aided process planning in aircraft manufacturing', *Computer Aided Design and Application*, 5 (6): 953–962.

Jansen, D. (2006) *The Electronic Design Automation Handbook,* Dordrecht: Kluwer Academic Publishers.

Khoshnevis, B. (2002) 'Automated construction by contour crafting – related robotics and information technologies', *Journal of Automation in Construction,* 13: 5–19.

Knight, T. and Sass, L. (2010) 'Looks count, computing and constructing visually expressive mass customized housing', *Artificial Intelligence for Engineering Design, Analysis and Manufacturing,* 24: 425–445.

Lee, M., Weil, F. and Shihadeh, E. (2008) 'The FEMA trailer parks: Negative perceptions and the social structure of avoidance', *Sociological Spectrum,* 27: 741–766.

Noguchi, M. and Friedman, A. (2002) 'Manufacturer-user communication in industrialised housing in Japan', *Open House International,* 27 (2): 21–29.

Noguchi, M. and Hernández, C. (2005) 'A "mass custom design" approach to upgrading traditional housing development in Mexico', *Journal of Habitat International,* 29 (2): 325–336.

Sass, L. (2006) 'Synthesis of design production with integrated digital fabrication', *Automation in Construction,* 16: 298–310.

Sass, L. and Botha, M. (2005) 'The instant house: A model of design production with digital fabrication', *International Journal of Architectural Computing,* 4: 109–123.

Smithwick, D. (2009) 'Architectural Design 2.0: An online platform for the mass customization of architectural structures', S.M. Thesis, Massachusetts Institute of Technology.

Stiny, G. (2006) *Shape, Talking About Seeing and Doing,* Cambridge: The MIT Press.

Stiny, G. and Mitchell W. (1978) 'The Palladian grammar', *Environment and Planning B,* 5: 5–18.

Wachsmann, K. (1961) *The Turning Point of Building,* Wurzburg: Reinhold Publishing Corporation.

16

Two case studies of mass customisation and digital fabrication in building industry

Ingrid Paoletti

ABSTRACT

Using two case studies, this chapter illustrates the application of mass custom-isation in the building sector. A particular focus will be given to the integration between new parametric software packages, with advanced production strategies (digital fabrication), and building technologies. The case examples, Gehry's IAC New York office building and Gramazio and Kohler's Winery in Switzerland, which are both based on an innovative interpretation of custom-isation for their customised building envelopes, will be discussed to explain how advanced technologies may be utilised to tailor-customise building elements to an extent comparable with craft production of a building envelope.

INTRODUCTION

Industrialisation has a very long history in construction. Mass production of specific building materials such as adobe bricks were some of the first examples of prefabrication during the industrial revolution. Throughout the twentieth century, and especially during a stage of extensive experimentation in the 1950s and 1960s, evolutions in the production process of building and construction products have taken place.

An example of a resulting technology has been dry assembly, an evolving common practice which developed into a foundation of modern 'prefabricated' elements. This method is characterised by the use of mainly mechanical interfaces for assembling the components, eliminating the need for wet connections. The construction method underlying dry assembly has prolonged over the entire evolution of a variation of techniques associated with different historical periods, from ancient stone structures, timber and wood constructions, when the use of local, vernacular and indigenous materials was a common practice, through to the first uses of wrought iron and steel in structures. After the industrial revolution, dry assembly techniques were outlined as a new paradigm for building construction. Benefiting from a shared heritage of material culture, they became a means of developing a concept of building radically different from traditional methods. Being uniform, repetitive and affordable, they represented the typical characteristics of industrialised mass production, allowing for rapidly increasing the quantity of the output while pertaining to a reasonable and controlled level of quality. As a result, dry assembly technologies witnessed an exponential growth in the early 1950s with the development of industrialised construction systems mostly due to high demand in the housing market after World War II. In the end, they became an expression of a "high-tech language" of architecture in the 1980s (Gann, 2000).

Today, industrialisation in the construction industry is associated with pre-assembly and is still continuing to develop further. Reasons for this development include:

- The nature of materials used and the need to enhance sustainability of the built environment
- The need to further reduce the complexity of the construction process to enhance the efficiency of the building process
- The arrival of advanced fabrication techniques that allow for a different kind of manufacturing and, hence, a new boost in industrialisation
- The growing market for high performance, high specification buildings which demands higher levels of flexibility and customisation, despite the continuous quest for low cost and stable quality.

One of the core ideas to bring the current level of industrialisation onto a higher level is building parts with a high degree of customisation, made at different places off site, delivered just-in-time and assembled on site. This combination of customisation with regard to the component and standardisation/industrialisation of its production process is a core characteristic of mass customisation – producing products to the specific needs and requirements of the end users at a reasonably comparable price to that of mass-produced products. While mass customisation is motivated by the trends outlined before, it is enabled by innovative design solutions, new production methods, advanced manufacturing processes such as digital fabrication or CNC technologies with flexible mechanical properties. A central technical enabler has been software based on parametric features which allow a direct link between design, engineering and production of each building component. The application of mass customised components can be from a building's structure to shell, and from its envelope to MEP and HVAC systems. In general, mass customisation can create advantages in construction methods where technical solutions require specific and personalised performance that can be achieved utilising functional layers, embedding the need for change during their life cycle, and enhancing the ease of maintenance.

In construction, this represents a real paradigm shift that may provide an answer on the current trade-off between the use of prefabricated components with dry assembly and the functional performance of a component. Mass customisation therefore conveys a twofold meaning. On one hand, it is the expression of a mature construction industry searching for a quality enhancement. On the other, it provides the designers with new construction choices, using the same information model from conception to completion. In other words, the formal complexity of many contemporary projects is offering the opportunity to reconsider the sequence of 'idea–project–site' based on engineering-to-propose instead of central explorative character of technological solutions through design (Campioli, 2005). In conclusion, an exponential diffusion of industrialised components due to market competition, improved performance and quality control, and the use of parametric software packages have resulted in a 'technological push' for new products and systems. At the same time, a new generation of designers in the building industry, who have been educated in the use of modern design software, has started to interpret these new components in an innovative way. This 'need pull' in search of satisfaction meets the 'technological push' resulting from the demand for more cost efficiency. This will lead to hybrid solutions: the genesis of a technology which can be found in an intermediate position between the necessity to satisfy a need and the availability of solutions for this need (Verganti et al., 2004).

DIGITAL FABRICATION AS A RESULT OF TECHNOLOGY TRANSFER

Digital fabrication is a manufacturing process developed in an industrial context where precision and direct production is requested, e.g. in automotive industries, furniture design and mechanical products. The main characteristic of digital fabrication is the combination of CAD design and flexible CNC machines, facilitated by parametric software packages.

The use of digital fabrication in the construction industry can be seen as a pattern for 'technology transfer' of innovative technologies from other disciplines, including chemistry, molecular biology, computing and material sciences as well as aeronautic and naval/marine industries. Examples of transferring the know-how from other fields in a building construction system can be found in different fields, from materials (shells, polymers, fibres), semi-processed products (profiles, accessories for the construction, gluing systems) to components (metallic nets, adhesive tapes) and lighting technologies (LED, optical systems, use of OLEDs (organic light-emitting diodes)).

All these elements can be regarded as being pervasive. They have been invented in sectors where high technology is of crucial importance, but are now being diffused transversally in sectors with a rather traditional structure where they have introduced important changes (Utterback, 1996). This is exactly what has happened in the building industry where innovative technologies are more and more placed upstream. This type of innovation transfer also suits the nature of small and medium enterprises (SMEs) which characterise the construction industry, merging craft competences with advanced technical skills (Barrett *et al.*, 2008).

TWO ILLUSTRATIONS OF ENVELOPE TECHNOLOGIES

The traditional form of buildings has been radically changing in the last decades due to a fast changing cultural context, new technological boundaries, innovative digital tools and industrial building components. One of the core enablers of this change has been the implementation of mass customisation models, systems and strategies for the digital fabrication of building envelopes. Envelopes are nowadays fully configurable as a consequence of high levels of industrialisation in fabrication processes of the buildings. Two examples of this development are Gehry's IAC New York office building and Gramazio and Kohler's Winery. The former is a perfect illustration of mass customisation, providing a cold curved unit facade system, while the latter is a product of digital fabrication with its facade having been built by a robot dry assembly brick technology. These two cases can express some of the recent achievements of innovative building technologies related to mass customisation and digital fabrication.

The IAC New York building, designed by Gehry Associates in 2007, is a glass office located in New York City, with a smooth, uniform appearance of the main facade. Horizontally fitted white bands line the windows and act as a decorative element to control the flow of light inside. The facade system always maintains a flat geometry in its forming compartments while representing, at the same time, a 'twist' in its overall form for the envelope of the building. Based on a design with parametric software, all units of the building have been mass customised in a central production unit. The envelope components are similar in their geometry but different in parameters that define their performance (Figure 16.1).

16.1 IAC building in New York by Gehry Associates, 2007 (Image courtesy of Permasteelisa Group)

Directly extracted from a file created using a parametric software tool, the curtain wall components have been optimised in relation to their position in the building, either for structural or thermal issues. In order to build this envelope with a 'curved' surface using a flat unit system facade, each component has to be able to epitomise part of the overall 'twist' within a certain range in order to keep in the correct position. This operation has been first modelled through software and then tested on site in order to verify the tolerances and the materials' flexibility. On site, each casement has been fitted in its final position using a manual installation process (Figure 16.2).

The IAC building is a perfect illustration of mass customisation technology. Its design has enabled an industrial facade construction system with a new way of conceiving and modelling its performances before production. This concept can be diffused on a wide scale allowing a mass customisation of flat glass building components, with a significant lower cost in comparison to a curved glazed facade.

The second project is the development and construction of the facade of Vineyard Gantenbei in Fläasch, Switzerland in 2006. Realised by Gramazio & Kohler Architects in cooperation with Bearth & Deplazes Architects, the building was realised as an extension of a small but remarkably successful vineyard

16.2 Parametric cell design and mock up test of the IAC building (Image courtesy of Permasteelisa Group)

(the following description has been taken from a research report by ETH Zurich, published at http://dfab.arch.ethz.ch/web/e/forschung/52.html). The wine producers wanted a new service building, consisting of a large fermentation room for processing grapes, a cellar dug into the ground for storing the wine barrels, and a roof terrace for wine tastings and receptions. The initial design proposed a simple concrete skeleton filled with bricks. The masonry acts as a temperature buffer as well as filtering the sunlight for the fermentation room behind it. The bricks are offset so that daylight penetrates the hall through the gaps between the bricks. Direct sunlight, which would have a detrimental effect on the fermentation, is, however, excluded. Polycarbonate panels are mounted inside to protect against wind. On the upper floor, the bricks form the balustrade of the roof terrace.

The robotic production method developed at Architecture and Digital Fabrication of ETH Zurich, by Professors Fabio Gramazio and Matthias Kohler, enabled the architects to lay each one of the 20,000 bricks precisely according to programmed parameters – at the desired angle and at the exact prescribed intervals. This allowed the design and construction of each wall in order to possess the desired light and air permeability, while creating a pattern that covers the entire building facade. According to the angle at which they are set,

16.3 AND 16.4 Brick wall by Gramazio & Kohler (Image courtesy of Gramazio and Kohler, Architecture and Digital Fabrication, ETH Zurich)

each individual brick reflects light differently and thus takes on different shades.

Creating the facade required the generation of a process: the studio started by digitally simulating gravity to make the grapes fall into a virtual basket, until they were closely packed, then the digital image data was transferred to the rotation of the individual bricks.

The wall elements were manufactured as a pilot project in the research facilities at the ETH Zurich, transported by lorry to the construction site, and installed using a crane. Because construction was already quite advanced, the construction time has been very tight: only three months before assembly on site. This made manufacturing the 72 facade elements a challenge both technologically and in terms of deadlines. As the robot could be driven directly by the design data, without having to produce additional implementation drawings, it was possible to work on the design of the facade up to the very last minute before starting production (Figures 16.3 and 16.4).

To accelerate the manufacturing process for the 400 square metre facade, Gramazio and Kohler had to develop an automated process for applying the two-component bonding agent. Because each brick has a different rotation, every single brick has a different and unique overlap with the brick below it, and the one below that. Together with the brick manufacturer's engineer, a method was established where four parallel bonding agent paths were applied, for each brick individually, at predefined intervals to the central axis of the wall element. Load tests performed on the first manufactured elements revealed that the bonding agent was so structurally effective that the reinforcements normally required for conventional prefabricated walls were unnecessary (Gramazio & Kohler, 2008). This project started as a pilot project but then developed into an advanced project with a concept of digital customisation of facades. Benefiting from digital fabrication, this technology will open new frontiers for mass customised cladding technologies.

CONCLUSIONS

Advanced methods of design and production will not entirely replace the traditional ones. For some materials and machining conditions, conventional planning and production processes (also on site) are necessary for proper work. However, it is likely that the site will become an increasingly less approximate location of the project construction, especially when dry processes and industrial components replace the traditional procedures. Digital fabrication offers a broad range of opportunities.

The two case examples allow us to draw two important conclusions. First, the collection, accuracy and availability of information become even more crucial than before. Ottchen (2009) speaks of the need to find a way to inform a project using 'soft data', i.e. a package of information that is neither excessive for the proposed architecture (e.g. Building Information Modelling; BIM) nor insufficient to meet the needs of a project (e.g. legislative consolidation of traditional materials). Another dimension of information is the capture of knowledge from different projects. Only when the experiences and methods of each individual project are collected, can greater knowledge be created.

Second, we must rethink the roles of different 'figures' (or role players) during the design and construction process. Traditionally, contractual roles were strictly defined. They, however, are giving way to less characterised and more trans-disciplinary roles which can enter the construction process at different levels with their competences. The relationships between these roles, and hence, between the human beings in a building project find an unprecedented importance. An issue of *Architectural Design* (March/April 2009) on the relationships between the various figures in this changing scenario of digital fabrication and customisation had the interesting title of 'Closing the Gap'. And indeed, there still often is a gap between the possibilities given to design by advanced tools and technologies and the construction process governed by traditional contracts (focusing on traditional on-site production methods). To realise the full potential of digital fabrication, the building industry has to close this gap. A major challenge for the coming years will be the creation of new roles connecting the modern design process with the building process. Only with this human facet, can the full potential of digital fabrication and mass customisation be realised.

BIBLIOGRAPHY

Architectural Design (2009) 'Closing the Gap', March–April.

Barrett P., Sexton M. and Lee A. (2008), *Innovation in Small Construction Firms*, Taylor and Francis, Abingdon.

Cagan, J. and Vogel Craig, M., (2002), *Creating Breakthrough Products*, Prentice Hall, New York.

Campioli, A. (2005) *Idea, Progetto, Cantiere*, in Pignataro Maria (ed.), *Innovazione di prodotto e architetture di forma complessa*, Milano: Clup.

Claudi de saint mihiel, C. (2005) *L'innovazione dei processi costruttivi*, in Losasso Mario (ed.), *Progetto e innovazione. Nuovi scenari per la costruzione e la sostenibilità del progetto architettonico*, Napoli: Clean, pp. 97–104.

Galli, R. (2005) *Innovazione. Le parole della tecnologia*, Roma: Ediesse.

Gann, D. (2000) *Building Innovation: Complex Constructs in a Changing World*, London: Thomas Telford Publishing.

Gramazio, F. and Kohler, M., (2008) *Digital Materiality in Architecture*, Zurich: Lars Müller Publishers.

Morin, E. (1985), *Le vie della complessità*, in Bocchi Gianluca and Ceruti Mauro (eds), *La sfida della complessità*, Milano: Feltrinelli.

Ottchen, C. (2009) 'The future of information modeling and the end of theory', *Architectural Design*, March–April: 22–27.

Paoletti, I. and Tardini, P. (2011), *Mass Innovation. Emerging technologies in construction*, Maggioli, Rome.

Patrick, B. and Cache, B. (2007), *Objectile: Fast-Wood: A Brouillon Project,* Wien, New York: Springer.

Pignataro, M. (ed.) (2005) *Innovazione di prodotto e architetture di forma complessa*, Milano: Clup.

Schodek, D., Bechthold, M., Griggs, J. K., Kao, K. and Steinberg, M. (2005), *Digital Design and Manufacturing: CAD/CAM Applications in Architecture and Design*, Hoboken, NJ: John Wiley & Sons.

Utterback, J. (1996), *Mastering the Dynamic of Innovations*, Cambridge, MA: Harvard Business School Press.

Verganti, R., Calderini, M., Garrone, P., and Palmieri, S. (2004) *L'impresa dell'innovazione. La gestione strategica della tecnologia nelle PMI.* IlSole24Ore, Milano.

PART **IV**

FUTURE TOPICS, NEW POTENTIALS, AND EMERGING CHALLENGES

17

Stylemachine – case study: mass tailoring the housing block apartments on the internet

Tomas Westerholm

ABSTRACT

Web-based services such as a data model of the business process, a database and virtual backend interface for managing the related information, related digital content (visualisation service), server and user interface on the internet seem to be an ultimate solution for customisation and personalisation in the building industry. This chapter is based on mass customisation projects devised to meet the need of our clients: the construction companies specialising in housing block apartments. The customer-driven thinking, which has been both a wish and a forced situation, is underlined, and we also explain how as a solution provider we have been assisting customers to formulate their ideas and combine them with ours in a web service. Chronological case studies including NCC's manual configurator (2005), Skanska's planning the future (2007), and YIT's prototype (2008) have been used and the most recent project, YIT's Stylemachine (2009), are also presented with prospects for future developments. Building on what has been learnt from this experience, some ideas for future development will be shared both for this specific purpose and generally for reinvigorating the concept of customisation within the building industry.

INTRODUCTION

3D Render's main goal is to deliver the best way to buy (and sell) new (non-built) mass customisable apartments by providing online mass tailoring tools for new home buyers. Customers of new apartments can visually tailor their homes before buying them and before they are built.

To have taken the customers' viewpoints into consideration, it was envisaged that an approach opposite to technology-oriented thinking was necessary and thus to be successful, all web-based 3D technologies were abandoned in favor of a Flash-based client.[1]

The first customer case in 2003 was also the construction company NCC's first dedicated internet page for a housing project. That turned out to be NCC's best-selling project of the year. For the first time NCC were able to fully tend to and answer the question: "How would my final choices look in reality?"

This chapter provides a chronological development of this technology, describes the current solution, and concludes with some ideas for future developments. The devised solution and the technologies behind it will be explained in principle as an independent case study with prospects for the future. This is because this presents exploratory research which attempts to investigate new concepts and new frontiers of customisation in the building industry.

3D RENDER LTD

3D Render Ltd is one of the oldest digital content creators for the building industry in Finland, serving architectural and construction businesses since 1997 by providing 3D images, animation and virtual models into core moments of design, decision making and marketing. An extensive knowledge base and skills in digital content production for the construction industry were the starting point for development of the company followed by an initial spark which came from customers and finally developed into a real internet-based project for 3D Render in 2007.

2003, NCC – SUDDEN SUCCESS

The configurator operation concept gestated at Render's Christmas party in 2002 from a conversation in the courtyard of the office, where the atmosphere was very informal and nobody seemed to have been interested in anything but getting into party mood on a dark Friday night in central Helsinki. One of the guests, a young project manager, was impressed by the visualisation images which were used as the screensavers of the office displays. The monitors had images of all kinds of projects, also of apartment construction. He had already thought how a construction company could boost its apartment sales with the help of the internet. He had thought that important apartment projects should have their own web pages. Now he also knew what could be presented on those web pages. The discussion in the courtyard went on, and an idea came up of a dedicated site where you could rotate the views of your future home and its material choices easily and visually. It was evident that this could be done with Flash. It turned out to become an informal brainstorming session about the idea and it was promised that they would get back to it as soon as possible. It was time to get back to the party.

Soon they started with the project. Render modeled and visualised a series of images of which simple room-specific configurators were compiled to the webpage, where the customer could change a limited number of choices i.e. floor materials and so forth. The implementation was narrow compared to the present versions, but at least it was carefully made, clear and well functioning. It was probably one of the first of its kind. After all, it was the first apartment-specific site of NCC's and it resulted in huge customer demand for the apartments. Terrace apartments on the top floor of the house were soon wanted by so many people that NCC decided – exceptionally – to hold an auction for the apartments. This was the best project of the year for NCC in terms of sales.

2005, NCC – MANUAL CONFIGURATOR

In the further developed vision, NCC wanted to increase the selection of con-figured details and their options. The style and quality definitions of an apart-ment were materialised to sell more quickly and more easily, from an individual apartment to an individual feature.

NCC borrowed well-established strategies from the car manufacturers and introduced them to their buyers: various ready-made interior decoration style configurations and optional features. It was easy for customers to choose the interior materials for their own home from ready-made entities with matching titles. Render produced (still manually) a series of images, where different rooms were visualised with different entities. The apartment sales agents used card series printed off the images for marketing and sale administration.

2006, SKANSKA – PLANNING THE FUTURE

Around this time there was wider interest by construction companies to represent a series of images in a more interactive way. The study carried out for Skanska was concerned with the available optional implementation methods regarding two critical views: the apartment buyer vs. life cycle cost. The evalu-ations ended up in focusing on the quality of the customers' experience. The first problem with the web applications – the installation of plugins and other possible programs – and the possible inoperability dropped the 3D-engine-based online solutions off the list. At the end, there was only the native HTML imple-mentation and Flash-based site left. Flash was found to be common enough back then when even large companies had adapted it to their webpage technology (see Figure 17.1).

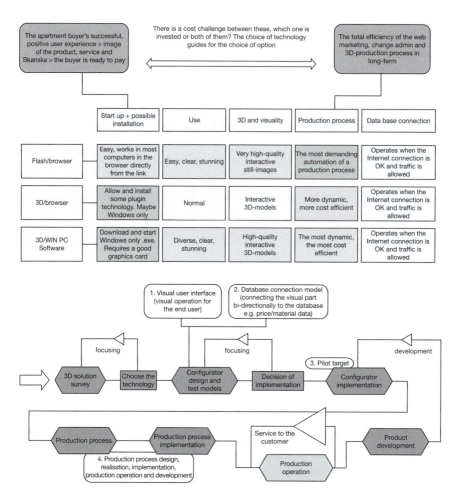

	Start up + possible installation	Use	3D and visuality	Production process	Data base connection
Flash/browser	Easy, works in most computers in the browser directly from the link	Easy, clear, stunning	Very high-quality interactive still-images	The most demanding automation of a production process	Operates when the Internet connection is OK and traffic is allowed
3D/browser	Allow and install some plugin technology. Maybe Windows only	Normal	Interactive 3D-models	More dynamic, more cost efficient	Operates when the Internet connection is OK and traffic is allowed
3D/WIN PC Software	Download and start Windows only .exe. Requires a good graphics card	Diverse, clear, stunning	High-quality interactive 3D-models	The most dynamic, the most cost efficient	Operates when the Internet connection is OK and traffic is allowed

17.1 Easy to use vs. easy to serve technology comparison: The second research outlined the main phases of a more robust platform implementation. The development of the actual system has progressed ever since according to this idea

2007, YIT – PROTOTYPE

Demand for an advertisement with a better quality and with more visual material had made a breakthrough. Realtors' advertisements in newspapers and magazines were full of fancy renderings. Something that was started ten years earlier as a luxury option for a major architectural competition had become a commodity – a striking visual impact.

YIT, as the biggest domestic construction company, felt the pressure and decided to find out how they could take the next step in quality and technology.

The first prototype was already larger than any previous implementation. It was felt that it was the time to start to push for this business. Render had

17.2 YIT Prototype: Printed visualisation play cards. 3D Render Ltd delivered the Internet configurator for YIT's As Oy Juontaja in summer 2007. Top: 2 images from same bedroom, Middle: 2 images from same bathroom, Bottom: 2 images from car configurator

recently decided to start moving into software business, so it was natural to look out for larger customers to give the ignition for a strategic change. A TEKES project was applied for to cover a part of the development costs.

The rapidly created initial technology showed its strengths in the very first trial. It was both fun and easy to move on and accomplish the relatively tightly scheduled project. YIT had chosen to pilot the solution at a single site in the Helsinki region (Figure 17.2).

2008 – DEVELOPING IDEAS

The planning of the new system went on. Several ideas for short- and long-term solutions were studied before the implementation was initiated.

It was still necessary to try to understand where the solution stands, who the users are, why they would use it, what its meaning is and what its role would be. As one of the major setbacks, Render was forced to drop early stage design ideas for configurations in construction business for three reasons.

Short time window

New home buyers move fast. They make their decisions and move in typically within 6 months. There is not enough time to participate in a 1–2 year planning process. Too many participants would face critical changes in their lives and they would discard the case. Examples are relocating due to work requirements or changes in the family sizes.

Pragmatic core business

Construction logistics and profitability currently favor the existing less dynamic model. Quick, massive changes are not expected.

Durable goods

Seldom are new home buyers professional designers. Pre-designed setups by professionals are more attractive and cheaper to implement than fully tailored apartments. Good architecture and professional design leads to higher quality production in general, which means higher total values for the apartment markets compared to the irrational 'over-tailored goods' that make the resell more challenging.

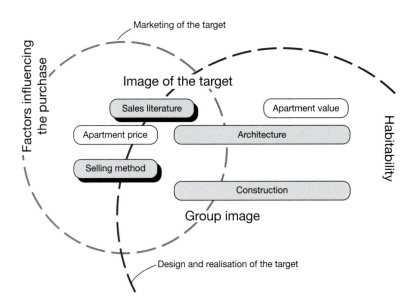

17.3 Influencing the decision process before the investment takes place

The core idea of the system was to deliver an excellent spatial experience including tailoring options, provided that it is naturally a challenge to convince someone to invest in a non-existing product (Figure 17.3).

The technology was, as a result of further developments in proof of concept, narrowed down to Flash for the client side, because of the high applicability within a range of browsers. Therefore, a system had to be developed that could cover up the technical compromise. Had a true 3D engine been chosen as the client server, it would have been easier to use the backend side. But since the end users in this market are very heterogeneous and not specifically IT-orientated, it would have been a recipe for disaster; almost an informed solution for failure.

Also, considering the smooth browsing of the space, pre-chosen quality views are still better than free navigation where one can end up staring at a corner.

Instead of bringing a full 3D model to the browser, a set of pre-defined views was provided for the browser. The benefits are:

- Fast start-up as the images are loaded on demand during the experience.
- Higher quality, as we can render each view with advanced off-line renderers that produce the highest visual quality as they can spend freely defined time per image, compared to online engines which have to be able to calculate a suitable number of frames per second (10–30 per second) to maintain a pleasantly smooth movement along the scenes.
- Spatial set of high quality images 'touches' the users' minds deeper than poor quality free navigation around the space. This has probably a lot to do with the perfect illumination and material simulation of images.

Out of the three core functions – navigation, configuration and communication – Render chose the first two for current implementation.

In addition to the core functions, several other optional features were considered, but they were left for future development at this point. The most interesting ones are those that enable bidirectional communication between the potential buyer and seller through the interface inside the virtual apartments.

2009 YIT – STYLEMACHINE

The YIT Stylemachine was launched in autumn 2009 and reached the technical-artistic level which was set as an objective a long time ago before starting the project. There were no intentions or willingness at Render to accept lower quality than the off-line renderers produce. This complicated task was combined with another ambitious goal to achieve: to produce millions of view combinations almost in real time.

17.4 Image of a room designed with YIT stailikone (Stylemachine)

YIT introduced a new dimension to its online apartment sales: the self-service enthusiasm of apartment buyers. Although we concentrated primarily on electrifying a limited part of the apartment sales engineers' material and change option process online, it was clear during the visualisation that the application will also create other added value. Along with the two critical parameters, another also received a good grade: the buyers had found the application and they could use it independently for configuration of their apartments (see Figure 17.4).

A user evaluation study was carried out to find out about the users' views and their required features for further developments. Some direct and important quotes from end-users' views are as follows:

- Easy – simple controls, the user is not supposed to lose one's way here.
- Fast – the server takes the burden, traffic to the client is minimised.
- Reliable – Flash is well spread, no other plugins or installations are needed.
- Multiplatform – Windows, also Mac and Linux are supported.
- Stunning – High quality images, bad quality is not allowed.

2012 – OTHER INDUSTRIES

Car industries and shoe manufacturers have introduced advanced and creative web configurators. Those businesses favor investments in web services for mass tailoring of big volume serial products whereas new apartments do suffer because of large overall individualism throughout the production.

State-of-the-art car configurators provide full exterior and limited interior visualisation. They provide an exact bill of materials including detailed pricing. Clothing does the same and instead of interior visualisation, used by the car manufacturers, they try to verify the fit to users' specifics.

The construction industry does a very repetitive task when it comes to building new homes but in contrast to other industries their products are more thoroughly tailored. In practice, almost all apartment block sites differ from each other, meaning that each site and even each apartment should have an unique configurator – or else if there is just one configurator, it should be extremely flexible and highly capable of taking care of all choice variations.

In Stylemachine Render's approach to this challenge was to limit the whole variation to the most relevant set of features, which for now has been the interior spaces. Stylemachine presents a set of prototypical yet generic rooms like kitchen, living room, bedrooms etc. with a set of choices provided by the construction company. Users can thus configure the individual spaces with individual choices out of millions of combinations.

The lack of exact individual floor plan and lack of being able to travel inside the apartment is compensated by high visual quality and well-chosen multiple viewpoints inside the rooms. Naturally individual floor plans and other information are provided as traditional documentation by the seller.

BUILDING VISION MANAGEMENT – THE PLATFORM

Building Vision Management is a background system or a 'platform', where the users define the configurable features of the space. This information will then be used by the configurator and the content providers in order to automate the permutation of image contents.

Due to processing power restrictions a set of images and image components are pre-rendered. They are then combined in real time into final hybrid images which present the individual choice combinations at each given moment of the user session. Pre-production is a script-driven process where database, 3D-model and rendering engine work together to produce the core material for online services.

Choice restrictions and dependencies are handled in rule data on the client side so that the server focuses only on serving the requested combined final images.

The benefits of this approach are that all the hard work is done before launching the service, there is no real-time 3D rendering happening. Compared to GPU-based real-time 3D services this approach is by far a lot faster and results in a smooth end-user experience.

FUTURE OF CONFIGURATORS AND VISUALISERS

A smooth interface that delivers a precise visual impact of the personalised apartment choices – "How would all my choices finally look in reality?" – is a benefit that is practically impossible to achieve by any other means. For the construction companies this is a professional dimension of the internet. Enabling the mass customisation (self) service for the buyers without using the traditional labor effort makes it also sensible businesswise.

An online tailoring system of non-built products can also be seen as a direct communication channel between the home buyer and seller. Besides the obvious user behavior data collecting, the interface could act as a feedback and polling system on a general level in regard to new apartment business.

Advanced options would enable participatory construction practice where the potential end users could get involved at early design stages starting from choosing the site. Participation could be arranged at various levels of commitment from open to purchased ownership share options, i.e. users could buy the apartments (options) already at the pre-planning stage and join the design team and thus more thoroughly influence the final result. The price and value of these options would develop accordingly along the process towards the final price of apartments and they would be free for transactions so that anyone interested could trade in or out at any moment at current market valuation.

Exposing the creation process for the end-user market would not only allow stronger buyer opinion influence per se but it would also create a new market of refining the products towards the real life execution. Market pricing of options should also reveal bad choices early enough, hopefully correcting the design before the building process starts.

Gifted participants could convert their talent into benefit of risen option prices along the development process. Business owners would benefit from a process where commitment happens earlier and deeper. End users would get to tailor their way of living.

Apartment blocks will be the major solution for housing in all metro-politan areas. The need for tailoring is not only for the individualism but also for the social common living experience in urban housing which could grow more personal and accommodated.

We believe that the future of mass tailoring of apartments is in a cloud-based SaaS-type web service containing: a data model of the business process segment, a database and virtual backend interface for managing the related information, related digital content (visualisation service and 2D/3D – hybrid production system), server and user interface on the net.

The future experience may be an interactive visual navigation around the apartment with a narrator explaining and helping with the tailoring options – in the big 3D holographic PC-TV screen of the would-be owner's living room.

NOTE

1   Flash is scheduled to offer major improvements in 3D soon while on the other hand HTML5 technologies have become widely popular recently.

18

Enabling mass customisation in construction – making the long tail work

Christian Thuesen, Jens Stissing Jensen, and Stefan Christoffer Gottlieb

ABSTRACT

The chapter discusses the development of construction management practices over the past 50 years outlining the academic and practical context for the adoption of mass customisation in construction.

Theoretically, the chapter builds on two fundamental insights: the Pareto principle and the Thomas theorem – a fundamental sociological principle. The Pareto principle is applied using the concept "the long tail".

Based on "the long tail" the three different production paradigms of mass production, mass customisation and individual customisation are identified. It is argued that construction in the 1950s and 1960s was driven by a "mass production" paradigm that gradually from the beginning of the 1970s was replaced by an "individual customisation" paradigm in which construction became a matter of tailoring unique buildings to each customer.

It is identified how these two different paradigms have been driven by two partial articulated myths. In the 1960s buildings were viewed as standardised while from the 1980s onwards they have been viewed as unique.

Based on the Thomas theorem it is argued that these myths have had a substantial impact on the way we build. Consequently, today's predominant view of buildings – as unique – implies that: 1) the nature of the construction processes is chaotic, 2) the buildings are realised through onsite project work rather than through offsite production; and 3) project management is the fundamental management principle.

The chapter further identifies how attempts to develop new construction practices like lean construction implicitly reproduce this myth. The result is that construction research in the past 25 years has been constructing the long tail in a way that hinders radical development of the construction industry.

The chapter concludes that if we allow ourselves to view buildings as both unique but also as standardised we can create a new platform for developing the construction industry – a mass customisation paradigm.

INTRODUCTION

A short analysis of different construction practices around the world based on Langford and Hughes (2009) illustrates a shared understanding of the building process as a heterogeneous assemblage of different professions, engaged in the realisation of buildings through projects, heavily regulated by the use of tendering systems and with project management as the primary management principle. Against these existing practices new industrialised ways of working are witnessing an increasing popularity within the construction industry – especially among practitioners. This development could to a very large degree be interpreted as a move towards the application of mass customisation strategies.

However, mass customisation as a strategy with the focus on standardisation, configuration and industrialisation is somehow incompatible with the existing practices (Jensen *et al.* 2011), so it is important to identify how mass customisation relates to the broader development of the construction industry.

The ambition of this chapter is to open a research agenda around mass customisation in construction by situating mass customisation in relation to the past, present and possible future of the construction industry.

The chapter opens with an introduction to the concept of the long tail, which is our fundamental framework for understanding different production strategies. This framework is subsequently used for understanding the development of production strategies in the construction industry. It is argued that these production strategies have developed simultaneously with a particular view or myths of buildings, which have tremendous influence on the way construction is practiced and developed today. The chapter concludes with an introduction to mass customisation as a design and production strategy that bridges the traditional mass production with today's construction strategy – individual customisation.

THE CONCEPT OF THE LONG TAIL

Based on the Pareto principle (the 80–20 rule) Anderson termed the concept "the long tail" (Anderson 2006). It gives an overview of a market by juxtaposing the volume/popularity of products with the number of product variants. The long tail refers to the tail of the Pareto distribution – that 80 per cent of the product variants represent only 20 per cent of the market. As we live in an

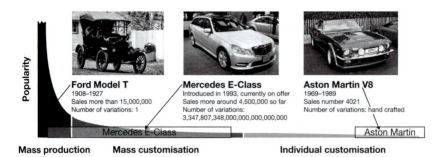

Popularity

Ford Model T
1908–1927
Sales more than 15,000,000
Number of variations: 1

Mercedes E-Class
Introduced in 1993, currently on offer
Sales more around 4,500,000 so far
Number of variations:
3,347,807,348,000,000,000,000,000

Aston Martin V8
1969–1989
Sales number 4021
Number of variations: hand crafted

Mercedes E-Class

Aston Martin

Mass production **Mass customisation**   **Individual customisation**

18.1 The long tail and production strategies

increasingly individualised society and as new technologies enable production and distribution of customised products – the tail part gets interesting.

Figure 18.1 relates the long tail to different production strategies (mass production, mass customisation and individual customisation) exemplified by the car industry. The figure should be read as a conceptualisation of where each production strategy's primary focus is regarding variation and market size.

Traditionally, industrial companies have focused on the small amount of products that are the most popular, as these can be delivered based on mass production strategies leveraging economies of scale. The most well-known example is the Ford Model T, which in the beginning only was produced in one variant – an extremely standardised product. As Henry Ford put it: "You can have all the colors you want, as long as it is black". Later Ford became one of the first customisers in the history of car production (Alizon *et al.* 2009).

The development of car manufacturing has evolved dramatically over the years. By the use of product platforms, customers can today design their own cars. This capability to deliver customer tailored cars increases the customers' perceived value of the car while the company can still leverage the economies of scale (e.g. Kruschwitz *et al.* 2000). In this way, car manufacturers have addressed the long tail, making it longer and bigger, by applying mass customisation strategies.

The last production strategy of the long tail is the "individual custom-isation" strategy, where every product is realised uniquely for each customer. Within the car industry this strategy is only adapted for certain extreme luxury cars such as the Aston Martin.

THE LONG TAIL OF THE BUILDING INDUSTRY

But what does the long tail of the construction industry look like? After the Second World War there were shortages of almost everything in Europe. People lacked not only basic foods, gasoline and coffee, but also homes, schools, hospitals etc. Within this context "mass production" strategies evolved in the 1950s and 1960s in the construction sector in order to rebuild societies (e.g. Bertelsen 1997). As the existing building practices could not meet the societal demands it was necessary to streamline the building industry. The chosen solution was to industrialise construction, and the inspiration came from scientific management (Taylor 1911).

The architectural basis for this change was the development of modern architecture. In 1852 the American sculptor Horatio Greenough coined the phrase "Form follows function" which later became the credo for modern architecture (McCarter 2010). The modern development was further fueled in the 1920s by the ideas of Le Corbusier. By his work and blessing, it became legitimate for architects to think of industrialisation, and the implementation of mass production principles in the construction industry began and buildings were erected for the growing population in the cities (Bertelsen 1997; Boxenbaum and Daudigeos 2007).

At the beginning of the 1970s the mass market for housing decreased and a revolution from upcoming architects against modernism's hard and angular shapes evolved (Boxenbaum and Daudigeos 2007). Architects would no longer build in solid squares, right angles and with an emphasis on simple shapes. They would use the forms, colors and lines they wanted to – finding inspiration in e.g. history and different cultures. In this new postmodern movement,[1] architects such as Bernard Tschumi, Jean Nouvel and Frank Gehry challenged Le Corbusier's ideas of "living machines" and under Tschumi's credo "form follows fiction" they developed a trend to produce buildings which were sensitive to the context in which they were built. Consequently, construction gradually became a matter of tailoring unique buildings to each customer and location. Figure 18.2 illustrates this shift in strategies.

Still today we are predominately and tacitly following this "individual customisation" strategy as every project starts from scratch trying to satisfy the customer's individual needs.

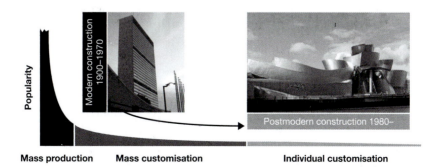

18.2 The long tail of the building industry

THE DRIVING MYTHS OF CONSTRUCTION

The two strategies treated above, mass production and individual customisation, have co-evolved with two more or less unarticulated myths which are discussed further below. First, we will, however, briefly explain the notion of myths as we use it here.[2]

It is a fundamental sociological principle that the way we view things matters. One of the conceptualisations of this is the Thomas theorem "If men define situations as real, they are real in their consequences" (Thomas and Thomas 1928: 572). Formulated in another way; if we believe that something is true, it will have an impact and eventually get true. This means that myths can possess tremendous power as long as they are well celebrated.

We suggest that the myths of the standardised and the unique operated as horizons for action. During the modernist period (up into the 1970s) buildings were generally viewed as standardised while in the postmodern era they have generally been viewed as unique.

We contend that these myths have had a definitive impact on the construction products and practices in each period. Recently the myth of individual customisation has thus been implicitly embedded in what some have come to define as the "nature" of the building process. As an example, the "lean construction" community often states that the nature of the building process is complex and even chaotic and consequently it follows that long-term planning is more or less impossible (e.g. Bertelsen *et al.* 2007). It is within this understanding that the development of the Last Planner System (LPS) for short-term planning should be understood, as LPS exactly enables managers to cope with a chaotic building process.

Lean construction was thus translated into an expression of a broader strategic field, governed by the myth of individual customisation, which focused on project management (PM) as the strategy for managing construction (e.g. PMI 2001).

This project management discourse generates tools and strategies for navigating in a chaotic and imperfect world. The "project" thus became the vehicle for realising buildings – and project management became the management principle. This, we argue, is still the predominant way of organising the building process today.

The development of lean construction illustrates how concepts that were originally developed to support mass production (lean production) have been reshaped by the logics of the myth of the uniqueness of buildings and tailored to support the perceived chaotic nature of "individual customisation". Table 18.1 summarises the differences of the two paradigms.

A limitation, as we see it in this perspective, is accordingly that most initiatives for improving performance in the construction industry implicitly

TABLE 18.1 Construction in the light of mass production and individual customisation

	Standardised	Unique
Societal frame	Modern	Postmodern
Timeframe	1900–1970	1980–?
Driver of identity	Social classes	Individualism
Architectural credo	Form follows function	Form follows fiction
Perceived nature of the building process	Known – complex	Chaotic – complex
Production paradigm	Mass production	Individual customisation
Value chain	Integrated	Fragmented
Vehicle for realisation	Prefabrication	Project
Management paradigm	Scientific management	Project management
Cost	Low	High
Implementation of lean	Long-term planning (line of balance)	Short-term planning (last planner system)

reproduce the myth of the unique and chaotic nature of construction. Consequently the construction industry is still struggling with inefficiency, high costs etc. To be provocative one could argue that most of the initiatives have been symptom treatment while not addressing the root causes of the problems.

However, despite the prevailing myth about the uniqueness of buildings, the buildings look paradoxically the same. How come it is produced as unique and in a chaotic way, when in the end it looks like the adjacent building? The answer could perhaps be found in the institutionalised practice-based learning processes where the different professions in their mutual interactions continuously reproduce the dominant order (Thuesen 2007) and are shaped in the image of the myth.

From an industrialised perspective it is, however, absurd not to take advantage of these similarities as benefits of economies of scale could be achieved. One could thus raise the question whether there exists a "right" way to view buildings. The short answer is that this is dependent on the cultural setting. In this way the so-called "nature" of the building process is socially constructed based on the myths. The interesting point is hence not whether there exists a "right" way to view buildings, but that our view of buildings have consequences. This implies that if we are able to reactivate the sedimented social strata, to experiment with our view of buildings as being both standardised and unique (instead of either standardised or unique), it will become possible to create a new "platform" for the development of the building industry – a platform which could be termed "mass customisation".

THE ROAD AHEAD – MASS CUSTOMISATION

The concept of mass customisation was first coined by Stan Davis (1996), and further developed by Joseph Pine (1993). Traditionally, customisation and low cost have been perceived as mutually exclusive. Mass production provided low cost but at the expense of uniformity. Customisation, on the other hand, characterised the products of designers and craftsmen and its cost generally made it a privilege of the rich. (It is tempting to state that the construction industry's customers today are stuck with this privilege.)

The basic idea of mass customisation is to bridge these two strategies by optimising the cost/value ratio – as illustrated in Figure 18.3. Tseng and Jiao (2001: 685) define it as "producing goods and services to meet individual customer's needs with near mass production efficiency".

The interesting point is that the field of mass customisation in construction is already in the making. Various actors are experimenting with mass customisation strategies.

The large contractors especially are moving towards mass customisation strategies. Both Skanska and NCC (Nordic Construction Company) have launched initiatives for leveraging their size through coordinated purchasing, supply chain management, development of standard solutions and platforms, etc.

Thuesen and Jonsson (2009) have evaluated two NCC initiatives (NCC Komplett and the German platform for housing), which both have aimed to implement the mass customisation paradigm. They found that there exists a

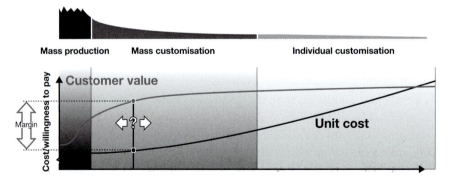

18.3 Optimisation of cost/value related to the long tail

key difference between the two initiatives – this being their point of departure. While NCC Komplett was trying to benefit from flexibility through industrialised manufacturing processes (mass production), the effort of the German platform was to manage flexibility in traditional construction (individual customisation).

So their point of departure was different, and so was the result. NCC Komplett seemed to do all the right things theoretically speaking and indeed developed a profoundly new approach for building. However, they lost control of the costs compared to normal construction practices and the NCC Board decided to abolish the investment. Compared to this, the German platform has managed to reduce the cost by more than 30 per cent over the past 10 years while still offering a high quality product carefully targeted at a specific market segment (Thuesen and Hvam 2011).

The German case is interesting as it contradicts the predominant understanding that a high degree of manufacturing is the way forward for the construction industry. Compared to NCC Komplett the German platform is extremely practical and low-tech as it takes its starting-point in existing, predominant in-situ construction practices.

The two NCC initiatives thus show that finding a successful mass customisation strategy is a challenge. Salvador *et al.* (2009) reach a similar conclusion in the analysis of 200 companies working with mass customisation. Their conclusion was that there is no best way to mass customise, but that "Managers must tailor [mass customisation] to an existing business – rather than vice versa" (Salvador *et al.* 2009: 79)

On a generic level, the movement towards mass customisation in construction can be seen as a development focusing on leveraging similarity. This is illustrated in Figure 18.4, combining the long tail with order decoupling points such as Match-to-Order, Configure-to-Order, Integrate-to-Order and Engineer-to-Order. Figure 18.4 should be read as showing how to integrate the ability to leverage similarity and still maintain the necessary flexibility. The more

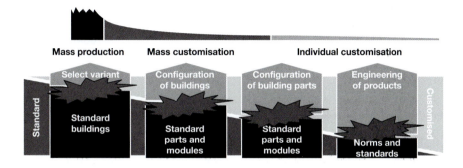

18.4 Leveraging similarity in the long tail – a "stair model"

you move to the left towards mass production the more you standardise your processes and products and reduce the flexibility towards the market.

A prerequisite for leveraging similarity is an integrated value chain. This implies that operating with mass customisation presupposes the development of strategic partnerships and even new types of companies integrating architectural, engineering and construction practices.

Today the institutional setup with fragmented value chains, short-term collaboration design/bid/build contracts and project-based production and management, however, hinders the application of mass customisation. It is therefore of utmost importance that the regulators of the industry start to be aware of what kind of structures they are enacting within the industry (Jensen *et al.* 2011).

RESEARCHING THE ROAD AHEAD

Despite an increasing interest in applying mass customisation principles in construction and the existence of plenty of cases of implementations – encompassing both failures and successes – the movement is more or less unsupported by formalised research. There is thus an urgent need for supporting the development with research.

In developing this support it is important to be aware of what kind of reality we are constructing by our research. As mentioned, construction is not driven by its own nature – although it sometimes could appear so. As practitioners and researchers we are constructing this nature ourselves while we are at the same time also constructed by it. Accepting this introduces a dilemma in terms of the validity of the research. A way forward is to legitimate research within construction in two ways – a constructive way and deconstructive way. Within the constructive area focus should not be on "finding the truth", but in what kind of "truth" we are creating with the research. Research within this area should be driven by the impact of the research.

But this paradigm cannot live without a deconstructive paradigm continuously operating to deconstruct the developed solutions and the nature/culture of construction. It is within the dialogue between these two paradigms that a fruitful research agenda for construction management and mass customisation can be developed.

CONCLUSION

This chapter has introduced the concept of the long tail as a framework for understanding the development of the building industry. It is argued that most of the construction industry today is driven by the myth of uniqueness of building. This myth is, together with other factors, inherently disabling the possibilities for fundamentally changing the construction industry into an effective and systematically innovative industry. It is further argued that if we allow ourselves to look at buildings as both unique but also similar we can create a new platform for developing the construction industry – a platform within the mass customisation paradigm. The industry is already developing and implementing strategies inspired by this approach, but research to back up and question this development is missing.

ACKNOWLEDGEMENTS

The argument of this chapter is developed based on input from anonymous reviewers of previous articles and colleagues. We are deeply grateful for all your input. Especially we would like to thank Marie Sofie Larsen for her valuable input on architectural issues in the argument. Furthermore we would like thank Emmauel Huybrechts, Autoviva, Brian Snelson, Kris Arnold and Dalbera for sharing their pictures under a Creative Commons license, enabling us to illustrate our figures with their photos of the cars Ford T, Mercedes E-class, Aston Martin V8 and buildings UN-headquarter in NY and Guggenheim in Bilbao.

This chapter is based on the paper "Making the long tail work: reflections on the development of the construction industry over the past 25 years" (Thuesen *et al.* 2009), which received the CIOB 175th Anniversary Prize at the ARCOM Annual Conference.

NOTES

1   Here the term "postmodern architecture" has been used as a collective term representing the different architectural movements, styles and schools following the modern period.

2   For a more detailed account of the notion of myth please refer to the original article (Thuesen *et al.* 2009).

BIBLIOGRAPHY

Alizon, F., Steven, B. S. and Simpson, T. W. (2009) 'Henry Ford and the Model T: Lessons for product platforming and mass customization', *Design Studies*, 30: 588–605.

Anderson, C. (2006) *The Long Tail: Why the Future of Business Is Selling Less of More*, New York: Hyperion.

Bertelsen, S. (1997) *Bellahøj, Ballerup, Brøndby Strand – 25 år der industrialiserede byggeriet*, Hørsholm: By og Byg.

Bertelsen, S., Koskela, L., Heinrich, G. and Rooke, J. (2007) *Construction Physics*, IGLC 15: Lansing, Michigan

Boxenbaum, E. and Daudigeos, T. (2007) 'Concrete innovations: Prefabrication in Denmark and France', in *Proceedings, Managing the Construction of Buildings Conference*, 15–16 November 2007, Copenhagen Business School, Denmark.

Davis, S. (1996) *Future Perfect*, 10th anniversary edition, Harlow: Addison-Wesley Pub Co.

Jensen, J. S., Gottlieb, S. C. and Thuesen, C. L. (2011) 'Construction sector development: Frames and governance responses', *Building Research and Information*, 39 (6): 665–677.

Kruschwitz, R., Schettler-Köhler, R. and Hoch, C. (2000) 'Product development and platform strategy at Volkswagen', *Slides, IBC Euroforumkonferens, Effektiv Produktutveckling med Modularisering*, Sweden.

Langford, D. A. and Hughes, W. P. (2009) *Building a Discipline: The Story of Construction Management*, Reading: ARCOM.

McCarter, R. (2010) *Frank Lloyd Wright*, 6th edn, London: Phaidon.

Pine, B. J. (1993) *Mass Customization – The New Frontier in Business Competition*, Boston, Mass: Harvard Business School Press.

PMI (2000) *A Guide to the Project Management Body of Knowledge (PMBOK1 Guide)*, 2000 edn CD-ROM, Philadelphia: PMI.

Salvador, F., Holan, P. M. de and Piller, F. (2009) 'Cracking the code of mass customization', *MIT Sloan Management Review*, 50 (3).

Taylor, F. W. (1911) *The Principles of Scientific Management*, New York: Harper & Brothers.

Thomas, W. I. and Thomas, D. S. (1928) *The Child in America: Behavior Problems and Programs*, New York: Knopf.

Thuesen, C. (2007) *Anvendelsen af den rette viden – et studie af byggeriets kulturelle organisering*, Published PhD Thesis, Byg-DTU: Technical University of Denmark. Online. Available at: http://orbit.dtu.dk/fedora/objects/orbit:82336/datastreams/file_4743791/content (accessed 22 May 2012).

Thuesen, C. and Hvam, L. (2011) 'Efficient on-site construction: Learning points from a German platform for housing', *Construction Innovation: Information, Process, Management*, 11 (3): 338–355.

Thuesen, C. and Jonsson, C. C. (2009) 'The Long Tail and innovation of new construction practices – Learning points from two case studies', in A. S. Kazi, M. Hanus and S. Boujabeur (eds) *Open Building Manufacturing: Key Technologies, Applications, and Industrial Cases*, Rotherham: Manubuild.

Thuesen, C., Jensen, J. S. and Gottlieb, S. C. (2009) 'Making the long tail work – reflections on the development of the construction industry over the past 25 years', in A. R. J. Dainty (ed.), *Proceedings 25th Annual ARCOM Conference*, 7–9 September 2009, Nottingham, UK. Association of Researchers in Construction Management, 2, 1111–1120.

Tseng, M. and Jiao, J. (2001) 'Mass customization', in G. Salvendy (ed.) *Handbook of Industrial Engineering: Technology and Operation Management*, 3rd edn, New York: John Wiley & Sons.

19

The application of game theory to customisation strategies in the construction industry

Ghashang Piroozfar and Poorang Piroozfar

ABSTRACT

As an interdisciplinary topic in architecture and the built environment, mass customisation has successfully flourished and thrived on technology and knowledge transfer both in its core concept from the manufacturing industry and in secondary concepts borrowed from other disciplines. This chapter uses game theory as an established mathematical theory in economics to show how informal rules can decrease willingness to take shortcuts in fulfilling rules, regulations and requirements while offering customisation; a higher choice for a better value to the end user, customer or client in the building industry. This will be initiated with an introduction to the concepts and an analytical review of the theory and how it works in a society. The discussion will then be followed by an analogical comparison between different perspectives in a society, in general, and the building industry, or in a more specific focus, construction economy, for the application of this theory. Finally the chapter concludes that this strategy works at a theory level and some proof of concept should be designed and implemented to demonstrate its practical application in professional practice in the building industry.

INTRODUCTION

According to Tseng and Jiao (2001), mass customisation denotes the technology and systems to deliver goods and services that meet individual customers' needs with mass production efficiency. This means fulfilling the purpose of optimising the resources, or more precisely minimising the cost and time of making products for each individual customer, while maximising the potential variability. Evidently, the most important fact behind mass customisation as a business strategy in the building industry is to minimise cost and time (which can be commoditised as cost) while maximising choices through enabling decision support systems and flexibility/adaptability. Achieving this goal in the built environment might be interpreted as taking shortcuts to reduce costs by some parties in the building industry, to be able to lower the final price of the product while increasing variation. These shortcuts can be referred to as lack of fulfilling requirement(s) L1 to reduce service and/or production costs. This chapter aims to use game theory in a comparable way to its application in the finance sector using the same underlying concepts and to make some suggestions to reduce or prevent the possibility of occurrence of such shortcuts. The chapter will use an analogical approach to test out an economics theory in the built environment. To achieve this, first of all we will go through a brief introduction to this theory, followed by an explanation of each introduced concept. Then, we will come up with a model which can further be developed and built into a customisation toolkit to assist in providing as varied a solution as possible in the expected cost brackets with no concerns about the shortcuts in dispute. So the question is:

> What if the requirement(s) L1 is (are) not met, yet the designer continues designing?[1]

We have built this study on the resemblance of this situation in the building industry to what is known as 'corruption' within a society. According to Macrae (1982), Kingston (2008), Vannucci (2011) and Piroozfar (2010) we can decrease corruption in different societies (regardless of the discipline) by adding informal rules to the structure of those societies. Thus here we will discuss how it is possible to reduce the disobedience in the building industry by adding informal rules to the design procedures.

CORRUPTION

Corruption affects resource allocation negatively and hampers the opportunities for economic growth (Gupta *et al.* 1998; Schaeffer 2002). The World Bank's definition of corruption is 'The abuse of public office for private gain', classified as the modern definition of corruption, which is its explicit definition, and according to this, bribery is a form of corrupt behaviour. According to Elliott (1997), Sanyal and Samanta (2000) and Treisman (2000) the most important factors of corruption (and extension of corruption) in a society are:

1. Amount of public benefits
2. Officials' power
3. The risks of corrupt activities
4. Briber and bribee power of bargaining.

An anti-corruption policy to restrain the above factors, therefore, should introduce changes such as:

1. Decreasing public benefits (governance of how public benefits are supplied)
2. Reducing officials' power (based on the assumption that the probability of abusing authority by the officials could be increased, when their power rises)
3. Increasing corruption costs and risks
4. Decreasing the bargaining power of briber and bribee.

Although all factors are more or less applicable to the construction industry, in this chapter we have chosen the third one to be able to present an in-depth analysis going through this factor. Therefore, increasing corruption costs to decrease corruption will be used to show how informal rules between people in the construction economy may help reduce corruption, or as indicated earlier taking shortcuts to cut costs.

In a society with informal rules, the corruption cost is higher than in a society without these rules. In such a society we can suppose that the individuals caught in a briber's dilemma also informally 'trade' with each other in a technologically unrelated game. Then, if the trade relationship is sufficiently valuable, they can threaten to punish bribery by suspending trade (Kingston 2008; Vannucci 2011). This means that informal rules will increase the total cost of corruption.

It will be discussed how these agreements among different parties enable them to benefit from not involving themselves in corruption, and by getting to this point how these rules change the corruption equilibrium point to an incorrupt one in a society, showing that the 'informal trade' between the members of the society is a factor of corruption cost's increment.

CAPACITY OF INFORMAL RELATIONSHIPS TO REDUCE CORRUPTION: A GAME THEORY APPROACH

Social capital (informal rules)

Social capital or informal rules are values of all social and professional networks both in their traditional form, such as communities of practice or trade unions, and in their modern forms, i.e. web-based professional or social networks such as LinkedIn, Academia, Twitter, Facebook, etc. Social capitals or informal rules are acknowledged and used by members of a society in persuasion to do things for each other in those networks. Social capital can be traced everywhere, from relationships between neighbours in a district, to colleagues and neighbouring countries. It can also play an important role in exchanging R&D knowledge between those countries and consequently increasing the production level in them (Westlund 2010; Allsopp 1995).

Game theory and the Nash equilibrium

Osborne and Rubinstein (1994) define game theory as 'a bag of analytical tools designed to help us understand the phenomena that we observe when decision-makers interact'. A game is understood as a combination of three different parts: players, action of the players, and pay-off (utility) function for each player. The Nash equilibrium as a set of strategies is an action profile which states none of the players will receive higher pay-off if they deviate individually from that profile (Gintis 2009; Wessels 2006).

Dominant strategy, prisoner's dilemma and the briber's dilemma

Dominant strategy is a strategy which provides the largest pay-off to the player no matter what the rest of the players' strategies are. Thus this strategy always works better than any other strategy of the other players, which they might adopt with respect to their different actions (Gintis 2009; Adams 2010).

The prisoner's dilemma is a game based on the following hypothetical situation (Leyton-Brown and Shoham 2008; Rapoport and Chammah 1965).

Two suspects are going to be interrogated separately. If one of them confesses and the other chooses not to, the latter will be sentenced to τ years in prison, while the former will be freed. If both confess they will be sentenced to $\tau-1$ years. The last option is when both of them do not confess, so they will only receive 1 year each. It is clear that although the best outcome for both criminals will obtain from the decision of 'Do Not Confess', each of them prefers the 'Confess' strategy. Thus, this leads to the unique Nash equilibrium solution of (Confess, Confess) for this game. In other words, there is a pair of decisions made by the two players which is jointly optimal for each of them, but that pair of decisions is not an equilibrium.

The briber's dilemma is a strategy based on making the agreement between competitors of not paying bribes for winning projects, receiving contracts, etc. for the fact that this compromise will result in a higher pay-off for all of them. In view of the briber's dilemma, every motivation that can stimulate making such agreements (on not paying bribes) in the society is important for the establishment of an incorrupt market institution. Informal rules can be mentioned as one of these motivations. The greater the number of these informal rules, the higher the possibility of giving up corruption by individuals in the economy.

The effects of informal rules on client society corruption

In a society with valuable informal trades between the clients, involvement in bribery will be equal to losing large benefits of participating in those trades. It will be shown how the presence of informal rules in a society will change the corruption equilibrium point to the uncorrupted equilibrium; changing disobedience to obedience of L1 requirement(s) between designers or service providers.

For this purpose the whole concept in a general society will be explained first and the theory behind the concept will be demonstrated. Then it will be depicted how this concept can correspond to the building industry and can be transferred to and utilised there.

Corrupt equilibrium conversion to incorrupt (Macrae 1982)

Consider a society with N firms (where Q is one of the firms), who are competing for receiving a project with value P. Here the chance of firm Q succeeding in getting the project in a corruption-free environment is $1/N$ or p.

The two following equations are the expected net incomes from a successful bid for the project (P):

$$EY_1 = p(x)P + \tilde{p}(1-x)P - p_F F - g \tag{1}$$

$$EY_2 = \bar{\bar{p}}(x)P + p(1-x)P - h \tag{2}$$

EY	is the expected income from the project
EY_1	is the expected income from the project for the corrupt firm
EY_2	is the expected income from the project for the incorrupt firm
P	is the project value
h	is the cost which has been made by the frustrated official who was not bribed, in the form of delays and difficulties of formalities
g	is the price for seeking bribe
F	is a legal sanction in a monetary format (fine)
p_F	is the probability of being punished
x	is the corrupt part of the society
$(1-x)$	is the innocent part of the society
$\tilde{p}$	is firm Q's chance of winning the competition and receiving the project, provided that Q could bribe the official
$p = 1/N$	is the chance of firm Q succeeding in getting the project in a corruption-free environment
$\bar{\bar{p}}$	is the probability of an innocent firm receiving the deal (contract).

To simplify the case we assume $g = h$ and F as a function of proportionality factor v and the project benefit P will be:

$$F = vP \tag{3}$$

In (3), where the value of a successful bid, P, is treated as a constant, F has a linear relation to v, i.e. $F{\uparrow} \Rightarrow v{\uparrow}$. This means that the proportionality factor is determined by the size of the fine.

So we can write $p_F F$ in the following format, where the society is divided into two parts: x: the corrupt part of the society and $(1-x)$: the incorrupt or innocent part. Thus in (4), p_{1F} is the probability of receiving a fine in a society where the rest of the agents are corrupt as well, and p_{2F} is the probability of being punished where the rest are incorrupt:

$$p_F F = p_{1F}(x)vP + p_{2F}(1-x)vP \tag{4}$$

p_{1F}	is the probability of receiving a fine in a society where the rest of the agents are corrupt
p_{2F}	is the probability of being punished in a society where the rest are incorrupt
$p_F F$	is the probability of receiving a fine no matter if the rest are either innocent or corrupt.

Consider p_{iF} as the probability of being fined, where $i = 1$ refers to the case when all other agents are corrupt, and $i = 2$ refers to the case when all other agents are honest or incorrupt. It is possible to use the proportionality factor, v, and multiply the p_{iF} probabilities to obtain the composite variable $\hat{p}_{iF}$ defined in (5):

$$\hat{p}_{iF} = (vp_{iF}) \tag{5}$$

$\hat{p}_{iF}$ is the multiplication of proportionality factor, v, and the probability of receiving a fine in a society with all corrupt rivals or all innocent rivals, i.e. p_{iF}, $i = 1, 2$, (vp_{iF}).

Also in (1) and (2) if we collect EY_i and g one side of the equation, and name their summation, Y_i^*, which yields:

$$EY_1 + g = p(x)P + \tilde{p}(1-x)P - p_F F \tag{6}$$

$$EY_2 + g = \overline{\overline{p}}(x)P + p(1-x)P \tag{7}$$

$$Y_i^* = EY_i + g, \quad i = 1, 2, \ldots$$

Thus:

$$Y_1^* = EY_1 + g \quad \text{and} \quad Y_2^* = EY_2 + g$$

By rewriting (1) and (2) in a matrix format we will have:

$$\hat{Y} = \hat{X}B \tag{8}$$

where we can compare corrupt and incorrupt strategies more easily.

In (8), $\hat{Y}$ is a [1*2] matrix with Y_1^* and Y_2^* as its elements:

$$\hat{Y} = [Y_1^*, \ Y_2^*]$$

$\hat{X}$ is also a [1*2] matrix with (x) as a corrupt part of the society and $(1-x)$ as an innocent part of society, as its elements:

$$\hat{X} = [(x), \ (1-x)]$$

And B is a [2*2] matrix, with the following structure:

$$B = \begin{bmatrix} (p - \hat{p}_{1F})P & \bar{\bar{p}}P \\ (\tilde{p} - \hat{p}_{2F})P & pP \end{bmatrix}$$

From B we can figure out that a corrupt strategy is a dominant strategy because $p > \bar{\bar{p}}$ and also $p > \tilde{p}$ (by comparing first column and the second column of the matrix B) (Piroozfar 2010). This strategy will be dominant except when the $\hat{p}_{iF}$ values are too large.

Thus in a society with informal rules for trade and interaction between the clients, the corrupt strategy will not be a dominant strategy any more.

We will show how the above approach can be applied in the construction industry in the following section.

DISCUSSION AND CONCLUSION

It was indicated that employing customisation strategies may fuel corruption in the construction industry by encouraging parties to take shortcuts in fulfilling requirements in an attempt to reduce costs and to increase choice. It was also discussed that the informal rules augment the monetary cost of corruption. This means, as we also showed in our discussion specific to the construction industry with reference to a trade between service/production costs and design/

configuration choices, that informal rules will increase the monetary cost of corruption. This will prevent any willingness for, or attempt on, procedures to take shortcuts on requirements in the hope of lowering costs (in the form of direct costs or as an implication of time spent on, and efforts dedicated to a job) while providing a greater choice of design, in the form of configuration, specification, flexibility and adaptation. This is what happens in a society with informal rules.

Therefore, if we consider a society with valuable informal trade rules between the clients, then involvement in bribery will be equal to losing the large benefits of participating in those trades. If we think of those benefits as monetary benefits, then we can infer that the main consequence of taking part in bribery in a society with informal trade rules will increase the monetary fine. So in equation (3), F will increase which leads to the v increment. Thus in (5) the v increment will lead to the surge of piF and finally according to the discussion we had in this chapter (where we explained that corrupt strategy will be dominant except when the piF values are too large) the corruption equilibrium will be contradicted and changed to non-bribery equilibrium.

This concept, and our discussion which took place in the setting of a society in general, can be transferred into the building industry as follows:

$$EY_1 = p(x)P + \tilde{p}(1-x)P - p_FF - g \qquad (1)$$

$$EY_2 = \bar{\bar{p}}(x)P + p(1-x)P - h \qquad (2)$$

$$F = vP \qquad (3)$$

$$p_FF = p_{1F}(x)vP + p_{2F}(1-x)vP \qquad (4)$$

$$\hat{p}_{iF} = (vp_{iF}) \qquad (5)$$

N	is number of designers/suppliers/contractors (where Q is one of the designers/suppliers/contractors) who are competing to win a project, a bid or a contract with value P
$p=1/N$	is a chance of Q as a designer/supplier/contractor to succeed in getting the project/bid/contract in a corruption-free environment
EY	is the expected income from the project/bid/contract
EY_1	is the expected income from the project/bid/contract for the corrupt designer/supplier/contractor
EY_2	is the expected income from the project/bid/contract for the incorrupt designer/supplier/contractor
P	is the project value
h	is the cost made by the frustrated official[2] who has not been bribed, in the form of delays and difficulties of formalities

g	is the price for seeking bribe
F	is a legal sanction in a monetary format (fine charged by court or by the accreditation body which might consequently blemish the reputation of the corrupt designer/supplier/contractor)
p_F	is the probability of being punished
x	is the corrupt part of the building industry
$(1 - x)$	is the innocent part of the building industry
$\tilde{p}$	is designer Q's chance of winning the competition and receiving the project, provided that Q could bribe the official
$\bar{\bar{p}}$	is the probability of an innocent designer receiving the deal (contract)
v	is the proportionality factor
p_{1F}	is the probability of receiving a fine in a building industry where the rest of the designers are corrupt
p_{2F}	is the probability of being punished in a building industry where the rest are incorrupt
$p_F F$	is the probability of receiving a fine no matter if the rest are either innocent or corrupt
$\hat{p}_{iF}$	is the multiplication of proportionality factor, v and the probability of receiving a fine in a building industry with all corrupt rivals or all rivals innocent.

By making such an analogy between a society, in general, and the building industry, in particular, it is evident that the presence of informal rules in the building industry as a society could change the corruption equilibrium point to the uncorrupted equilibrium between designers/suppliers/contractors. This shows the effectiveness of these rules to decrease corruption in the form of bribery. This means that the existence of informal rules in communities of practice within the building industry will decrease disobedience of rules and requirements and even help replace it by obedience and a higher rate of compliance.

FUTURE WORK

The future scope of the work would be to validate the theoretical findings of this research on real cases. However, because of the nature of the problem, this might be a challenging task to do. Since real collaboration can be much more complicated and measuring corruption could also be rather difficult, there might be some limitations on further developing and testing the model. This can be addressed by restricting the scope of test cases while increasing the number of cases to cover all foreseeable forms of corruption. This will enable us to reach a point where evidence-base generalisation can be deployed to formulate a theory in this area. Although the authors have already started articulating on informal rules within construction professional networks in other research projects, this can form another slightly different trajectory for further research with special reference to game theory and its application to control corruption when customisation strategies are introduced.

NOTES

1 In an earlier paper we used an example of designing a customisable solution for building facades where the thermal performance of the building was to be fulfilled. We presented three generic requirements to be met to fulfil Approved Document Part L. For further reading please refer to: Piroozfar *et al.* (2009)

2 Official here means people who check whether L1 requirements have been fulfilled or not.

BIBLIOGRAPHY

Adams, E., (2010), *Fundamentals of Game Design*, 2nd edn, Berkeley, CA: New Riders, Pearson Education.

Allsopp, V., (1995), *Understanding Economics*, London: Routledge.

Cadot, O., (1987), 'Corruption as a gamble', *Journal of Public Economics*, 33: 223–244.

Cameron, L., Chaudhuri, A., Erkal, N., and Gangadharan., L., (2009), 'Propensities to engage in and punish corrupt behaviour: experimental evidence from Australia, India, Indonesia and Singapore', *Journal of Public Economics*, 93: 843–851.

Dutta, P. K., (1999), *Strategies and Games: Theory and Practice*, Boston, MA: MIT Press.

Elliott, K. A., (ed.), (1997), *Corruption and the Global Economy*, Washington DC: Institute for International Economics.

Gintis, H., (2009), *Game Theory Evolving: A Problem-Centered Introduction to Modeling Strategic Interaction*, 2nd edition, Princeton, NJ: Princeton University Press.

Grootaert, C., Narayan, D., Nyhan Jones, V., and Woolcock, M., (2004), *Measuring Social Capital: An Integrated Questionnaire*, World Bank Working Papers, Washington DC: World Bank Publications.

Gupta, S., Davoodi, H., and Alonso-Terme, R., (1998), *Does Corruption Affect Income Inequality and Poverty?*, IMF Working Paper, WP/98/76 , International Monetary Fund.

Halpern, D., (2005), *Social Capital*, Cambridge: Polity Press.

Hodgson, G. M., (2006), 'What are institutions?', *Journal of Economic Issues*, 40(1): 1–25

Huang, P. H., and Wu, H., (1994), 'More order without more law: a theory of social norms and organizational cultures', *Journal of Law, Economics & Organization*, 10(2): 390–406.

Kingston, C., (2008), 'Social structure and cultures of corruption', *Journal of Economic Behavior & Organization*, 67: 90–102.

Leyton-Brown, K., and Shoham, Y., (2008), *Essentials of Game Theory: A Concise, Multidisciplinary Introduction*, Morgan & Claypool Publishers.

Macrae, J., (1982), 'Underdevelopment and the economics of corruption: a game theory approach', *World Development*, 10(8): 677–687.

North, D. C., (1985), 'The growth of government in the United States: an economic historian's perspective', *Journal of Public Economics*, 28: 383–399.

Osborne, M. J., and Rubinstein, A., (1994), *A Course in Game Theory*, Boston, MA: MIT Press.

Piroozfar, A. E., Popovic Larsen, O., and Piroozfar, G. (2009) '*Mass matching: developing a quasi-game toolkit for a customer-driven process in building industry*'. In F. T. Piller and M. M. Tseng (eds) *Proceedings of 5th International World Congress on Mass Customization and Personalization (MCPC2009)*. The University of Art and Design, Helsinki, Finland.

Piroozfar, G., (2010), 'Game theoretical aspects of corruption reduction', MSc Thesis, Copenhagen: KTH Royal Institute of Technology.

Rapoport, A., and Chammah, A. M., (1965), *Prisoner's Dilemma: A Study in Conflict and Cooperation*, Ann Arbor: University of Michigan Press.

Sanyal, R. N., and Samanta, S. K., (2000), 'Corruption across countries: the cultural and economic factors', *Business & Professional Ethics Journal*, 21(1): 21–46.

Schaeffer, M., (2002), *Corruption and Public Finance*, United States Agency for International Development (USAID) and Management Systems International (MSI)

Treisman, D. (2000), 'The causes of corruption: a cross-national study', *Journal of Public Economics*, 67: 399–457.

Tseng, M. M., and Jiao, J. (2001) 'Mass customization'. In G. Salvendy (ed.) *Handbook of Industrial Engineering, Technology and Operation Management*, 3rd edn, New York, NY: Wiley, pp. 684–709

Tuccillo, J. A., (1998), *The Eight New Rules of Real Estate: Doing Business in a Consumer-Centric, Techno-Savvy World*, Real Estate Education Co., Dearborn Financial Publication, Inc.

Vannucci, A., (2011), 'The informal institutions of corruption: A typology of governance mechanisms and anti-corruption policies', Working Paper, *For a Culture of Integrity on the Public Sector*, Scuola Superiore della Pubblica Amministrazione (SSPA), Available online at: http://integrita.sspa.it/wp-content/uploads/2011/04/sspa_papern3_Vannucci.pdf (accessed on 07-04-2012).

Weimer, D. L., (ed.), (1995), *Institutional Design*, Norwell, MA: Kluwer Academic Publishers.

Wessels, W. J., (2006), *Economics*, Hauppauge, NY: Barron's Educational Series Inc.

Westlund, H., (2010), *Social Capital in the Knowledge Economy: Theory and Empirics*, Berlin: Springer.

20

A shift in the order of use – 'user informed objects'

Assa Ashuach

ABSTRACT

The concept of 'Digital Forming' was first coined by Assa Ashuach in 2005 and later developed into a commercial company in 2009 with the aim of unlocking product design and co-creativity online. Digital Forming facilitated the design of everyday products, using synthesis of innovative 3D software solutions, through the online personalisation and shape modification of products. In addition considerable saving can be made by utilising the concept of postcode production, where products can be produced locally via the intelligent assignment of the user's submitted designs. By enhancing the end-user's participation in relation to the product design process and linking it to that of a designer, key benefits can also be derived. These include both optimised, tailor-made and therefore better-fitting products and an increased attachment to owned artefacts. This architecture also provides producers with the means to capitalise on their redundant production capacities, by ensuring that their otherwise non-used machine space is utilised. In addition, this benefits users with improved delivery times resulting from an optimised production and supply chain. This in turn reduces carbon footprint, and with an on-demand production process, the conventional storage and logistic issues for mass produced items are removed. Finally, the concept and work carried out within 'training objects' (an intelligent platform for the use of personal data to design and produce optimised product) is introduced.

INTRODUCTION

The notion of 'objects open within boundaries' was first introduced during a research fellowship granted to the author by London Metropolitan University in 2005. During this time the Digital Forming® concept and workflow was first conceived and later fully defined in a patent. This novel workflow was created based on the assumption that 3D objects are fundamentally a line of code, which can be stored, embedded and rendered as a 'virtual open product'. By 'open' it is meant that objects and the interactive experience of designing them are achieved in an 'unlocked' state by the original designer, while the fundamental functional parts are 'locked' and protected to co-designers. These restrictions relate to the areas of the object that can be manipulated, the ways in which they may be adapted and the degree of adaptation allowed. A key consideration here is to design objects that are extensible enough for industrial production, without jeopardising the products' functional soundness and their properties.

To make this possible, a team of dedicated developers at Digital Forming introduced two new file formats: ODO – Original Designed Object and CODO – Co-Designed Object, offering users and designers/brands a platform solution to 'open' their products for personalisation through shape modification and re-configuration. These file formats contain the data that defines the anatomy of virtual 3D objects created by the designer and co-designer within the platforms' graphical user interface (GUI). They consist of binary data describing geometric forms defined by point coordinates and can therefore be translated into a production format and reconstructed as products via Additive Manufacturing (AM). The translation process is necessary to convert the co-designer experience and created object into 3D mesh files utilised in AM. They are file formats therefore that bridge between the virtual experience and machine ready production files.

It was a process pipeline devised to introduce a new form of dialogue and an innovative industrial solution within the triangle of designer, manufac-turer and user; a previously less-explored territory. Here, there is no middleman any more and designers can connect to home users directly from their desktops. Brands can directly connect to their user communities and by staying in touch can convert their users into partners. This is a new industrial reality where the consumer becomes a user, and a user becomes a partner. It is a long-held vision and the supporting platform for the scenario of 'postcode production' and local manufacturing, as its core concept, is in continual refinement.

BACKGROUND AND PHILOSOPHY

We should own less but with more value, and things we own need to perform better for us. Design, therefore, should be seen as a strategy for questioning and modifying traditional notions of the aesthetics and functions of products. A considerable part of our practice today is dedicated to re-examining and developing new design methodologies as a means of achieving new forms of connections between the object and its future owner. Design is a technological catalyst and can be used as an enabler and a problem solver. Through the work undertaken a technology was introduced that will enable designers to add a new layer of 3D user design experience on top of the digitally designed object. This workflow was developed as a new industrial design method to enable users direct and personal input to their daily functional object collections at home.

By using 3D codes as a means to devise and develop new tools, it is possible to find new solutions and to continue investigating and evolving forms and contemporary aesthetics. An interest in giving an open access to users' input has always been an important part and aim of the work. Whether a mechanical action or a virtual opportunity, the user's choices are an essential element that must be incorporated into the final designed object, and not only in the act of purchase. This vision, in tandem with technological advancements enables this shift in the order of use, whereby a user is informing the functions and aesthetics of the future object-to-be. Instead of being solely an end-user, the purchaser becomes an active contributor to the final shape and function of his/her product. The industrial revolution introduced mass production and millions of affordable and identical products, which turned us into the mass consumers of low value, short shelf life products. We now should begin the move away from this rigid model. It is about improved communication; a phenomenon that started with voice exchange in the telecom industry and continues today with the streaming and embedding of interactive 3D data online/offline. This reality opens a world of new possibilities.

A SHORT MONOLOGUE ON THE CONCEPT

Back in the late 1990s, 3D drawings and modelling were more of a planning and rendering tool used mainly by the automotive and the film industries. As an enthusiastic BA product design student as I was then, the power of visualisation of a 3D rotatable object was always a big fascination for me. Many hours were spent modelling sketches into this joyful 3D experience, where one would sit back and just turn the finished design around and around to be able to experience it from different angles in real time.

'Mind materialisation' magic

The repetition of two-dimensional forms can be arranged in such a way as to give a 3D visual experience. This was one of the main 3D production/ prototyping routines at that time: slice your 3D geometry, produce 2D layers and join them up together for the full 3D form. 3D printing completed this 'mind materialisation' magic process. This directness immediately opened up a multitude of new opportunities, for both design and manufacturing. The idea

20.1 'PolyPix' the magic material, a hybrid of polygons and pixels, data ready for production

was to keep these products virtual for as long as possible. They were air until someone pays for them to be made.

Studying at the Royal College of Art (RCA) in the early 2000s provided the perfect laboratory for experimental and theoretical development. 3D design software was not just a visualisation tool any more but a clever new way to form real objects of various sizes; blurring the boundaries between the physical and virtual domains (see Figure 20.1).

At this time it was realised that by production of what was originally 'alive', unconstrained 3D virtual object, several opportunities were being missed. These identified opportunities were then defined within the following concepts:

1. Object 'DNA' – seeing a virtual object as a point cloud, a collection of points that exist in space that can be grouped into a sensible and meaningful representation of an object. Points can be tagged and grouped again into functions; for example defining a surface as flexible and 'unlocked' and in the specification of the degree of transition into a solid 'locked' area, setting physical rules and behaviours to the object geometry ensuring a successful materialisation and transition from virtual to actual reality.
2. Object 'evolution' – where an object is open to user input and is evolving. It is a passive or active interaction that can drive a virtual object, shift and

evolve it into a new form with better function and fit for its user/owner. An object or a surface can be conformed to the user's body shape, where some elements of an object can be evolved through time. Here objects and sub-elements can learn how to become better. For example: the runner's shoe can be made to be lighter and with enhanced foot support and bespoke porosity, allowing the runner to perform better due to having footwear with optimised fit and mechanical properties.

3. Object 'lexical' – the notion of object language: an assembly of parts with identity, address and impact. Like words making up a sentence, virtual parts can be defined as a root or a seed that can have a functional impact but also a behavioural impact. Something that dictates the way the overall assembly behaves in relation to a user's selections or behaviours.

4. Object as 'air' – virtual, made of no material, achievable, ownable and producible, but yet actualised only if really needed.

Through work and research undertaken to date, these core concepts have been developed into actual objects and technologies. What follows is a small selection of the work that has been informed by these underlying drivers.

RELATED WORK

Omi.mgx (2004/5)

The Omi.mgx light for 'Materialise' was one of the first products to be produced entirely as a single nylon part and distributed to the masses straight from the Selective Laser Sintering (SLS) machine tank (see Figure 20.2). Its form, together with the natural flexibility of polyamide, creates the joint-less form of a biological mechanism. The object was designed to be transformable as a result of direct manipulation by the user bending or twisting the structure, which allows for the sculpting and re-sculpting of the form to create new and personalised sculptural elements. This permeated but yet powerful form of interaction offered the user access into the design process. By letting the user change some of the object's sculptural elements the embedding of personal values is enabled and by this the object's value for its user/owner is increased.

SLS technology facilitated the manufacture of a single skeletal-like structure, a feat unachievable by any other manufacturing process of that time. Here, the fundamental aspects of 'no assembly' together with the instant digital materialisation of 3D geometry proved to be a successful concept and was therefore used as a foundation for further design innovation and software development. This product was awarded the Red Dot award for product design in 2006 and is now part of the Israel museum's permanent collection.

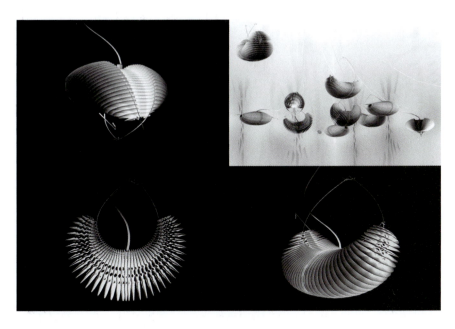

20.2 The OMI.mgx, one of the first objects to be sold to the mass market straight from the SLS machine tan

Osteon Chair (2006)

The Osteon Chair was the first chair to be designed using a combination of 3D tools and Artificial Intelligence (AI). Utilising a 'DNA' code containing all the information required to ensure that the object will transform perfectly from a virtual design into a 3D object, the Osteon Chair achieves the optimum strength whilst maintaining the desired visual aesthetic (see Figure 20.3).

Produced by Electro Optical Systems' (EOS) laser sintering in collaboration with Complex Matters the chair design consisted of a cosmetic skin and an intelligent internal structure. The AI software was used to analyse the designed surfaces to generate sufficient internal support structures by providing additional mass for the user's and the chair's stability, similar to the structure and mechanism of biological mechanisms such as a human bone/muscle. The Osteon Chair was designed as an 'intelligent' product. Here, instead of manipulation by an end-user to affect the form of the product, algorithmic computation was utilised to generate optimised structures capable of bearing varying degrees of load at different points. An ideal set of end results were formulated as the starting point and the optimal structure was created by working backwards to achieve that goal. The final outcome met all of the mechanical requirements while only using one-third of the anticipated material. The Osteon Chair is now part of the DHUB (Design Museum) Barcelona permanent collection.

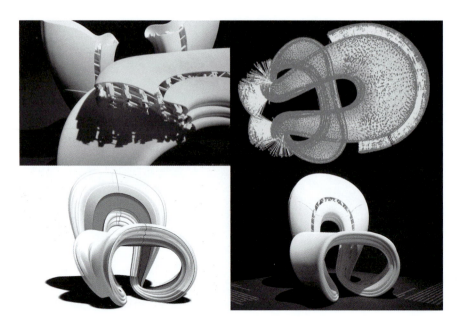

20.3 The Osteon chair, first use of AI (artificial intelligence) for the simulation of internal microstructures similar to human bone structure, the end product

The invaluable ongoing support from EOS, the laser sintering machine producer, and then Alias Wavefront's (acquired by Autodesk in 2006), the inspiring and incredibly innovative 3D software house, had both allowed building the perfect R&D Lab: a combination of advanced software and hardware that together enabled the concept generation of the digital forming workflow; a reality where an object is defined as a file, open to user's input within the boundaries set by the original designer, and ready to be locally produced via a postcode manufacturing network.

The digital forming technology: 'open within boundaries'

A 3D virtual object can be seen as a point cloud with an embedded DNA code. It contains all the required structural and visual characteristics and has a 3D point grid, open to be tagged and assigned with physical attributes at selected points. Here, any 3D object may have a basic topology, but more than this it may have pre-programmed instructions that dictate its behaviour under certain conditions. Otherwise it can be called an object with no boundaries or a virtual code that is without limits.

Within the context of the ODO file format, as designers we can specify a design within the ODO interface that will enable 'certain' operations at certain points on the ODO object. This may be manipulated by a user via the CODO

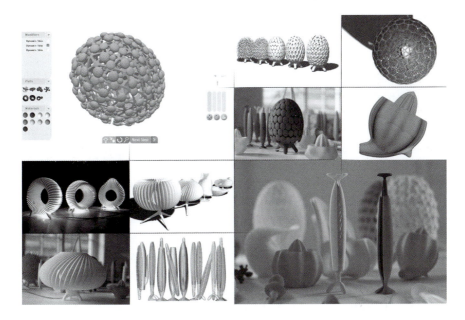

20.4 The CODO user interface and a collection of co-designed objects showing the personalisation and shape modification of original design (ODO)

interface (see Figure 20.4). Here, the notions of locking and unlocking come into place. For example, you can resize the handle (to some specified degree) on a CODO vessel design. However, the surrounding geometry where the handle meets the main body of the vessel can be locked so that manipulation is not possible. This then avoids any negative impact and provides a safe co-designing environment ensuring the sensitive production process constraints enforced by AM are respected. These include issues such as maintaining a minimum wall thickness as well as a safe distance between adjacent but separate moveable elements, to provide the product with adequate strength and to prevent powder fusion (as in the case with closely positioned parts such as gears) during the AM process, respectively. This creative freedom with varying degrees of pre-programmed control is the concept behind 'openness within boundaries'. Users can shape, modify, assemble, select colour, texture and choose the object's material only within the safe boundaries set by a designer to ensure that the design remains functional and producible (see Figure 20.4).

This new reality empowers the user and offers the opportunity to create objects with greater embedded value. This is due to them being an integral part of a co-designed creative process that produces personalised and/or optimised products which therefore results in a greater investment and attachment to owned artefacts. Moreover, this has the effect of empowering the owner by elevating them from their role as simply a consumer to a co-designer. With a simple and intuitive CODO interface, people with no modelling or design experience are able to express their creativity without any concern for the underlying technical issues and complexity associated with traditional 3D design.

In terms of the mechanics of the production and delivery aspect of this technology, when a user's order is received, the request is fed into an intelligent machine allocation system. Here, based upon the postcode of the user an automated enquiry is sent to the nearest corresponding bureau within the network. In response from the bureau, data is given pertaining to the availability of their machine space. Should a suitable space be present the production file is transferred, and produced within a previously agreed timeframe. Should no space be found at the nearest bureau to the user's address, the next nearest will be queried, as will others in succession.

This model works for both end-users, and producers. End-users receive cheaper products built within fully utilised machine spaces due to the fact that chargeable machine costs such as machine energy consumption and manpower are the same even if 1 or 100 parts are produced within a single job run (with SLS and other rapid manufacture machine costs, operational costs are always much larger than those of material costs). The owner of a single small part built in one machine run will still lock up that particular machine and its resources for the time required to complete the part and will therefore incur all associated costs. This is not the case when the cost is spread with others. Conversely, for the producer too, running a machine for one small part is not a practical or cost effective scenario either. Production bureaus can therefore maximise their machine costs. This way, end-users are given speedier product delivery turnaround times due to the fact that production is carried out locally meaning that the distribution times are considerably lower, hence lower carbon footprint.

Within this framework the original designs (ODO) chosen are products of a relatively small scale that can fit within an acceptable volume. This is because, when a user decides to have their design produced, the system needs to locate a local manufacturing bureau that has sufficient capacity to house it, and therefore, the probability of this increases when the object is small. In addition, as the size and thickness of a part increase, so does its cost. Therefore, in order to make products financially accessible this strategic decision was made from the outset. With an ethos of keeping objects virtual and 'alive' until they are wanted, huge impacts in terms of waste reduction can be made. As long as the files are not produced there is zero energy, no material consumption, no warehouse storage and no shipping or other logistic costs of mass produced products and packaging. Keeping your favourite objects on a 'virtual shelf' therefore, means zero waste, zero energy, zero transportation and zero storage.

CONCLUSION

From the early ventures in primitive user interaction with the OMI.mgx light through to the formation of the digital forming technology and UCODO co-creation platform, I have been working on the development of new ways and methods to embed personal user data and values into daily designed objects. The digital forming ODO side software offers a new design method. It is a virtual composer that allows designers to build the interaction experience delivered to the user by the CODO side user interface. This new design method enables designers to design virtual production equipped with a built-in user interaction experience and ready to allow the user to personalise and co-design the product better for themselves at home.

Within this new scenario brands and manufacturers can stay better 'in touch' with their user communities, demonstrating a greater degree of care and responsibility which in turn enables them to be more closely connected with their user communities (once called 'consumers'). This converts the concept of consumer from a purchaser/user of a 'thing' to a partner of a 'company'. As such they can participate in an exchange of information that in time will result in better products where there is less waste and overall needless consumption. It can be an active or passive exchange. This new industrial reality can be seen as a live stream of bidirectional information and a way to directly connect with users. It is about owning less but with more value and enhanced performance.

THE NEXT STEP 'TRAINING OBJECTS' ADDING THE ELEMENT OF TIME

The ongoing research includes current activities that are a natural evolution of some of the key concepts introduced in this chapter, and involve the real-time collection of user data that can then be harnessed into a feed of essential information. Here, personal sensor data is streamed into predesigned 3D virtual, production ready objects. These virtual objects are 'living' and 'evolving' within an intelligent environment where the live stream of personal user data is driving the objects' evolution, adaptation and optimisation (see Figure 20.5). There is the potential to produce objects and processes that result in significant energy and financial savings as a consequence of the shift to the notion of 'objects as a file'. This is in support of the perception and use of 3D virtual geometry assigned with physical attributes.

This is followed in the hope of harnessing the user's selective and collective consciousness, the optimisation of products through the processing of users' behaviour patterns.

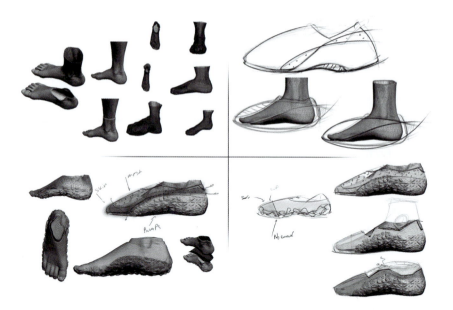

20.5 Concept sketches of a personalised shoe, with a better fit to the user's ergonomics and characteristics

This new workflow introduces not only an inverse design thinking but a new technology which enables the embedding of users' data into a phase of the 'no object' or the 'object abstract'.

ACKNOWLEDGEMENTS

The author wishes to thank Nicolas De Cordes for his beautiful mind, the Digital Forming team, London Metropolitan University and research assistant Daniel Hilldrup for their support in providing this chapter. Special thanks also go to EOS for their invaluable support throughout the years.

Index

117; advanced management/ organisation 123–4; advanced paradigm/philosophy 124–5; advanced product structure 123; advanced production technology 122–3; best-practice industrialisation 116–21; Enterprise Resource Planning 115, 116, 117, 159; flexible on-site automation 118–19; flexible on-site robots 119–20; hyper-flexible systems 124–5; Japanese customised fabrication 116–17; mass customisation 124; modular automation 118–19; off-site building re-customisation 121; on/off-site combined fabrication 117–18; production networks 4; reverse logistics 125; robot-oriented design 123; supply chain design 123–4; systemised deconstruction 121; value chain integration 121–2; wall and facade painting **120**

robust process design 18, 21–3

row houses: Taiwan 142

Royal College of Art (RCA) 233

Royal Danish Academy of Fine Arts, School of Architecture (KA) 106–7

Rubinstein, A.: and Osborne, M.J. 222

Rugg, G.: and McGeorge, P. 36

sales and marketing: apartments 129–30

Salvador, F.: et al. 215

Sanyo homes **168**

Sass, L.: and Botha, M. 177; and Smithwick, D. 174–83

SCANIA: system products 67, 68–9

schemata 36

Schneider Electric LK 67

Schreier, M. 25

Sekisui Chemical Co Ltd 169

Sekisui Heim 117, 121, 157, 159, **161**; Heim Automated Parts Pickup System (HAPPS) 159

Sekisui House *160*, 161, **161**

Selective Laser Sintering (SLS) machine tank 234, 235

service/manufacturing industry lessons: built environment 31–41

shading lamellas: ceramic **86**

shape grammars 178

shelters: relief 174–83

Shimizu: horizontally moving smart factory **118**

shoes 84

showroom display **48**

Shui On Land 134–7, **135**

Simpson, T.W 34

Siza, A. 178

Skanska **119**, 199–200, 214

skylights 86–91

Smithwick, D.: and Sass, L. 174–83

social capital 221–2

social construction: housing personalisation 43–4

Sol Ca building **135**

solar power systems: photovoltaic 167–70, *168*, **168**, *169*

SOLIDS projects: Amsterdam 49

solution space development 18, 19–21; conjoint analysis 19–20; customer experience intelligence 20; modularity 20; Netnography 20; product family approach 21

spatial mass customisation 53–64; adaptive urban spaces 58; compartment 61; components **62**; customisable entities 61–2; customising characteristics 61–2; definition 55–7; element 62; furniture 62; implications 54–5; infrastructure 61; interactive urban spaces 59; mixed-use development 57; objective 56–7; specification 62; versatile urban spaces 59

specification: spatial mass customisation 62

Sriram, R.D.: and Zha, X.F. 35

standard products 79–80; digital design considerations 81; pre-configuration 82–3; user-side configuration 80–1; variation creation 80–1

Stone, R.: et al. 35

Stylemachine 203–5

sunrooms 45

SUNTY Development Company (Taiwan) 49

supply chain: strategy *151*; Taiwan apartments 143, **143**

supply chain design: robot-oriented construction management 123–4